Economic Public Policy and Jewish Law

by

AARON LEVINE

KTAV PUBLISHING HOUSE, INC.
HOBOKEN

YESHIVA UNIVERSITY PRESS
NEW YORK

THE LIBRARY OF JEWISH LAW AND ETHICS
VOLUME XIX
EDITED BY NORMAN LAMM

Jakob and Erna Michael Professor of Jewish Philosophy
Yeshiva University

Economic Public Policy and Jewish Law

by

AARON LEVINE

KTAV PUBLISHING HOUSE, INC.
HOBOKEN

YESHIVA UNIVERSITY PRESS
NEW YORK

Library of Congress Cataloging-in-Publication Data

Levine, Aaron.
Economic public policy and Jewish law / by Aaron Levine.
p. cm. -- (Library of Jewish law and ethics ; v. 19)
Includes bibliographical references and index.
ISBN 0-88125-437-1
1. Jewish law. 2. Economics--Religious aspects--Judaism.
3. Judaism--Economic aspects. I. Title. II. Series.
LAW
296.1'8--dc20 93-16847
CIP

Manufactured in the United States of America

In loving memory of my dear parents.

Contents

Foreword

This volume is the third work by Professor Aaron Levine to be published as part of the Library of Jewish Law and Ethics. In it, our author continues to explore the interface between economics and Jewish tradition, in both its halakhic (legal) and aggadic (ethical) dimensions. Rarely has the dismal science been infused with so much exciting and novel content!

Economic Public Policy and Jewish Law focuses more on government than on the individual. This calls for a different perspective than that which informed Dr. Levine's previous works. The reader, whether professional or casual, will undoubtedly learn a great deal from this volume no matter which end he comes from: economics or Halakhah. The layman will probably find this an easier text than Rabbi Levine's earlier books, but he is bound to learn a great deal from it about a subject (economic public policy) which is more and more engaging the interest of all alert and sensitive people in these tumultuous times.

September 15, 1992 NORMAN LAMM

Acknowledgments

The present volume is the product of research I conducted over the past five years into economic public policy from the perspective of Halakhah (Jewish law).

Portions of this work originally appeared in slightly different form in other publications. Chapter 7, "Resale Price Maintenance," was first published as "The Moral Climate of Society and Government in the Torah Community: The Case of Resale Price Maintenance," in Ruth Link-Salinger, ed., *Torah and Wisdom: Studies in Jewish Philosophy, Kabbalah, and Halacha; Essays in Honor of Arthur Hyman* (New York: Shengold, 1992), pp. 129–143; chapter 8, "Unauthorized Copying and Dubbing," was first published as "Veiled Misconduct and Government in the Torah Society: The Case of Unauthorized Copying and Dubbing," in *National Jewish Law Review* 5 (1990–91): 115–143; chapter 5, "*Hakkarat Hatov* and the Making of the Moral Personality," was first published as "*Hakkarat Hatov* (Gratitude) and the Moral Personality," in *Tradition* 25, no. 2 (Winter 1990): 42–53; chapter 2, "Minimum Wage Legislation," as "Minimum Wage Legislation: A Halakhic Perspective," in *Tradition* 24, no. 1 (Fall 1988): 11–27; and chapter 3, "Comparable Worth," as "Comparable Worth in Society and in Jewish Law," *Tradition* 23, no. 1 (Summer 1987): 1–32.

This volume is the third work which I am privileged to have included in the Library of Jewish Law and Ethics. To the editor, Rabbi Dr. Norman Lamm, president of Yeshiva University, my heartfelt appreciation for his warm encouragement and for the many kindnesses he has extended to me over these many years. My debt of gratitude for his critique of my present work, especially his incisive comments on an earlier draft of chapter 5.

Dr. Yaakov Elman, associate editor at Ktav and distinguished colleague at Yeshiva University, scrupulously read the entire manuscript and made many valuable suggestions, both substantive and editorial. As production manager of this project,

Dr. Elman gave generously of his time and talents beyond the call of duty. My debt of thanks to him.

My debt of gratitude to Rabbi Shalom Carmy, consulting editor at *Tradition* and distinguished colleague at Yeshiva University, for the benefit of his wide-ranging scholarship, and his editorial and technical assistance.

To Dr. Joel Wolowelsky, associate editor at *Tradition*, for the thoughtful critique and editorial assistance he provided for the portions of this work which originally appeared in *Tradition*.

For the past thirteen years I have offered a course dealing with the interface between economics and Halakhahh at both Stern College and Yeshiva College. Much of the material in this volume has been woven into the curriculum of that course.

Dr. Norman Rosenfeld, dean, Yeshiva College, played a key role in introducing the subject of economics and Jewish law into the curriculum of Yeshiva University. My gratitude to him for his superb academic leadership, for the many kindnesses he has extended me to facilitate my research, and for the personal interest he has taken in my work.

To Dr. Karen Bacon, dean, Stern College, my appreciation for her outstanding academic leadership, for her encouragement, and for the personal interest she has taken in my work.

My gratitude to a number of very able and devoted students who provided research and technical assistance in the preparation of this volume. Lawrence Burian, Michael Olshin, Avi Posen, Geoffrey Rochwarger, Jonathan Rochwarger, and Ben Weiner verified references and extended bibliographies of earlier drafts of this work. Jonathan Rochwarger also rendered valuable service in computer technology at critical junctures.

Dov Kesselman extended himself in an extraordinary manner in providing valuable research, technical, and computer assistance throughout the project.

Shimon Horn meticulously prepared the name and subject indexes of this work.

Professor Mareleyn Schneider gave generously of her time and talents in assisting this project in computer technology. Many thanks also to Mr. Leonard Brandwein and Professor Aizik Leibovitch for their timely advice on computer technology.

Throughout this project, my research was aided by the professionalism and the many amenities extended to me by the library staffs of Yeshiva University. In particular, I would like to thank Zalman Alpert, Zvi Erenyi, Chaya Gordin, Rabbi Theodore Lasdun, and Rabbi Berish Mandelbaum of the Mendel Gottesman Library; John Moryl and Marilyn Winn of the Pollack Library; and Professor Edith Lubetski (head), Sarah Leah Gross, and Vivian Moskovitz of the Hedi Steinberg Library.

The manuscript of this work was typed by Harriet Nachmann. My gratitude to her for her competence, efficiency, courtesy, and extreme patience.

To my beloved wife and life companion, Sarah, a special note of appreciation. For me and for our cherished children she is yesterday's fondest memories, today's happiness, and the inspiration for tomorrow's dreams.

New York — Aaron Levine
11 Tishrei 5753

• 1

Economic Public Policy in the Torah Society: An Overview

THIS WORK WILL FOCUS on economic public policy for a society which is bound by Halakhah (Jewish law). Throughout this work we will refer to this society as the Torah society.

The major theme of this work is that public policy provides an appropriate setting for an interface between economic theory and Halakhah.

One important factor to be considered is efficiency. In economic terms, efficiency results when the problem-solver manages to maximize benefits and minimize costs within the constraints set. In the Torah society, efficiency is never an absolute value in evaluating the merits of any particular policy. It will be rejected when it comes into conflict with some value or ideal which Halakhah seeks to advance. Nevertheless, within its proper halakhic sphere of operation, efficiency takes on the character of a religious duty both in the formulation and the implementation of economic public policy.

The second factor is the imperative of *imitatio Dei*. This tenet of Judaism sets God's attribute of mercy as the guidepost for interpersonal human conduct.

These two themes—the demands of and constraints on efficient operation, and the requirement of *imitatio Dei*—will determine the specific issues explored in this volume.

Before introducing the above two building blocks of this work, several preliminary comments regarding the legislative process in the Torah society are in order.

It should be noted at the outset that communal legislation enjoys no halakhic sanction when it comes into conflict with ritual prohibitions.[1] In matters of civil and criminal law, however, communal enactments are generally recognized even if they come into conflict with a particular rule of Halakhah.

Communal legislation is further linked to religious law by the requirement that all communal enactments must be approved by the loally recognized religious authority and communal leader (*adam ḥashuv*). Should an individual blessed with these attributes not be present locally, communal legislation is fully valid without any outside approval.[2]

The following baraita quoted at Bava Batra 8b provides a basic source for the nature of this authority:

> The townspeople are also at liberty to fix weights and measures, prices and wages, and to inflict penalties for infringement of their rules.

Espousing the majority view, R. Isaac b. Jacob Alfasi (Algeria, 1013–1103) and others understand this communal legislative authority as coming into force by means of a majority-decision rule.[3] Indicative of the limitations of the coercive power of the majority over the minority is the observation that all the actions the baraita speaks of have a community-wide welfare basis. Consequently, in matters not pertaining to a community-wide interest, the majority may not pass legislation favoring one group at the expense of another, as is clearly stated by R. Joseph Colon (Italy, ca. 1420–1480).[4]

In this vein, R. Solomon b. Abraham Adret (Barcelona, 1235–1310) ruled invalid a community edict calling for the taxation of a resident on the basis of his ownership of assets located in a different town. Majority decision, as R. Adret points out, cannot legitimize robbery. Since the edict effectively subjected a segment of the community to double taxation, the provision amounted to outright robbery.[5]

In the Torah society, certain functions are mandated on the public sector. Mandated functions entailing major tax implications include: (1) security (defense) measures; (2) social welfare programs for the poor; (3) religious-education institutions for the young; (4) a variety of communal projects of a religious character; (5) maintaining public roads; and (6) water-supply projects. Minority sponsorship of any of the public sector's mandatory functions is sufficient to confer legal sanction upon it, making it binding on all, including a protesting majority.[6]

Efficiency And Economic Public Policy

The concept of efficiency enters the arena of economic public policy on two different levels. On one level it demands that alternative means for accomplishing a given objective must be explored and the least-cost method be adopted. As an ideal for economic public policy, this concept of efficiency is free of controversy.

Alternatively, efficiency moves from the realm of means to the realm of ends, and itself becomes the tool for evaluating the worthiness of economic public policy. Called the Pareto Optimality criterion, this principle would call for the adoption of a legislative proposal only if it offered the reasonable prospect of improving the economic well-being of at least one person without reducing anyone else's well-being. If improvement for A can only be accomplished by reducing the welfare of B, the status quo condition must remain intact.

Since legislative action will almost invariably entail gains for some but losses for others, the Pareto rule is too austere to be of any operational use. A less stringent efficiency criterion, called the Kaldor-Hicks rule, has accordingly been advanced as an appropriate operational guideline in legislative and judicial decisions. What this rule entails for decision- makers is that they assess the proposed change in terms of what value gainers would assign to their gain and what value losers would assign to their losses. If the gains exceed the losses in monetary value, the proposal enhances society's wealth and should therefore be adopted.

Kaldor-Hicks does not require the gainers to compensate the losers. Nevertheless, any proposal which meets this criterion carries with it the potential of enhancing the well-being of the losers in the long run even if compensation was not given to them at the time the legislation was passed.

This result obtains because the increase in *aggregate* income which Kaldor-Hicks makes possible sets into motion a whole series of rounds of spending and income creation. Called the multiplier effect, this expansionary process obtains regardless of how the original gainers choose to dispose of their increment in income between savings and spending.Suppose A, the gainer, decides to spend his increment, then A's spending increases B's income, which, in turn, triggers an increase in income for C. Since in each successive round of income creation, some portion of the increment is saved, the expansionary process must eventually come to a halt. Suppose, however, that A opts to save the increment in his income. Because A's action, other things being equal, increases the supply of loanable funds relative to its demand, A's savings lowers the borrowing cost for B. B's borrowing will then set into motion the multiplier effect described above.[7]

Efficiency And The Legislative Process

In the Torah society, the duty for political decision-makers to search for the least-cost alternative in the pursuit of a given objective is not just a matter of idealized conduct, but constitutes a religious imperative. This proposition follows from an analysis of the legal basis of political authority in Halakhah. Three views on this have been advanced.

One school of thought regards political authority as rooted in an agency relationship between the holder of political authority and society.[8]

An agency relationship carries with it an implicit charge by the principal to his agent: *letakunai shelaḥtikh velo li'avutei* ("I have commissioned you to advance my cause and not to impair it").[9] The implication this has for efficiency can be seen from a point in the law on *ona'ah* (overreaching).

The ethics of the price terms of a transaction concluded within the framework of a competitive norm is governed in Halakhah by the law of *ona'ah*. This prohibits an individual from knowingly concluding a transaction at a price which is more favorable to himself than the competitive norm.[10] Depending on how widely the price of the subject transaction departs from the competitive norm, the injured party may have recourse to void or adjust the transaction. Provided the price discrepancy is assessed to be within the margin of error,[11] the plaintiff's right to void the transaction is recognized when the difference between the sale price and the competitive norm is more than one-sixth.[12] When the differential is exactly one-sixth, neither of the parties may subsequently void the transaction on account of the price discrepancy. The plaintiff is, however, entitled to full restitution of the *ona'ah* involved. [13] Finally, third-degree *ona'ah* occurs when the sale price differs from the market price by less than one-sixth. Here, the transaction not only remains binding, but in addition, the complainant has no legal claim to the price differential.[14]

When a transaction is contracted through an agent and the agent is victimized by *ona'ah*, the principal is conferred with nullification rights even when the amount of the *ona'ah* is merely third-degree. The principal's nullification rights proceed from the fact that an agreement concluded through an agent derives its legitimacy from the presumption that power of attorney (*sheliḥut*) was in effect when the transaction was consummated. Given the financial loss an *ona'ah* agreement imposes on the principal, the latter may protest that his agent had no authority to enter into such an agreement on his behalf. This protest is regarded as legitimate, for it is presumed that an agent is commissioned to benefit his principal and not to impair his cause (*letakunai shelaḥtikh velo li'avutei*). Since abuse of authority on the part of the agent forms the basis of the principal's nullification rights, the latter may exercise this right even when the degree of *ona'ah* transacted on his behalf was merely third-degree.[15]

To make the connection between *ona'ah* and efficiency, we need merely point out that what stands at the basis of the *ona'ah* claim is the availability of a better market opportunity for the plaintiff at the time he entered into the disputed transaction. If the plaintiff's claim that he was ignorant of the better alternative at the time he entered into the disputed transaction was reasonable, the *ona'ah* complaint is validated.[16]

As the foregoing discussion indicates, recognition of an *ona'ah* claim expresses a halakhic attitude that, to a certain degree, inefficient market search does not forfeit for a plaintiff a chance for legal redress in respect to the disputed transaction. Thus, the higher *ona'ah* standard Halakhah imposes on an agent translates into a more thorough market-search expectation for him.

If political authority is rooted in agency, the political office-holder must strive for policies which operate efficiently. This is so because the agency relationship here is not established separately for each decision, but rather is in the nature of a proxy for all decision-making during the term of office. The *letakunai shelaḥtikh* charge for the political authority should therefore go beyond a responsibility for allocational efficiency in pubic expenditures and extend to the obligation to thoroughly explore alternative means to achieve given ends.

Another school of thought regards political authority as rooted in judicial status.[17] Sitting in supervision over the affairs of both the public at large and private individuals gives communal officials a judicial character.[18]

Conceiving political authority as rooted in judicial status, R. Ben-Zion Meir Ḥai Ouziel (Israel, 1881–1953) posits that trustees of a charitable organization also take on a judicial character. What leads him to this conclusion is the explanation by R. Joseph Caro (Safed, 1488–1575) of why the distribution of charity requires a committee of three.[19] This requirement is called for, according to R. Caro, because determining the measure of support and relief for each recipient is a distinctly judicial function.[20] By extension, R. Caro's comment explains why political authority assumes judicial status. Given that the ambit of Jewish communal legislation will invariably entail income redistribution, legislation takes on a distinctly judicial character.

Conceiving political authority as rooted in judicial standing will also result in an implicit efficiency mandate for political decision-makers. This is evident from another point in *ona'ah* law relating to the division of property by brothers or partners. Ordinarily, if the appraisal upon which the division of property was made is later found to be inaccurate, the division of property is subject to adjustment and even possibly to nullification in accordance with the rules of *ona'ah*.[21] But if the parties, instead of appraising the property themselves, entrusted the task to a Bet Din (Jewish court), and the appraisal was off the mark by one-sixth, the original division of property becomes null and void and must be done again.[22] Thus, when a task is entrusted to a court, the level of exactitude expected of it in carrying out the task is greater than the standard the parties would set for themselves had they executed the matter themselves.

Finally, still another school of thought regards political authority as occupying the status of sovereignty.[23] This too results in an implicit mandate for efficiency, as witness the following comment of R. Aaron ha-Levi (Barcelona, 1235–1300) in connection with the Torah's charge to the king: "He shall not accumulate very much silver and gold" (Deuteronomy 17:17). This charge, says R. Aaron, prohibits the king from accumulating treasure for his own personal storage or use. Accumulating treasure for the benefit of the nation is, however, permissible. Standing at the basis of this law is the presumption that the entire nation depends and relies upon the king. The king, therefore, may not devote his energies toward self-gratification. Instead, he must totally direct himself toward advancing the public welfare.[24]

Moreover, Halakhah generally imposes an efficiency standard on employees. This standard takes on two dimensions. One aspect is the instruction not to idle on the employer's time.[25] The second is the duty to apply oneself to the task at hand with the utmost energy.[26] Since energetic dedication entails both physical exertion and mental concentration, satisfaction of this latter aspect of the efficiency mandate, so it would appear, requires the worker to summon whatever resourcefulness and creativity he has to pursue the objective at hand through the most efficient means available.

The Kaldor–Hicks Rule And Legislation

As a criterion for evaluating the worthiness of legislative proposals, the Kaldor-Hicks rule itself is subject to a constraint in a Torah society. Before it comes into play, the ramifications of a legislative proposal must first be thoroughly explored in order to ensure that its implementation would not work to undermine Torah values. In this context, given the paramountcy of economic analysis as a tool in discovering possible conflicts between legislative proposals and Torah values, it becomes a matter of religious duty to integrate economic analysis into the legislative process of the Torah society, since legislation is not recognized when it comes into conflict with ritual prohibitions

Once legislators are convinced that a proposal will not work to undermine Torah values, evaluating its worthiness in terms of Kaldor-Hicks becomes admissible. Moreover, one could well argue that at this stage, Kaldor-Hicks becomes an important requirement for the legislative process of the Torah society. This follows from the comment of R. Moses Isserles (Poland, 1525 or 1530–1572) that voting in the political process must be done *le-shem shamayim* ("for the sake of heaven").[27] As a definite matter, what R. Isserles' criterion disallows is voting on the narrow basis of self-interest. Since Kaldor-Hicks represents a potential Pareto gain for the current income stream and, in addition, expands the economic pie for the community in the long run, use of this criterion in the legislative process promotes the best interests of the community as a whole and is therefore consistent with *le-shem shamayim*.

The Conflict Between Equity and Efficiency

Efficiency is not the only consideration in evaluating proposals in the Torah society. Equity, or what society regards as fair, must also enter the decision-making process. That Halakhah takes matters of equity into account in the legislative process can be seen from the principle of *darkhei no'am*.

Darkhei no'am (i.e., the promotion of a harmonious social order) is one of the ultimate aims of the Torah's precepts and commands. This goal, according to Rav Joseph (4th cent.), is expressed in the verse *Derakheha darkhei no'am* ("Her ways are ways of pleasantness"; Proverbs 3:17).[28] It is reflected in the many ordinances introduced by the sages with the motivation of either defusing or preventing communal dissension.[29]

Examination of a sample of the ordinances rooted in *darkhei no'am* reveals that the rabbis understood the import of a harmonious social order on different levels.

On a fundamental level, *darkhei no'am* means the averting of disputes. Avoiding strife and the disruption of the public order was, for instance, the basis for recognizing the minor's legal title to a lost article he picks up.[30] By pentateuchal law, a minor has no legal capacity to acquire property unless an adult confers the property to him (*da'at aḥeret maknah*).[31] This state of affairs, however, fosters strife. Since the minor does not acquire title, it can be expected that people will try to wrest the article away from him, coming in conflict with the child[32] and/or with his relatives.[33]

On a different level, *darkhei no'am* legislation makes an award of a property right not just for the sake of minimizing strife, but because such action conforms to society's notion of fairness, notwithstanding the lack of a legal basis for the award. Illustrating this aspect of *darkhei no'am* is a rabbinical enactment relating to an agricultural entitlement of the poor called *shikheḥah* (forgotten sheaf). By pentateuchal law, a poor man acquires legal title to the forgotten sheaf only if he first takes hold of it and thereby performs the necessary symbolic act of acquisition (*kinyan*).[34] Accordingly, should poor man A climb to the top of an olive tree and beat its branches for the purpose of releasing the fruit, the olives which fall to the ground will not automatically become his. If another poor man (B) takes hold of the fallen olives before A gets a chance to do so, B's legal claim to the olives is fully recognized. But this state of affairs assaults society's notion of fairness. The sages, therefore, by force of formal enactment, awarded the olives to A and declared that it is theft if anyone else takes them.[35]

Standing at the basis of this enactment, according to R. Mordecai b. Hillel (Germany, 1240–1298), is that it is unfair for A to lose out to B after he had exerted himself to acquire the forgotten sheaf and also had fully expected that his toil and effort would culminate in his taking possession of the fruit.[36]

R. Mordecai b. Hillel's concept of the *darkhei no'am* principle in the forgotten-sheaf case provides a precedent for introducing notions of equity into the legislative process of the Torah society. Provided these notions of equity do not directly contradict Torah values, legislators may not ignore them.

Given the admissibility of both equity and efficiency in the legislative process, economic analysis becomes essential in providing direction. Specifically, when economic analysis demonstrates that certain positions are rooted in false premises, and exposes other opinions as espousing values which are alien to the Torah society, informed economic public policy is promoted. Economic analysis as a tool for the legislative process of the Torah society finds its most potent impact, of course, when it demonstrates that the very group which common sense dictates will gain from a legislative proposal will in actuality be hurt by it.

In chapters 2 and 3, the issues of minimum wage and comparable worth will be taken up. Economic analysis will be brought to bear to determine how these proposals impinge on various Torah values.

In chapter 2 our focus will be on how the minimum-wage concept meets various halakhic antipoverty goals and its impact on teenage Torah study. We will then turn to a comparison of the minimum wage with the concept of wage-rate subsidy.

In chapter 3 our focus will be on how the comparable-worth proposal would affect the institution of marriage. Moreover, economic analysis will demonstrate that the proposal's goals are self-defeating.

Imitatio Dei and Economic Public Policy

In Judaism, the guidepost for interpersonal conduct is the duty to emulate God's attribute of mercy. This behavioral norm is called *imitatio Dei* ("imitation of God"). In this section, we will develop the thesis that *imitatio Dei* is also the guidepost for economic public policy in the Torah society. We begin with an exposition of what this behavioral imperative denotes for interpersonal conduct:

> "After the Lord your God shall you walk" (Deuteronomy 13:5). [R. Ḥama b. Ḥanina asks]: Is it then possible to "walk after" the Divine Presence? Has not Scripture already said, "for the Lord your God is a devouring fire" (Deuteronomy 4:24)? But it means, walk after the attributes of the Holy One. Even as He clothes the naked [clothing Adam and Eve with the garments of skins (Genesis 3:21)], so must you provide clothes for the naked. The Holy One visited the sick [appearing to Abraham after his circumcision (Genesis 18:1)]; so must you visit the sick. The Holy One consoled the bereaved [blessing Isaac after Abraham's death (Genesis 25:11)]; so must you console the bereaved. The Holy One buried the dead [interring Moses (Deuteronomy 34:6)]; so must you bury the dead.[37]

> "To walk in all his ways" (Deuteronomy 10:12). These are the "ways of the Lord": as it is written, "The Lord, the Lord, God, merciful and gracious, long-suffering and abundant in

> goodness and truth, keeping mercy unto the thousandth generation, forgiving iniquity and transgression and sin" (Exodus 34:6–7).[38]
>
> "And it shall come to pass that whosoever shall call on the name of the Lord shall be saved" Joel 3:15). Is it, then, possible for a man to be called by the name of the Holy One? But this means: Just as He is called "merciful and gracious," . . . so must you be merciful and gracious, and give of your gifts freely to all; just as the Holy One is called "righteous," . . . so must you be righteous. The Holy One is called loving," . . . so must you be loving. That is why it is said, "And it shall come to pass that whoever shall be called by the name of the Lord shall be delivered" (Joel 3:5). And it also is said, "Everyone that is called by My name, and whom I created for My glory, I formed him, yea I made him" (Isaiah 43:7). And it also is said, "The Lord has made everything for His own purpose" (Proverbs 16:4).[39]

At the outset, let us take note that Maimonides (Egypt, 1135–1204) counts *imitatio Dei* as one of the 613 precepts.[40] The significance of this, as Professor Yiẓḥak Twersky points out, is to make *imitatio Dei* not just a theological concept but a halakhic imperative.[41]

R. Naftali Ẓevi Yehudah Berlin (Russia, 1817–1893) derives this selfsame point from the proof-texts cited above, Isaiah 43:7 and Proverbs 16:4. These texts make *imitatio Dei* not merely a matter of nobility of spirit but a God-given duty, its practice being the very goal of creation.[42]

As a behavioral imperative, *imitatio Dei* extends beyond a duty to emulate those aspects of God's mercy explicitly enumerated at Exodus 34:6–7. By the exegesis of Joel 3:5, a duty to emulate every manifestation of God's mercy is established.[43]

In R. Joseph B. Soloveitchik's thinking, *imitatio Dei* imposes specific conduct and sets a standard for character. Sotah 14a directs man to engage in *imitatio Dei* conduct. Sifrei, however, sets a standard for human character. Not only should man's conduct be God-like, but he must nurture a God-like character, becoming worthy of being called by the names of God. Engaging in God-like actions naturally and with no sense of burden demonstrates a God-like character.[44]

The Social Component of Imitatio Dei

While the source texts cited above all relate to *imitatio Dei* in connection with interpersonal conduct, this behavioral imperative, according to Maimonides, applies not only to the private citizen but to the ruler in his capacity as ruler. It requires that his criminal-justice system should not be based on the passion of the moment, but on a careful consideration of equity with the aim of promoting social welfare. Since the sovereign must perforce be involved in the administration of justice, *imitatio Dei* requires him to mete out punishment in the manner that God metes out punishment.[45] Man as a private citizen, however, is bidden only to emulate God's attribute of mercy. Emulating attributes of God relating to punishment is strictly forbidden.[46]

Supporting the proposition that the *imitatio Dei* concept has a social component is Abba Saul's dictum, expressed by his exposition of the verse *Zeh E-li ve-anvehu* ("This is my God and I will glorify Him"; Exodus 15:2), Abba Saul understands *ve-anvehu* as consisting of two words, *ve-ani ve-hu,* with the import being: "I will be like Him. Just as He is *raḥum* (merciful) and *ḥanun* (gracious), so too will I be merciful and gracious" (Shabbat 133b).

In light of the *imitatio Dei* lesson derived from Deuteronomy 10:12, Abba Saul's exegesis appears superfluous. Closer examination of the dictum reveals, however, that Abba Saul adds a social component to the principle of *imitatio Dei*. This follows from the consideration that the circumstance which inspired the Jewish people to proclaim *zeh E-li ve-anvehu* was the miracle of the splitting of the Red sea. No one was singled out to experience the miracle. Quite to the contrary, God wrought this miracle for the Jewish people in its entirety. In contrast to the manna, whose benefit manifested itself on different levels according to individual merit,[47] the miracle at the Red Sea benefited the Jewish people as a whole,[48] making no distinctions between the deserving and the undeserving.[49] Hence Abba Saul advances *imitatio Dei* beyond interpersonal relations, making it man's duty to incorporate God's attributes of mercy into the community's social fabric and legal environment.

Imitatio Dei and the Moral Climate

One aspect of God's mercy is the weakening of the power of the evil inclination which He effects for those who strive for moral betterment. Expressing this dimension of God's mercy, Resh Lakish states that "if one wishes to defile himself [with sin] the door is merely opened for him; but if one comes to purify himself, he is assisted."[50] Divine assistance is not triggered only by great human initiatives. An unexceptional act of spiritual striving also merits Divine assistance, and so too, perhaps, does an unarticulated spiritual search. Evidencing this is the talmudic dictum that the Almighty demands only that we present to Him an opening of repentance no bigger than the eye of a needle. If we can manage this, God promises us, He will respond by widening our opening so that even wagons and carriages can pass through.[51]

The immense degree of compassion inherent in God's assistance in our battle against the evil inclination is expressed by Resh Lakish in the following dictum:

> The evil inclination renews its attack on man with increasing force every day, and tries to kill him, as it says: "The wicked one watches for the righteous and seeks to execute him" (Psalms 37:32). Were it not for God's assistance, no man could survive the onslaught, as it says: "But God will not forsake him to his power, nor let him be condemned in his judgment" (Psalms 37:33).[52]

The seductive power of the evil inclination is greatest when man is thrust into a setting involving either a conflict of interest or an opportunity to engage in hidden misconduct. It is here that cunning and shrewdness can often camouflage deceitful and fraudulent conduct and at the same time enable the perpetrator to avoid both legal consequences and social outrage.

To be spared the challenge of a test of piety is regarded in Jewish religious doctrine as ideal. Witness both the warning of the sages not to deliberately enter into a situation which will involve us in a test of piety[53] and the plea we make to God in our daily prayers not to thrust us into a test of piety.[54]

As private citizens we are very limited in what we can do to assist our fellow man in his battle against the evil inclination. But *imitatio Dei* is a mandate for government too, and government can accomplish much in this area. The government's duty here is to ensure that society's legal environment minimizes settings for hidden misconduct.

Support for the thesis that the government in the Torah society must be concerned with the elimination of hidden wrongdoing is the interpretation of R. Judah's dictum by R. Menaḥem b. Solomon Meiri (Perpignan, 1249–1316).

> "The secret things belong unto the Lord our God, but the things that are revealed belong unto us and to our children forever" (Deuteronomy 29:28). Why are the words *lanu u-lebanenu* [unto us and to our children] and the *ayin* of the word *ad* [forever] dotted? To teach that God did not punish for transgressions committed in secret until the Israelites had crossed the Jordan: This is the view of R. Judah. Said R. Neḥemia to him: Did God ever punish [all Israel] for crimes committed in secret; does not Scripture say forever? But just as God did not punish [all Israel] for secret transgressions [at that time], so too did He not punish them [corporately] for open transgressions until they had crossed the Jordan.[55]

Meiri rules in accordance with R. Judah's view. The practical implication of this view, he says, is that society's judges, sages, and leaders must do more than simply deal with the issues brought to them. Rather, they must search out and deal with hidden wrongdoings and take measures to remedy the misconduct they discover. Failure to search out hidden wrongs makes the entire community vulnerable to punishment for the sins of evildoers.[56] It follows that government has the duty of ensuring that society's legal environment minimizes settings for invisible misconduct.

Lifnei Iver and Legislation

Another aspect of the government's responsibility for the moral climate is the prohibition against the enactment of laws which inherently generate settings for veiled misconduct. An analysis of the following dictum by Rav, recorded at Bava Meẓia 75b, bears out this prohibition.

> Said R. Judah in the name of Rav: Whoever has money and lends it without witnesses violates the prohibition of "Do not place a stumbling block before the blind" (*lifnei iver lo titen mikshol*; Leviticus 19:14). Resh Lakish said: He brings a curse upon himself, as it is written, "Let the lying lips be put to silence; which speak grievous things proudly and contemptuously against the righteous" (Psalms 31:19).

When a loan transaction takes place without the formality of witnesses, the borrower can eliminate his debt by denying that the transaction took place. This being so, lending money without witnesses is prohibited. To do otherwise, explains Rashi (R. Solomon b. Isaac, Troyes, 1040–1105), would effectively tempt the debtor to repudiate his lawful debt and hence the lender would be in violation of the interdict against *lifnei iver*.[57]

Picking up on Rashi's remarks, R. Joel Sirkes (Poland, 1561–1650) and R. Joshua b. Alexander ha-Kohen Falk (Poland, 1555–1614) understand Rav's dictum to be rooted in the concern that the debtor will *willfully* repudiate a debt which he knows to be a lawful one.

In the event the debtor is a *talmid ḥakham* (rabbinical scholar), the above concern does not exist. Therefore lending money to a *talmid ḥakham* without the formality of witnesses does not violate the *lifnei iver* interdict. The latter action is, nonetheless, prohibited by Resh Lakish's dictum. The concern here is that the *talmid ḥakham*'s preoccupation with his studies might cause him to forget his indebtedness and consequently lead him to deny the creditor's claim. Given the *talmid ḥakham*'s stature, his denials will find credence and the public will curse the lender.[58]

Disputing the preceding opinions, R. Abraham b. Moses di Boton (Salonika, 1545–1588) and R. Jacob Moses Lorberbaum (Lisa, 1760–1832) understand Rav's dictum to be rooted in the concern that the debtor might forget the loan and consequently deny the debt, all along convinced that the creditor's claim is false. This rationale applies whether or not the debtor is a *talmid ḥakham*.[59]

In defending his position that the concern for willful repudiation cannot stand at the basis of Rav's dictum, R. Boton invokes the talmudic principle that exhortations are never directed at those who are predisposed to willfully violate them (*atu b'reshiei askinan*). The basis of the application of the *lifnei iver* interdict to the making of an unwitnessed loan must therefore be the concern that the debtor might come to forget his obligation and consequently be led to deny it.[60]

A narrower understanding of *atu b'reshiei askinan*, however, follows from Rashi et al. Given the inherent futility of exhorting the willfully evil who do not care if their misconduct is discovered, the Torah never ascribes this character trait to the subjects of its exhortations. This is what is meant by the talmudic phrase *atu b'reshiei askinan*. The Torah does, however, direct its exhortations to the willfully evil who want to avoid social disapproval by covering up their misconduct. Witness that the phrase *ve yareta me-Eloheka* ("and you shall fear your God") is employed by the Torah specifically in connection with those of its prohibitions which man convinces himself he can violate without detection.[61]

Supporting the narrow interpretation of *atu b'reshiei askinan* is the connection the Talmud makes between this phrase and the *ve yareta me-Eloheka* exhortation employed in relation to the duty to give deference to a *talmid ḥakham* by standing up for him as he approaches.[62] Invoking *atu b'reshiei askinan*, The Talmud rejects the possibility that *ve yareta me-Eloheka* adjures against closing our eyes and pretending that the *talmid ḥakham* is not in our presence. Rather, *ve yareta me-Eloheka* forewarns against closing our eyes just before the talmid hakham arrives. Here, the willful sinner might be tempted to show the *talmid ḥakham* disrespect and yet imagine that by claiming that he simply did not notice his presence he will escape social outrage for the misconduct. Thus, the Torah forewarns that the Almighty knows man's true circumstances and true intentions.[63]

Proceeding from this concept of *atu b'reshiei askinan* is the following refinement of Rav's dictum: Lending money without the formality of witnesses is prohibited because such action generates for the debtor a setting for hidden misconduct. Since denying the debt outright brands the debtor an ingrate, there is no concern that the debtor will adopt this tactic. Such a brazen approach is unthinkable by dint of the principle of *atu b'reshiei askinan*. Rather, the concern is that the unwitnessed transaction will lead the debtor to shrewdly evade payment by pleading ignorance of the indebtedness.[64] By taking an oath affirming his ignorance of the debt, the defendant avoids the stigma of being branded an ingrate and at the same time gets out of paying.[65]

We see an application of Rav's dictum in the prohibition against government in a Torah society enacting a law which inherently generates settings for veiled misconduct.

Legislation In The Moral Sphere

Imitatio Dei makes government the guardian of the moral climate of society. One implication of this mandate is that it provides a rationale for government regulation of advertising. This point will be taken up in chapter 4.

Another implication of this mandate for government is the duty to design policies with the aim of fostering the moral personality. This topic will be the subject matter of chapter 5.

What *imitatio Dei* denotes for government in respect to specific economic issues is, however, somewhat problematic. The difficulty arises out of the consideration that the implementation of any particular rule of conduct is at the expense of the moral climate which would have been fostered under an alternative rule. In consequence, keen economic analysis to determine the opportunity cost of alternative courses of action is required. Moreover, God's mercy is designed for man's ultimate good.[66] Hence *imitatio Dei* disallows the confinement of economic policy-making to a short-run analysis. The long-term consequences of alternative courses of action must be evaluated. Given the limitations of extrapolating the direct and indirect consequences of any particular policy, the onus of persuasion facing those who propose change is imposing.

Notwithstanding these difficulties, *imitatio Dei* offers the following prescriptions for economic public policy:

1. The distribution of property rights which Halakhah calls for in any particular situation should not be altered legislatively when such a change would inherently create conflict of interest and veiled misconduct. Applications of this proposition arise in regard to insider trading and resale price maintenance. We take up these topics in chapters 6 and 7, respectively.

The government of the Torah society should not *subsidize* a social institution which fosters or allows conflicts of interest and hidden misconduct. An application of this principle, which we have dealt with elsewhere, is the treatment of the phenomenon of the leveraged buyout.[67]

2. When a choice must be made among competing policy alternatives and none of them will affect the distribution of property rights, the policy which fosters the superior moral climate must be preferred. An application of this proposition, which is taken up in chapter 8, is the treatment of unauthorized copying and dubbing.

In chapter 9 we offer the proposition that full employment and price stability are legitimate functions of government in the Torah society. Various nuances of *imitatio Dei* are developed in the course of the discussion.

•2
Minimum Wage Legislation

SINCE ITS ENACTMENT IN 1938, minimum wage legislation has been an integral part of the social welfare program of the United States government. Its underlying philosophy has always been to provide the working poor with a "living" wage. Our purpose here will be to consider the minimum wage concept from the perspective of Halakhah.

The Minimum Wage And Jewish Communal Legislation

Halakhah's attitude toward the minimum wage concept begins with a consideration of whether such a policy falls within the legislative prerogative of the Jewish community. Since the Jewish community is empowered to fix prices and wages,[1] setting a minimum wage falls squarely within its legislative prerogative. But since Halakhah does not mandate the minimum wage for Jewish society, the appropriateness of enacting such legislation must be considered carefully.

Halakhic Antipoverty Goals

The stated goal of minimum wage legislation, ensuring the working poor a "living" wage, is an objective Halakhah would fully embrace. In Jewish law, poverty prevention is an aspect of the charity obligation.[2] Indeed, preventing a faltering individual from falling into the throes of poverty is given first ranking by Maimonides (Egypt, 1135–1204) in his eight categories of charity. The position of someone in that predicament must be stabilized, with his dignity preserved, by either conferring a gift upon him, extending him a loan, entering a partnership with him, or creating a job for him.[3]

Minimum wage legislation, of course, takes the "invisible charity" concept beyond voluntarism to the level of a legislative mandate. Government involvement in the charity obligation, is, however, an integral part of the social welfare program of the Torah society. Specifically, Judaism's obligation of giving has both a public and a private component. In talmudic times the public component consisted of a variety of coercive levies for the purpose of attending to the full range of needs of the poor.[4] Public communal levies, however, were never entirely relied upon to relieve poverty. Evidence of this is the rule that a person in need may not apply for public relief until his relatives and neighbors have first helped him as best they can; only then is the community required to make up the deficiency.[5]

Another consequence of minimum wage legislation that Halakhah would embrace is the influence it exerts on the work-leisure trade-off. By setting the wage rate above the level it would attain if market forces were left to their own devices, minimum wage legislation influences the would-be welfare recipient to choose gainful employment over idleness. Judaism attaches a positive value to work.[6] Indicative of its disdain for idleness is the teaching that idleness brings on immorality.[7] Discouragement of idleness follows also from the halakhic disapproval of the "welfare mentality," as enunciated in Rav's advice to R. Kahana: "Flay carcasses in the marketplace and earn wages, and do not say, I am a priest and a great man, and it is beneath my dignity."[8]

Talmudic Precedents

The minimum wage concept apparently finds its counterpart in the product market in the talmudic ordinance which sets a one-sixth profit-rate limit for vendors dealing in commodities essential to human life (*ḥayyei nefesh*).[9] R. Joshua ha-Kohen Falk (Poland, 1555–1614) explains that this is based on the biblical injunction, "and let your brother live with you" (Leviticus 25:36).[10] According to this interpretation, the seller of essential foodstuffs should sacrifice some part of the potential profits he could realize so as to lessen the drain on the buyer's resources that a higher sales price would generate.

Hence, interfering with the natural workings of the marketplace for the purpose of promoting social welfare finds historical precedent in the talmudic essential foodstuffs ordinance.

Economic Analysis

Notwithstanding the agreement of the minimum wage concept with halakhic goals, economic analysis demonstrates that this goal cannot be achieved. Moreover, examination of the distributional consequences of the minimum wage law places this rule in conflict with the equity rules Halakhah sets for financing social welfare projects. Finally, economic analysis uncovers a basic difference between the minimum wage concept and the talmudic foodstuffs ordinance. This distinction will, in turn, dispel any notion that the minimum wage concept finds precedence in the ancient foodstuffs ordinance.

Economists generally have been critical of minimum wage legislation. The primary argument against such legislation is its effects on employment opportunities. As the wage rate is increased, employers' demand for labor will fall. There will be fewer job opportunities. Those who remain employed do gain a higher wage rate, but at the expense of those who are no longer employed.

The negative employment effects occur in direct response to various measures employers undertake to counteract the higher labor costs the minimum wage entails for them.

One response might be to cut back on the production of goods and services. For example, in response to the boosts in the minimum wage between 1977 and 1981, many fast-food restaurants cut back on off-peak work crews. With fewer employees working at certain hours, this meant that some customers had to wait longer to be served. A few of the large restaurant chains decided to close earlier at some locations.

Another way to cut back labor usage is to have customers perform more services for themselves. Many fast-food restaurants, for example, have eliminated table service. Customers, in effect, wait on themselves. Many service stations have installed self-service gasoline pumps. Customers are given the option of pumping their own gasoline at a reduced price or getting full service at a higher price. The elimination of many delivery services is yet another example.

A third method designed to reduce the use of labor services is automation—the use of machinery in place of people. For example, it is thought that the shift from manually operated to automatic elevators was spurred by a rising minimum wage.[11]

We should note that the brunt of the unemployment effect described above is borne by teenagers. This occurs because about 40 percent of the teenagers who work are working at the minimum wage. In addition, at the higher minimum wage, employers are often able to attract adult workers to take the place of teenagers. Older workers are generally more productive and stay on the job longer. By hiring older workers, employers can cut both hiring and training costs.[12]

The Minimum Wage as an Antipoverty Program

The major goal of minimum wage legislation, as mentioned earlier, is to reduce poverty for the working poor. Available evidence suggests, however, that the minimum wage has had little net effect on poverty and the distribution of income. A combination of three factors points to this conclusion. First, the wage gains resulting from minimum wage legislation, as indicated earlier, are somewhat offset by the negative employment effects. Second, the wage gains are small relative to the total income of the poor; and third, many of those who gain from the minimum wage are children or other secondary earners in reasonably well-to-do families, families where the household head has a well-paying job.[13]

The Minimum Wage and On-the-Job Training

Minimum wage legislation also has a negative impact in regard to on-the-job training. Higher minimum wage rates give employers incentives to reduce on-the-job training. Unless an employer captures 100 percent of the benefit of such training, a portion of its cost is usually paid for by the worker in the form of a lower wage (but not below the legally binding minimum). Thus younger workers get fewer jobs, and those who get jobs have fewer opportunities over the years to convert an essentially flat income stream to one that is rising because of the improved productivity that on-the-job training stimulates.[14]

The Minimum Wage and Discrimination

Still another adverse effect of minimum wage legislation is that it exacerbates the problem of discrimination. With the number of workers wanting to work at the minimum wage exceeding the number of workers firms want to hire, employers who harbor prejudices will be able to discriminate at zero cost.[15]

The Minimum Wage and Job Security

Finally, with the option of cutting wages eliminated under minimum wage legislation, the job security of low-income workers becomes more vulnerable during an economic downturn.[16]

Thus, despite its widespread perception as a humanitarian gesture, minimum wage legislation is a poor means of promoting the interests of low-income workers.

The Minimum Wage and Distributional Justice

The preceding analysis points to another halakhic objection to the minimum wage. Since the *raison d'être* of the minimum wage is its antipoverty objective, Halakhah would apparently call for this measure to be financed by the same equity benchmark it invokes for all social welfare legislation. This benchmark consists of a broad-based proportional wealth tax.[17] Far from mandating the practice of "invisible charity" in a broad-based fashion proportional to wealth, the minimum wage imposes this obligation only on employers. They, in turn, can be expected to attempt to minimize the burden of higher labor costs by either reducing labor usage or raising prices. The negative employment effects of the minimum wage are, of course, borne by low-income households. The same households bear a disproportionate burden of any increase in the price level occasioned by the minimum wage law. This follows from the fact that any inflationary consequence resulting from the minimum wage is effectively a tax on consumption, and consumption spending is a declining fraction of income as income rises.

The Profit Constraint On Foodstuffs Vendors

It was earlier stated that the minimum wage apparently has a halakhic precedent in the talmudic constraint on the profits of vendors of foodstuffs. Just as economic analysis attacks minimum wage legislation as self-defeating, the same conclusion is in order with respect to the talmudic foodstuffs ordinance. We need only point out that interference with market forces carries with it the danger of creating a shortage, with the consequence of making completely unavailable to the poor the very items we want them to obtain at low prices. This condition will obtain when the price ceiling inherent in the profit constraint fails to coax out a supply equal to the demand. With price deprived of its rationing function, substitute mechanisms will emerge to allocate the available supply among the demanders. In the absence of governmentally supervised rationing, queuing and/or a black market will emerge to correct the imbalance between supply and demand. The latter two mechanisms will all but ensure that the poor will disproportionately go without the regulated items. Since the sages did not attach a rationing provision to the ordinance, the regulation would be expected, at times, to work against the interests of the poor.

The affinity between the foodstuffs ordinance and the minimum wage concept, however, dissipates when we examine various details of the talmudic edict. The exact design of the foodstuffs ordinance is both a matter of dispute and subject to interpretation. Adopting a particular viewpoint with respect to several critical details of this regulation minimizes the prospect that its operation would generate shortages.

Market Forces

One critical issue is whether the ordinance was directed at individual vendors in the foodstuffs sector or was translated into a price-fixing obligation for this sector by the Jewish court. Adopting the former view, R. Jacob b. Asher (Toledo, 1270–1340), R. Joseph Caro (Safed, 1488–1575), and R. Jeḥiel Michel Epstein (Belorussia, 1829–1908) regard the role of the court with respect to this ordinance to consist of the enforcement of the one-sixth profit-rate constraint on individual vendors.[18] Moreover, these decisors take the position that the regulation does not work to prohibit vendors from selling at the current market norm.[19] If, for instance, market forces push the price of wheat above its harvest-time level, vendors may sell at the current price, despite any windfall above the one-sixth profit constraint they will realize thereby. Taken together, these two elements of the ordinance lead to the thesis that the edict was never designed to intentionally create a disequilibrium price. What the profit constraint amounts to, then, may be nothing more than a maximum mark-up directive to vendors of foodstuffs, which can be suspended if market forces so dictate.

If the foodstuffs ordinance allows market forces free rein, then its practical significance is merely to prohibit sellers from collusively restricting supply for the purpose of raising their profit margins above the one-sixth level. Hence the ordinance restricts both cartelization and restraint-of-trade practices by the monopoly firm in the essential foodstuffs industry.

We should note that the authorities cited above all record that the foodstuffs ordinance called for the appointment of market commissioners by the court to monitor the regulated sector.[20] If the ordinance was never intended to countermand market conditions, then the role of the market officials, it appears, must merely have been to enforce the competitive norm. Without this monitoring, ignorance of market conditions could have resulted in transactions concluded in divergence from the competitive norm.

To be sure, judicial redress is often open to victims of price divergence of this sort in the form of an *ona'ah* (overreaching) claim.[21] But the *ona'ah* claim is at best an ex post facto remedy. Legal technicalities often make it difficult for a complainant to legally recover losses on account of *ona'ah*. Moreover, many instances of *ona'ah* go undetected by the victim. Out of concern for the subsistence needs of the masses, the sages added another layer of consumer protection in the foodstuffs sector. Price commissioners were assigned for the purpose of enforcing market price and preventing instances of *ona'ah*.

Preventing and breaking up collusive arrangements among sellers would be another role assigned to the price commissioners in the essential foodstuffs sector.

Labor Costs

Another critical issue is whether an allowance for the implicit labor costs of the owner is included in the cost base against which the one-sixth profit-rate constraint is calculated. The widely held view is that if the owner provides his labor services on a continuous basis, i.e., a retailer, an allowance for the labor services is included in the base.[22] Presumably the return is limited to the competitive rate for the type of work performed. Inclusion of implicit wages in the cost base may amount to a "safety margin" to ensure that the foodstuffs ordinance does not work to create shortages.

Since the sages did not call for any allowance for implicit wages for the wholesalers, the safety margin is apparently absent for this segment of the foodstuffs market. The failure to make provision for implicit wages here was probably due to a conviction on the part of the framers of the ordinance that wholesalers provided no useful social service.

The preceding assertion is explicitly invoked by R. Jeḥiel Michel Epstein in rationalizing a related talmudic ordinance which prohibited middlemen dealing in essential commodities in the Land of Israel from earning a mark-up unless they in some way processed the products they purchased.[23] Standing behind this ordinance, according to R. Epstein, was the conviction that producers themselves were capable of handling the function of supplying the market for the entire year.[24] The ordinance was accordingly meant to drive middlemen out of the market, thus promoting lower prices for essential foodstuffs in the Land of Israel.

It follows from R. Epstein's thesis that Halakhah would today adopt quite a different attitude toward wholesalers in the agricultural sector. In sharp contrast to talmudic times, when agricultural production served a predominantly local market,[25] agricultural production today is mainly for the regional, national, or international market. Warehousing and distribution are clearly differentiated from production. Without middlemen performing the former two functions, the economic viability of the agricultural sector could not be assured. Given the social usefulness of wholesalers in the agricultural sector today, Halakhah would apparently regard as legitimate an expansion of the wholesaler's cost base to include a return for his labor services.

Unprocessed Foodstuffs

One final aspect of the design of the foodstuffs ordinance which would work to minimize the prospect of shortages is the possibility that the price of unprocessed foodstuffs is entirely unregulated. This point emerges from the analysis of the following talmudic passage at Bava Batra 9a by R. Simeon b. Samuel of Joinville (12th–13th cent.):

> Our rabbis taught: It is not permitted to make a profit in eggs twice. [As to the meaning of "twice"] Mari b. Mari said: Rav [d. 247] and Samuel [d. 254] are in dispute. One says: Two for one [100 percent profit margin], and the other says: [selling] by a dealer to a dealer.

Commenting on the opinion that limits the profit rate in the egg industry to less than 100 percent, Tosafot ask why the egg industry is set apart from other industries dealing in essential foodstuffs, wherein the profit constraint is one-sixth. Addressing himself to this dilemma, R. Simeon posits that unprocessed foodstuffs are usually not subject to any mandatory profit limitation. The egg industry, however, provides an exception to this rule. Egg farmers must limit their mark-up to less than 100 percent.[26]

If the price of unprocessed foodstuffs is unregulated, then yet another "safety margin" exists for the foodstuffs ordinance to ensure that its operation would not work to produce shortages.

Consideration of the various features of the foodstuffs ordinance outlined above suggests that the profit ceiling was never meant to interfere with what the suppliers could earn in their next-best market alternatives. Economic theory calls these earnings "opportunity cost earnings," and earnings above that level "economic rent." If the ordinance was intended only to set a maximum for economic rent, its operation presents no problem of economic inefficiency.

Maimonides on the Foodstuffs Ordinance

Examination of Maimonides' presentation of the foodstuffs ordinance makes the thesis just discussed difficult to sustain. Unlike the authorities cited above, Maimonides specifically identifies the foodstuffs ordinance with a price-fixing obligation on the part of the Jewish court.[27] Accordingly, the role of the market commissioners is to enforce the official prices set by the court.

Moreover, in his own conceptualization of the ordinance, Maimonides does not mention that the Jewish court is required, or at least has the discretion, to upwardly adjust the price when it is evident that the prevailing norm is creating shortages. Finally, in his treatment of the cost base, Maimonides makes no mention of a return for the labor services of the owner. Noting the later lacuna, R. Joel Sirkes (Poland, 1561–1650) posits that the one-sixth profit rate, in Maimonides' view, is the return the owner receives for his labor services.[28]

The inefficiency inherent in Maimonides' formulation of the foodstuffs ordinance is somewhat attenuated by the fact that he regarded the community's price-fixing authority as superseding any price requirement proceeding from the foodstuffs ordinance. That the price requirement proceeding from the ordinance is not inviolate in Maimonides' view is seen from the following ruling:

> The residents of a city may agree among themselves to fix a price on any article they desire, even on meat and bread, and to stipulate that they will inflict such-and-such penalty upon one who violates the agreement.[29]

Price-fixing legislation in the foodstuffs sector obviously may come into conflict with the prescribed one-sixth profit constraint. Maimonides' failure to qualify communal legislative authority in this regard clearly indicates that, in his view, communal price-fixing authority is absolute and may, if necessary, supersede the profit-rate constraint rabbinically mandated for foodstuffs. Hence the community's price-fixing authority represents a means of correcting any commodity shortage that may arise out of the operation of the foodstuffs ordinance.

The Minimum Wage And Teenage Unemployment

Of all the adverse effects of minimum wage legislation, the negative impact on teenage employment is perhaps the most serious. In America a high value is placed on teenage employment. By getting and keeping jobs, teenagers learn the crucial importance of good work habits. For many of them, these simple work habits do not come naturally and are often not learned at home. Employers are aware of this, and as a result some record of employability—even at a "dead end" job—is often essential in order to get a better job. Before employers will risk investing in employees through an on-the-job training program, they will typically want some evidence of successful past performance.

By contrast, teenagers who do not hold steady jobs often fail to learn even the most basic work habits essential to any career. Instead, they may adopt a life-style detrimental to their long-run self-interest. The welfare syndrome and a life of crime are often very real alternatives to productive work, and the minimum wage law may be a major factor influencing the choices that generations of young people are making.[30]

Concern for teenage employment played a key role in shaping the design of the 1989 change in the minimum wage law. While raising the minimum wage to $3.80 per hour in 1990 and $4.25 in 1991, it provided for a "training" wage (equal to 85 percent of the minimum wage) for inexperienced teenagers during the first ninety days on the job.

While American society places a premium on teenage employment, the Torah society regards Torah study as the ideal occupation for teenagers. This proposition follows from the central role Judaism assigns Torah study in the life experience.

Expressing the ideal that Halakhah establishes regarding Torah study are the guidelines of R. Mosheh Isserles (Poland, 1525 or 1530–1572):

> And man should not entertain the thought that he can preoccupy himself in Torah study as well as acquire wealth and honor. Anyone who entertains such thoughts will not merit the crown of Torah. Instead, Torah study should be his main preoccupation, and the pursuit of a livelihood secondary. And he should minimize his livelihood activities and preoccupy himself in Torah study; and remove from his heart the lure of the blandishments of the moment, and should work sufficiently every day for his subsistence in the event he does not have what to eat, with what remains of the day and night devoted to Torah study. It is a mark of high distinction if one supports

himself from his own toil, as it says: "The labor of your hands, when you eat of that, then you shall stride forward and the good will be yours" (Psalms 128:2).[31]

If the ideal is to maximize the time spent on Torah study, it follows that in the absence of economic pressure to support a family, an individual must opt for Torah study instead of gainful employment. Indeed, Halakhah generally recommends that young men should postpone marriage in order to fully concentrate on Torah study without the necessity to pursue a livelihood.[32]

Encouraging unmarried males to choose Torah study over gainful employment follows from another consideration. One aspect of the miẓvah of Talmud Torah is the obligation of the father to teach his son Torah.[33] This miẓvah continues to devolve upon the father even after his son has reached adulthood, i.e., thirteen years.[34] While public funds cannot be used to finance Talmud Torah for adults,[35] encouraging the father to support the Torah studies of his teenage son is certainly in order.

We should note that the ideal of Talmud Torah includes Torah study for women as well. Notwithstanding the generally discouraging attitude of the sages of the past in respect to teaching Torah to women, changing social conditions have convinced modern-day halakhists of the dire need to organize Torah study in a formal setting for girls.[36]

Providing a historical precedent for a social-engineering policy designed to maximize Torah study is the analysis of the talmudic ordinance regarding the preferential commercial rights of rabbinical scholars by R. Asher b. Jeḥiel (Germany, ca. 1250–1327). The special treatment consists of disallowing competing firms to offer their wares on the market until the rabbinical scholar has managed to sell out his inventory.[37]

Why rabbinical scholars are conferred special trading rights is a matter of dispute. Maimonides posits that the courtesy proceeds from the biblical obligation to confer honor on rabbinical scholars.[38] R. Asher, however, views the measure as a means of minimizing the time lost from Torah study. Rabbinical scholars, in contrast to their commercial competitors, normally spend their time in Torah study. Extending the rabbinical scholar a temporary monopoly license allows him to minimize the time he must devote to earning a livelihood, thereby maximizing the time he spends on Torah study.[39]

Minimum wage legislation, as we discussed earlier, will bias employers in favor of heads of households at the expense of teenagers. Hence the incentive system of the marketplace under minimum wage legislation promotes the halakhic goal of inducing teenagers to engage in Torah study. The flip side of this proposition is that a subminimum "training" wage for teenagers sets in motion, from the standpoint of Halakhah, a perverse incentive system.

The Minimum Wage and Jewish Law

The minimum wage represents a noble attempt to raise the living standards of the working poor. Its work-incentive effect on the poor as well as its "invisible charity" intent are antipoverty goals Halakhah would readily embrace. Economic analysis, however, demonstrates that the minimum wage will not achieve these goals. Moreover, its regressive distributional consequences lead to another halakhic objection. On the other hand, one consequence of the minimum wage, namely, its effect of biasing employers in favor of heads of households as opposed to teenagers, would find favor in the halakhic society. Available jobs would be allocated to those under the greatest economic pressure to earn a livelihood. While teenagers are shut out of the labor market, they are simultaneously induced to devote their time to fulfilling their obligation to engage in Torah study.

The Wage-Rate Subsidy and Halakhah

In this section we will discuss a variant of the minimum wage concept called the wage-rate subsidy. We will demonstrate that it offers the prospect of meeting the halakhic concerns, discussed earlier, for a program aimed at improving the economic well-being of the working poor. John Bishop has written extensively on the wage-rate subsidy.[40] The design of the wage-rate subsidy which we present below draws on his work.

The wage-rate subsidy is a government supplement of a worker's hourly wage. The per-hour payment is equal to a percentage (the subsidy rate, r) of the difference between some target wage

(*TW*) and the worker's actual wage (*W*). The total payment would then be: subsidy = $r(TW - W)$ x hours worked.

With the aim of having the wage-rate subsidy serve as an antipoverty program for the working poor, eligibility could be restricted to heads of households. To ensure that the subsidy would be adequate, the targeted wage would be made to increase with the number of children in the household.

Since the wage-rate subsidy is financed by means of an income tax, it satisfies Halakhah's equity benchmark for the financing of an antipoverty program. Unlike the minimum wage, which mandates the practice of invisible charity only on employers, the wage rate subsidy enlists the support of the entire society.

While the antipoverty objective of the wage-rate subsidy requires that the government subsidy be higher for low-paying jobs than for higher-paying ones, a work-incentive feature can easily be incorporated. This is done by so structuring the program as to allow the higher-paying job to attain higher final earnings than the lower-paying job. To illustrate: A earns $3.50 per hour. His subsidy is $1 per hour. B earns $4.50 per hour. His subsidy is only $0.75 per hour. While B's subsidy is $0.25 less than A's, B's final earnings of $5.25 per hour are higher than A's final earnings of $4.50 per hour.

Since the economic-incentive feature encourages recipients to make themselves qualified for the higher-paying jobs, wage-rate subsidy fosters the value of self-help in societal efforts to relieve poverty. Elsewhere we have developed the thesis that self-help is an essential component of Judaism's antipoverty program.[41]

From the standpoint of Halakhah, the wage-rate subsidy has several other attractive features as an antipoverty program. These include the preservation of the dignity of the poor and the promotion of marital stability. Since the worker receives the subsidy as part of his paycheck, being the beneficiary of a governmental supplement will escape stigma. Moreover, raising the wage of the family's breadwinner will magnify the importance of his contribution to the family. Social-psychological theory predicts that this should promote marital stability in families holding traditional views of man's role.[42]

• 3

Comparable Worth

ONE OF THE MOST EXPLOSIVE current civil rights issues is the "equal pay for comparable worth" movement. This doctrine demands that work be compensated in accordance with its inherent worth. Instead of giving market forces free rein, comparable worth advocates would set relative wage rates on the basis of such criteria as skill, effort, responsibility, and working conditions. More than 150 initiatives are underway to force this wage policy on government in forty states and fifty-two municipalities.

In this chapter, we will first delineate the inroads the comparable worth movement has made thus far in the American economy and then extrapolate the perspective Halakhah takes on this issue.

Comparable Worth In American Society

Comparable worth finds its legislative beginning in the United States with the passage of the Equal Pay Act of 1963. This act prohibits employers from compensating women less than men when both are performing equal work on the employer's premises, except when the greater pay is justified by a widely accepted standard, such as seniority, merit, or output. Title VII of the Civil Rights Act of 1964 reinforced the basic intent of the Equal Pay Act by setting forth a general ban on employment practices that discriminate on the basis of race, color, religion, sex, or national origin.

Judicial interpretation of the Equal Pay Act has developed a two-pronged standard for deciding whether two jobs are equal: they must have a substantial common core of work tasks, and they must require equivalent skill, effort, and responsibility for the work tasks they do not have in common.[1]

Court interpretation of the comparable worth dimension of the above criteria has worked to limit the operational significance of the Equal Pay Act. In *Hodgson* v. *Brookhaven General Hospital*, the court held that two jobs are not equal if one of them involves additional tasks which consume a significant amount of the time of those receiving the higher pay and have economic value commensurate with the pay differential.[2]

In *Hodgson* v. Robert Hall Inc., the employer was paying male salespersons a higher wage than female salespersons who were performing equal work. The court ruled that the wage discrimination did not violate the Equal Pay Act. Merit was found in Robert Hall's contention that the differential was justified on the basis of the greater economic value of male salespersons. Specifically, the men's clothing department had a greater average sales volume and profit per salesperson than the women's department.[3]

In the 1980s comparable worth advocates attempted to push this doctrine beyond its recognition in the Equal Pay Act, demanding that dissimilar work should be subject to job evaluation. Jobs scoring equal points on the basis of skill, effort, responsibility, and working conditions should be compensated equally.

Comparative worth advocates scored a major victory in a 1983 case, *AFSCME* v. *State of Washington*. Relying on an earlier state-sponsored study which found that jobs that tended to be filled by women systematically earned 20 percent less than comparable jobs held by men, the federal district court ruled that 15,000 Washington state employees were entitled to immediate raises and back pay to remedy years of discriminatory treatment.[4] In 1985, however, a federal appeals court in San Francisco reversed the district court's decision, noting that market forces, and not government, were responsible for the wage disparities. The court ruled that the state was under no obligation to "eliminate an economic inequality which it did not create."[5]

The Equal Pay Act And Jewish Law

Sex-based discrimination in employment is treated in Jewish law as part of the broader issue of wage discrimination. The ethics of paying workers unequal wages for performing the same tasks is discussed in the talmudic literature under the rubric of *ona'ah* (price discrepancy).

Before relating the law of *ona'ah* to the labor market, we take note that Halakhah classifies an employee as either a day laborer (*po'el*) or a piece-worker (*kabbelan*). What distinguishes the *po'el* from the *kabbelan* is the provision for fixed working hours. While the *po'el*'s contract obligates him to perform work for his employer at specified hours over a given time period, no such clause is included in the *kabbelan*'s agreement.[6] Given the controlling nature of the fixed-hours factor, the absence of this provision retains *kabbelan* status for an employee even when his contract calls for him to complete the project by a specified date.[7]

In his discussion of the law of *ona'ah* as it pertains to the labor market, Maimonides (Egypt, 1135–1204) rules that *ona'ah* applies only to a *kabbelan* and not to a *po'el*.[8] Several strands of *ona'ah* law underlie this ruling. Exegetical interpretation of the source of the *ona'ah* prohibition, "When you sell property to your neighbor, or buy any from the hand of your neighbor" (Leviticus 25:14), establishes that the prohibition applies only to something which is acquired (by being passed) from "hand to hand"—excluding land. Since slaves are assimilated to land,[9] the exemption extends to transactions involving slaves.[10]

Another point of the law of *ona'ah* is that the prohibition applies not only to an outright permanent sale but to rental and hire. The rationale for this extension is that rental and hire are in effect a "sale" for the duration of the lease.[11] Consequently, whenever the law of *ona'ah* does not apply to a particular sales transaction, it also does not apply to the corresponding rental transaction. Given that the status of a *po'el* is regarded halakhically as akin, in certain respects, to slavery, the law of *ona'ah* does not apply to the hiring of a *po'el*.[12]

Another authority who formulates the *po'el*'s *ona'ah* exemption in blanket terms is R. Israel b. Pethahiah Isserlein (Germany, 1390–1460). Advancing his own rationale, R. Isserlein avers that the exemption is rooted in the impossibility of assigning a precise market value to the *po'el*'s services, as the employer would pay a premium for the services of a *po'el* when the work at hand requires immediate attention, failing which a material loss (*davar ha-avud*) would result. Similarly, finding himself in economic straits, a job seeker would presumably accept a less than competitive wage.[13]

While blanket exclusion of the *po'el* from the law of *ona'ah* follows from both Maimonides and R. Isserlein, the issue is far from conclusive. Maimonides, as will be recalled, ultimately bases the *po'el*'s *ona'ah* exclusion on the assimilation of slaves to immovable property. While Maimonides holds that the immovable-property *ona'ah* exclusion is absolute,[14] many other Rishonim do not share this view. R. Eliezer b. Samuel of Metz (ca. 1115–ca. 1198) and others, for instance, take the position that a price variance of more than 100 percent allows a plaintiff to void the immovable-property transaction.[15] R. Jacob Tam (ca. 1100–1171) and others vest the plaintiff with this right even if the price discrepancy is exactly 100 percent.[16] Finally, "some authorities," quoted by R. Isaac b. Jacob Alfasi and R. Asher b. Jeḥiel, allow the plaintiff to invalidate the agreement even when the price discrepancy is more than one-sixth.[17] Thus, if the *ona'ah* exemption of the *po'el* ultimately rests on the immovable-property exclusion, blanket exclusion for the *po'el* does not obtain.

However, Naḥmanides, in his discussion of the immovable-property exemption, asserts that the exemption pertains only to the restitution procedure normally prescribed, but not to the prohibition against knowingly contracting into *ona'ah*.[18] Now, if the *ona'ah* exemption of the *po'el* is rooted in the immovable-property exclusion, both the *ona'ah* prohibition and the restitution procedure, albeit in truncated form, may very well apply to this segment of the labor market.

We should note that despite the diversity of opinion as to whether the *ona'ah* claim is to be honored in the immovable-property market, and, if so, to what extent, R. Shabbetai b. Meir ha-Kohen (Poland, 1621–1662) rules in accordance with Maimonides.[19] The import of this ruling is to deny the plaintiff judicial remedy for an *ona'ah* claim in the *po'el* labor market as well. Judicial nonintervention in respect to *ona'ah* claims in the *po'el* labor market effectively leaves compliance to the prohibition against contracting into an *ona'ah* agreement, as formulated by Naḥmanides, i.e., to a system of voluntary compliance.

Voluntary compliance may, however, prove ineffectual in preventing widespread violations of *ona'ah* in the *po'el* labor market.

Correcting the abuses of Halakhah by means of remedial legislation may therefore be indicated. In order to determine the appropriate design of such legislation, however, we must first discover the basis of the *ona'ah* claim. Elsewhere, we have developed the thesis that the availability of a better market opportunity for the plaintiff at the time he entered into the disputed transaction stands as the basis of the *ona'ah* claim.[20] Regulating the internal labor market of a firm would therefore appear to be the primary target for legislation designed to end perceived widespread abuses of *ona'ah*. Legislation pertaining to *ona'ah*, accordingly, would prohibit a firm, during a given hiring period, from engaging in wage discrimination with respect to a particular job title. Coverage under the legislation would apply when both the job title and the qualifications for the job are well-defined. Under these conditions, anyone hired for the position could legitimately compare himself to other people hired by the firm for the same position. If a complainant was hired at a lower wage than his colleagues, the opportunity-cost basis of his *ona'ah* claim would be readily apparent. Had the plaintiff known that his employer was paying someone else a higher wage for the same job title, intensive bargaining might very well have raised the employer's offer.

We should note that *ona'ah* legislation in no way constrains a firm from instituting a pay scale based on such criteria as seniority, merit, or output. Such criteria merely identify differentiation within the firm's own internal labor market. Establishing pay increments on the basis of artificial or vague criteria, however, amounts to no more than a circumvention of the law of *ona'ah*.

Ona'ah and the External Labor Market

An *ona'ah* claim based on the external labor market runs into two difficulties. It is necessary to defend the appropriateness of regarding the comparison job and the job at hand as belonging to the same labor market. In addition, the plaintiff must prove that he incurred an opportunity cost.

Illustrating the difficulty of proving an opportunity cost when the *ona'ah* claim is based on the external labor market is the following case: Mesader, a recent law school graduate, secures a job at Emet (a small, newly established law firm) at a salary of $60,000. Subsequent to learning that the starting salary at Yatsiv (a large, well-established law firm) is $75,000, Mesader lodges an *ona'ah* claim against Emet. Emet counters that employment at Yatsiv was not a viable alternative for Mesader, as this firm hires only the top graduating students from the most prestigious law schools. Mesader's credentials, Emet contends, would not even gain him an interview with Yatsiv.

Slightly changing the assumptions of our model demonstrates the difficulty of identifying the relevant labor market for the purpose of adjudicating the *ona'ah* claim. Suppose Mesader's credentials qualify him to be hired at Yatsiv. Instead of applying at Yatsiv, Mesader interviews with Emet and manages to negotiate a salary higher than what Yatsiv pays for the same job title. Subsequently, Emet lodges an *ona'ah* claim against Mesader. The defendant counters that as far as the *ona'ah* claim is concerned, Emet and Yatsiv should not be considered to be in the same labor market. Given the marketplace's aversion to risk, Yatsiv employees would only be interested in working for Emet at the same higher salary he negotiated for himself. Yatsiv employees purposely trade off the prospect of a higher salary for the security, prestige, and possibilities for advancement that employment at Yatsiv entails.

We should note that in respect to one segment of the internal labor market, Halakhah specifically mandates a discriminatory wage scale. Compensation for a religious functionary hired by the community must be in accordance with his need.[21] Need takes into account both family size and the cost of living.[22]

R. Jacob Tam, however, limits the operational significance of this imperative. In his view, it applies only when the arrangement calls for the functionary to devote his time exclusively to the communal religious duties.[23]

Revealed Preference and the Ona'ah Claim

Within the framework of a differentiated labor market, a job seeker may find a particular feature of an employment opportunity so appealing that he is willing to accept the offer, forgoing the possibility of securing a higher salary elsewhere by continuing the search process. If a job seeker exclaims at a job interview that a particular feature of the employment opportunity at hand makes the salary offer well worth it, this may work to nullify any subsequent *ona'ah* claim. Analysis of the following talmudic text at Bava Meẓia 58b is most relevant in this regard:

> R. Judah said, . . . an animal or a pearl is not subject to *ona'ah*, because one desires to match them. Said they [the sages] to him, but one wishes to match up everything! And R. Judah? These are particularly important to him [the purchaser]; others are not. And to what extent? Said Amemar: up to their value.

Interpreting R. Judah's argument that "one desires to match them," Rashi (R. Solomon b. Isaac, 1040–1145) comments that the productivity of a strong, healthy work animal is adversely affected when it is teamed together with a weak, indolent beast. Realizing this, the owner of a strong work animal seeks to harness his beast with an animal of like nature. Similarly, the owner of a precious jewel seeks to enhance its beauty by combining it in the same setting with another stone.[24] Given the strong likelihood that the acquisition of an animal or a pearl affords the purchaser this advantage, R. Judah denies the plaintiff's *ona'ah* claim.

The sages reject R. Judah's reasoning on the grounds that the purchase of any commodity may involve complementarities in consumption. Just as price-discrepancy claims are normally not denied on the basis of possible complementarities in consumption enjoyed by the injured party, so too should the *ona'ah* claim not be discarded on these grounds when the sale object is an animal or a pearl. The import of R. Judah's rejoinder is clear. Compared to other commodities, the likelihood that the purchase generated complementarities in consumption is much stronger when the sale object is an animal or a pearl.

While most talmudic decisors reject R. Judah's position in favor of the sages' view,[25] R. Aaron Walkin (Pinsk, 1865–1942) suggests that perhaps R. Judah's view should not be discarded entirely. What leads him to this hypothesis is the ruling by R. Yom Tov Ishbili (Spain, 1270–1342) that the buyer forfeits any subsequent *ona'ah* claim if he declares at the time he enters into the transaction that the purchase is subjectively worth to him the entire sum demanded.[26] Rather than understand R. Ishbili's view as following R. Judah's minority position,[27] R. Walkin posits that when a buyer makes an explicit declaration of subjective equivalence at the time he enters into the transaction, everyone is in agreement that the declaration amounts to a waiver of any possible *ona'ah* claim.[28]

Reconciliation of R. Walkin's insight with the opportunity-cost basis of the *ona'ah* claim is readily possible under the assumption that the declaration of subjective equivalence nullifies a subsequent *ona'ah* claim only when the product market involved is heterogenous. Here, the declaration amounts to a statement of willingness to discontinue further market search for the item at hand out of fear that continuation of the search may result in making the exact item at hand unavailable. If the product market is homogeneous, the declaration of subjective equivalence cannot be understood as an expression of fear that further market search might jeopardize the availability of the item at hand. Rather, it merely amounts to an admission on the part of the buyer that for him the purchase entails a windfall. Given the availability of the identical item elsewhere, the purchaser's declaration of subjective equivalence should not nullify a subsequent *ona'ah* claim, as the purchase entailed an opportunity cost for him.

Let us now apply R. Walkin's insight, along the lines we have suggested, to the labor market. Suppose that in the course of his interview with Emet, Mesader expresses initial dissatisfaction with their $60,000 salary offer. Upon learning that Yashar, his former law school professor, is now a partner at Emet, Mesader changes his attitude sharply. Recalling his brilliant academic record in Yashar's class as well as the close personal relationship he established with him, Mesader excitedly exclaims that working under Yashar makes the salary offer well worth it for him. Subsequent to accepting Emet's offer, Mesader learns that Yatsiv pays $75,000 for the same job title. While there is no denying that Mesader qualifies for the Yatsiv position, his statement that he attaches a monetary value to working under his former professor amounts to a declaration that this feature of the Emet position makes it worthwhile for him to end his search for a job. The possibility of landing a higher-paying job is traded off for the elimination of the risk of ending up with a job with an unpredictable work environment. The *ona'ah* claim is hence denied.

Labor Exploitation In Economic Theory And Halakhah

In a competitive labor market, the firm has no control over the price of labor and therefore takes the wage rate of a particular labor skill as a given. To maximize profits, it hires workers of a particular skill up to the point where the anticipated increase in total revenue it stands to gain by the hiring, called the marginal revenue product of that worker (MRP), is just equal to the increase in total cost the contemplated hiring entails.

Labor exploitation occurs when the worker is remunerated in accordance with his minimum wage demand rather than with the MRP of the last worker of his skill hired. One circumstance that produces this result is the monopsony case. Here, only a single employer bids for the services of all the workers in a given labor market. Since the labor force does not benefit from competitive bidding among employers, the wage rate declines to the wage demand of the last worker hired.

Monopsony power similarly occurs when employers band together into a cartel and act as a single unit in hiring a particular skill, e.g., electricians. Here, too, the wage rate the workers receive will fall below the MRP of the last worker hired.

Adopting the view that *ona'ah* is essentially an opportunity-cost claim leads to the rejection, from the standpoint of Jewish law, of the kind of labor exploitation just described. Provided the worker did not incur an opportunity cost in his industry of employment as a result of entering into his present job, paying him below his MRP is not unethical per se. Moreover, if the job seeker is aware that the salary offer was tendered out of conviction that his MRP for the firm does not exceed that figure, this works to invalidate an otherwise legitimate *ona'ah* claim.

Supporting this argument is the case of the exemption from the law of *ona'ah* called selling on trust (*nose be-emunah*). Selling on trust occurs when the vendor divulges to a prospective buyer both his cost price and his proposed profit margin. Should the buyer agree to these terms and consummate the transaction with a *kinyan*, a subsequent finding that the final price involved *ona'ah* does not allow plaintiff to modify the original transaction in any manner.[29] By agreeing to allow the vendor a specified profit margin, the buyer demonstrates a lack of concern about the objective value of the commodity. Since realization of the agreed-upon profit rate required the sale to be concluded at the stipulated price, subsequent *ona'ah* claims are denied.[30]

The analogue of the above case in the labor market entails the following elements: Mesader, our promising recent law school graduate, interviews with Emet, the smaller law firm. While praising his credentials, Emet points out that it will not be able to bill clients for more than $50 an hour for Mesader's services. If they were to charge a fee above this figure, they would run the risk of pricing themselves out of their market. With the $50 an hour fee as a basis, Emet makes a $60,000 salary offer to Mesader. Subsequent to accepting the offer, Mesader learns that Yatsiv, the larger, more prestigious law firm, offers $75,000 for the same job title. Mesader lodges an *ona'ah* claim against Emet. While not denying that Mesader's credentials qualify him for employment at Yatsiv, Emet counters that Yatsiv bills clients at $75 an hour for the type of legal work Mesader does. Since Mesader's MRP is higher at Yatsiv than it is at Emet, the *ona'ah* claim should be denied, despite the opportunity cost he incurred by entering into employment with Emet.

Class Discrimination And Jewish Law

A variant of the cases discussed above occurs when wage discrimination for a particular job title is not sporadic but reflects a systematic bias against a particular class of people. To illustrate, suppose accounting firms are found to systematically pay blacks lower salaries than whites for the same job title. Since blacks are systematically discriminated against, the *ona'ah* cannot be viewed as an opportunity-cost claim, even in respect to the intrafirm case. Barring wage discrimination by class by means of legislative edict, therefore, cannot find its inspirational source in the law of *ona'ah*. While elimination of this practice falls within the price-wage legislative prerogative of the Jewish community, a case must be made that halakhic norms demand such legislation.

Voting on legislative proposals, according to Halakhah, must not be dictated by self-interest, but rather should be guided by one's perception of what is in the public interest.[31] The public interest entails both equity and efficiency considerations. Toward the end of building a halakhic case for legislation designed to eliminate wage discrimination by class, we will present arguments based on equity and efficiency. First, the equity argument:

When systematic wage discrimination for equal work against a particular group is rooted in some *irrelevant* personal trait, such as race or national origin, it generates strong feelings of frustration, bitterness, and resentment among those victimized by the practice. Societal toleration of the practice not only gives legitimacy to meanness in economic relations, but also does violence to the values of humaneness, decency, and fairness. An expression of outrage against class discrimination in the form of legislation banning the practice is therefore appropriate on the basis of *darkhei no'am*, discussed in chapter 1.

We now turn to the economic efficiency argument. Let us assume an initial condition of wage discrimination in the field of carpentry. Whites are compensated at $25 an hour, a wage rate equal to their MRP. While the MRP of blacks is equal to that of their white counterparts, blacks receive only $15 an hour. Discrimination has the effect of driving blacks to enter related fields, such as masonry, where their incomes will be higher than their expected earnings in carpentry.

Within the framework of a competitive marketplace, this dual wage rate cannot persist for long. It will be quickly learned that maintaining a prejudice is an expensive proposition. Profit-maximizing behavior will drive firms to substitute black carpenters for white ones. This substitution will continue until the MRP of black carpenters is no more than the firm pays them. As the above adjustment process unfolds, the relative scarcity of the different categories of labor changes. With the profit motive driving employers more and more to view black and white carpenters as interchangeable, the relative scarcity of carpenters diminishes and the $25 wage rate for this category of labor is driven below its initial level. Simultaneously, the exit of blacks from the masonry industry increases the relative scarcity of workers in that industry and should result in a higher wage there.

Notwithstanding the change in relative wages, the primary source of the increased income for black carpenters is not the reduced income of white carpenters. Rather, the extra income for black workers primarily comes from the extra output that their higher productivity in their new employment brings, compared with the lower productivity enforced by discrimination. Hence, society as a whole benefits from the elimination of wage discrimination. Banning wage discrimination for equal work, accordingly, merely accelerates the disappearance of a practice which economic self-interest would have in any case worked to eliminate.

Statistical Generalization And Wage Discrimination

Systematic discrimination against a class of people is, however, not always rooted in bigotry and erroneous beliefs. Statistical sex discrimination provides a case in point. This occurs when hiring decisions are based on differences between male and female averages on predictions of productivity. If women, for example, have higher turnover rates than men, employers will hesitate to hire women in jobs in which they provide expensive training, screening out even those women who would have stayed for decades. Since men and women have overlapping distributions on virtually all characteristics, using sex-group means to estimate the productivity of applicants results in mistaken predictions for individuals above or below the mean for their sex.

Notwithstanding the mistaken predictions that result from statistical generalizations, the use of this method, as Englard points out, is an efficient approach to hiring for the firm. How is an employer to predict how long an applicant will stay with the firm, or how successful a managerial style he or she has? Because of this uncertainty and the cost of information, basing predictions on averages for easily recognizable groups may save more in screening costs than is lost by the nonoptimal work force that results.[32]

When unequal pay for equal work is rooted in statistical generalizations, banning the practice works to bias employers against candidates whom they perceive to have a lower MRP than the general pool of applicants they face. Ironically, for workers suffering under the bias, wage discrimination may be preferable.

Under the Equal Pay Act, consistent differences in the employment costs, productivity, and training participation of men and women constitute justifiable grounds for paying unequal wages for what appears, on the surface, to be equal work. Statistical sex discrimination does not, however, qualify as an exception, as the courts have held that the higher cost or lower productivity must be shown for each individual female employee.[33]

While an Equal Pay Act gives the impression of worsening the marketability of below-average-MRP candidates for a particular job, the plight of these workers, as it appears to this writer, does not necessarily deteriorate under this legislation. Considerations of profit maximization drive the firm to substitute cheaper labor for more expensive labor. If the law prohibits a dual wage rate within the framework of a single job title, the firm has every incentive to redefine job titles.

To illustrate, if statistical generalization tells the firm that women are less attached to the labor force than men, the various duties of the subject job title would be analyzed in terms of job attachment. Such an analysis might indicate the appropriateness of creating a new job title. The new job title would only retain components of the old job title whose performance would not suffer appreciably on account of intermittency. Should the surviving contents prove too meager to justify a job title, additional duties could be found by reorganizing other jobs on the work scene.

Under the Equal Pay Act, the courts have ruled that the requirement of equal pay extends even to jobs that are only substantially the same. In *Wetzel* v. *Liberty Mutual Insurance Company*, for instance, the court ruled that the difference in working conditions between claim adjustors (men) and claim representatives (women) was insignificant and therefore did not justify "unequal" pay. Men typically used their cars to examine claims in various locations, while women handled claims from an office building.[34]

In his critique of the Equal Pay Act, Fogel contends that the operation of the law now limits the ability of firms to create variations of old job titles, with the result that the goal of minimizing labor costs has been hampered. A case in point is *Shultz* v. *Wheaton Glass Company*.[35] Wheaton is a large manufacturer of glass containers. The operation in question involved the inspection and packaging of glass bottles manufactured in the company's plant. This job was performed by "selector-packers" who picked glass containers by hand from a conveyor belt, visually inspected them, and packed those accepted into adjacent cardboard cartons. In late 1967, 230 of the selector-packers were women, employed at $2.14 an hour; 276 were males, employed at $2.35 an hour. The males had sixteen additional duties not required of females (according to the trial court's opinion). The additional duties included lifting of cartons in excess of 35 pounds, mechanical adjustments to equipment, and other miscellaneous tasks. The differentiation of male and female jobs was the result of a collective bargaining agreement.

In bringing this case, the U.S. Department of Labor alleged that the male and female selector-packers performed equal work and that the occasional performance of additional tasks by males was merely incidental to the total job cycle and did not make the male and female jobs unequal. The district court rejected these contentions, finding instead that Wheaton had proven the jobs unequal by showing that "men are required to exert additional effort, to possess additional skill, and to have additional responsibility." The decision of the district court was reversed by the Court of Appeals. Cited among the various reasons for the reversal were: (1) the district court had made no finding that all male selector-packers performed many or all of the additional tasks; (2) the additional duties performed by male selector-packers were also carried out by thirty-seven "snap-up" boys who did these heavy duties exclusively and were paid only $2.16 an hour for doing so, just 2 cents more than the rate paid females; and (3) the motive for the creation of two jobs from the original single one "clearly appears to have been to keep women in a subordinate role."

Critical of the appellate decision on all three counts, Fogel regards the first reason for the reversal as far too restrictive.

What made the male and female jobs different and unequal in Wheaton Glass is that the male job required the capacity to perform the extra duties, and this capacity had to be paid for, regardless of variation in its actual use by job incumbents.

The second reason for reversing the Wheaton trial court, in Fogel's view, was also faulty. First, in deciding whether a pay differential between two job titles violates the Equal Pay Act, the only relevant comparison is between the subject job titles. Bringing into play the duties of a third, unassociated job stretches the coverage of the act beyond its intent. Moreover, Wheaton may very well have regarded the position of snap-up boy as relatively unimportant compared to male selector-packer.

Finally, the circuit court's conclusion that Wheaton's original motive for bifurcating the selector-packer job was to keep women in a subordinate role is, in Fogel's opinion, wrong. The company created the female job (with the union's acquiescence) in order to tap a new source of labor. The duties of the new job were circumscribed because the union wanted to maintain job security for men, because the company probably believed that few women were capable of heavy lifting, and because the circumscribed duties provided a visible justification for attaching a lower rate to it.

Whether Wheaton also wished to subordinate women because it believed that women, in the nature of things, should be subordinate cannot be determined. Since a purely business motive was well served by the company's actions, it is doubtful that an insidious discriminatory motive, whether present or not, played a significant part in the job specialization Wheaton created.[36]

While coverage of the equal pay requirement beyond the identical job case is understandably necessary if the law is not to be emasculated, extending coverage to jobs that are only substantially the same may seriously compromise economic efficiency. To avoid economic inefficiency the act must not work to interfere with the freedom of the firm to give MRP a controlling role in differentiating job titles and setting pay scales.

Comparable Worth And Jewish Law

We now turn our attention to Judaism's attitude toward the issue of comparable worth.

Given that the proposal entails the comparison of essentially dissimilar jobs, the law of *ona'ah* is entirely irrelevant in evaluating the merits of this issue from the standpoint of Jewish law.

The comparable worth proposal does, however, fall squarely within the legislative purview of the Jewish community. Legislative proposals in the Torah society, as will be recalled, must be considered on the basis of their impact on communal welfare rather than from the perspective of self-interest. Aspects of the comparable worth proposal relevant to Halakhah include the issue of equity, its effect on employment, and its effect on the institution of marriage. Economic analysis is helpful in elucidating each of these issues.

Equity

Pay equity, according to comparable worth advocates, demands that dissimilar jobs of equivalent worth be paid the same wages. If this is not done, the holder of the lower-paying job is justified in claiming that he or she is a victim of illegal discrimination. One of the most important findings of the evaluation tests of dissimilar jobs is that women employed in female-dominated occupations are significantly underpaid as against men in male-dominated occupations. Applying the pay-equity criterion of comparable worth leads, therefore, to the conclusion that widespread illegal sex discrimination exists in the United States today.

The above conclusion is, however, unwarranted. Unequal pay for jobs of comparable worth, as Killingsworth points out, is not inherently discriminatory. Even in a gender-neutral labor market wherein gender is entirely irrelevant to market outcomes, there is no reason why individuals in jobs of comparable worth should necessarily receive the same wage. Consider the job of translator. On the basis of the comparable worth criterion, the jobs of Spanish-English translators and French-English translators would, in all probability, be deemed equal. But if market forces were allowed free rein, the compensation of the two jobs would not necessarily be equal. This is so because relative scarcity is what determines price in the marketplace. Accordingly, if the employer was located in Miami, the supply side of the labor market would work to depress the earnings of Spanish-English translators relative to the earnings of French-English translators. Nevertheless, the Spanish-English translators would, in the final analysis, command a higher remuneration if the demand for their services was substantially higher than the corresponding demand for French-English translators.[37]

The occupational choices women make are another consideration in evaluating the claim that women are victims of systematic employer discrimination in the labor market. In 1983, for instance, roughly four-fifths of all women worked in only 25 of the 420 job categories listed by the Department of Labor.[38] Occupational choice results in women being crowded into certain jobs. The relative abundance of the particular skills women have is, hence, what ultimately accounts for their lower earnings relative to men.

Women's occupational choices differ from men's because their expected lifetime labor force commitments differ. Men expect to remain in the labor force their entire working lives. Women, on the other hand, expect that their patterns of labor force participation will be characterized by intermittency due to childbearing responsibilities and other familial obligations.

Because women generally regard their labor force commitment as intermittent, they choose occupations which are most compatible with childrearing and familial obligations. Most attractive to them, therefore, are occupations characterized by such features as easy entry and exit and availability of flexible hours and part-time work. Women crowd into such professions as nursing, elementary school teaching, operative and sales work, and household work.

Adding refinement to this insight is Polachek's analysis of the phenomenon of occupational depreciation and appreciation. Occupational depreciation refers to the rate at which the skills a job requires depreciate when not in use. Occupational appreciation refers to the rate at which new skills are learned on the job. Those occupations with low appreciation rates, i.e., jobs which allow for very little or no skill advancement, have relatively flat earnings curves. Wages rise very little as one's experience in that occupation increases. Those occupations with high appreciation rates have steep earnings curves. Because of the costs associated with training, wages are relatively low at the beginning of the work experience. Skills are enhanced with experience, and wages respond accordingly.

Because women often regard their attachment to the labor force as intermittent, they naturally are drawn to occupations with low depreciation rates and those with the highest starting salaries, whose payoff comes quickly, not at some future date when they likely will be out of the labor force.

Extending the above line of reasoning, women do not find it optimal to invest in as much on-the-job training as men or in as much quality of schooling.[39]

What follows from Polachek's theory is that it is erroneous to attribute low wages in women's occupations to discrimination when it is really women themselves who, by their rational behavior, are bloating supply and keeping their own wages low.

Another consideration in regard to equity and comparable worth is William's finding that the earnings gap between the sexes is in reality a marriage gap rather than a gender gap. Men and women who are equally attached to the labor force do receive equal pay for comparable work. Women who have never married show much stronger labor market attachment than women who are married and living with their husbands. To be specific, never-married women with a college education spend 88.9 percent of their working years in the labor force, while married women with the same education spend only 36.4 percent of their working years in the labor force. Among men and women who have never married, women earn 99 percent as much as men, while among people who are married and have never been divorced, women earn only a third as much as men.[40]

In comparing male and female incomes in the Canadian economy, Block also found that marital status almost entirely accounted for the earnings gap. That is, marriage increases male earnings and reduces female earnings.

Research has brought to light a variety of reasons for this. Wives, more often than husbands, take on a higher and disproportionate share of child care and homemaking. A woman is more likely to give up her job if her husband gets a better job elsewhere, to interrupt her career for domestic reasons, to place her home and family ahead of her job or profession, and even purposely to keep her earnings below her spouse's. While it is impossible to quantify the effects of such phenomena on the increasing disparity between married male and female incomes, there can be little doubt that their influence is substantial.[41]

The findings summarized above call into question the proposition that employers discriminate against all women simply because some married women pull down women's average degree of labor market attachment. Instead, it appears that never-married men and never-married women, whose degree of labor market attachment is about equal, earn about equal pay.

Given the crucial role marital status plays in explaining the earnings gap, the gap could very well reflect society's tendency to pay a price, as it were, to maintain the traditional role differentiation between men and women. Drawing upon the economic literature that theorizes that societal perceptions of fairness influence relative wages, Sorensen suggests that the current advantage employers enjoy with respect to women's work reflects the cultural bias against women participating in the labor market as equals with men. Accordingly, the earnings gap would be totally in accord with societal notions of fairness.[42]

Effects On Employment

Raising the relative pay of low-paid jobs held predominantly by women may very well represent a mixed blessing for the target group. While the welfare of those hired at the higher wage would improve, employers, in all probability, would reduce their demand for such jobs. Take the case of nurses. With nurses' pay higher, other things being equal, hospitals would have less incentive than before to substitute nurses' work for doctors'. At the same time, they would have more incentive to substitute the work of nurses' aides and orderlies for that of nurses. They would also buy more automatic equipment to allow each nurse to handle more patients. Fewer nurses would be hired, and some already on the job might be laid off. Presumably, those who kept their jobs would tend to be from the best nursing schools or perhaps the ones with the most experience. Thus, implementation of comparable worth would be most helpful to those who least need the help.

Another likely effect of comparable worth would be to attract men into occupations such as nursing and secretarial work now dominated by women. Under the new, more competitive conditions, some women would prosper. These would be the women with the best educations, strongest job skills, and fewest distracting family commitments.

Finally, as comparable worth raised pay in women's occupations and attracted men into them, the characteristics of those occupations that attracted women into them in the first place would change. Many American women work to help their families, which are their chief concerns. This motive steers them into work with such features as easy entry and exit and availability of flexible hours and part-time work. But if jobs like nursing and secretarial work paid more, employers would have less incentive to tailor them to suit the needs of such women. They would begin to insist on stronger job attachment, just as they have in occupations dominated by men. Experience and training would begin to count for more. With fewer positions open and people of both sexes applying for them, employers would be more likely to pass over women who wanted to work just to help their families.[43]

Implementation of comparable worth will, in all likelihood, lead to an overall rise in wages and hence in prices. Thus, if the work of a firm's clerical staff is found to be comparable to that of its higher-paid truckers, it is unlikely that pay cuts will be forced on the truckers. Instead, the salaries of the clerical workers will be raised to a comparable level. This means that the firm's overall costs of production will rise. Rising labor costs exerts upward pressure on the price level.

The inflationary impact described above is reinforced in consideration of the implications comparable worth has for incentive wages. At present, if an employer, say a municipality, wants to attract a particular skill which is in short supply, say, electrical engineers, it will raise its wage offer for electrical engineers. But under comparable worth the wages of comparable jobs, say city planners, must also be raised. Raising the wages of city planners along with the wages of electrical engineers not only substantially increases the cost of attracting electrical engineers, but also removes entirely any economic incentive in the long run for people to train to become electrical engineers.[44]

The Institution of Marriage

One final factor in considering the merits of the comparable worth proposal, from the perspective of Jewish law, is its impact on the institution of marriage. In Jewish teaching, marriage and family life are regarded as integral parts of the divine plan.[45] All human beings are necessarily incomplete without a mate, and it is through marriage that completeness is achieved.[46] Notwithstanding that women, unlike men,[47] are not commanded to marry,[48] Judaism regards marriage as the ideal lifestyle for both sexes.

Rabbi Samson R. Hirsch (Germany, 1808–1888) derives the above dictum from the following biblical verse: "And God said: it is not good that man shall be alone; I shall make him a helpmate unto him" (Genesis 2:18). Take note, R. Hirsch points out, that the Torah does actually not say that it was not good for man to be alone, but rather (translating the Hebrew literally): "This is not good, man being alone." As long as man stands alone it is already not yet good; the goal of perfection which the world is to attain through him will never be reached as long as he stands alone.[49]

On a most basic level, marriage is an ideal even for women, who are not commanded to marry, because it is within this relationship that *ḥessed* (loving-kindness) can achieve its highest form. *Ḥessed* is the basis of all Jewish ethics and is the character trait that must underlie all interpersonal relationships. Realization of the ideal of *ḥessed* obtains when an individual gives to another out of a sense of closeness and identification with the other's needs. One who gives out of *ḥessed* does so because the other's need is as real to him as his own. Marriage realizes *ḥessed* in its highest form when the relationship becomes to the partners a oneness in the form of existential commitment and a metaphysical fusion of souls.[50]

In his analysis of the Torah perspective on women, R. Moshe Meiselman develops the theme that Halakhah regards woman's intrinsically valuable role to be that of builder of the Jewish home. In this capacity, two missions are thrust upon her. First, she must assume the role of enabler. In Judaism, this role is regarded as the highest form of spiritual fulfillment. Second, she must develop the personality trait of *ẓeniut* (modesty) to its very heights.[51]

The role of woman as enabler is given particular stress in connection with the miẓvah of Talmud Torah. In this regard, the sages declared that in the merit of encouraging and urging her husband and children to study Torah, woman shares in their reward.[52]

Beyond the role of enabler, Halakhah assigns a vital role for the mother in the Talmud Torah experience of her child. Maternal involvement in the actual learning experience proceeds from the miẓvah to transmit the Torah to posterity (Deuteronomy 4:9). This miẓvah, according to Naḥmanides (Spain, 1194–1270)[53] and R. Baḥya b. Asher (Saragossa, 13th cent.)[54] consists of two components: (1) the obligation to pass on the experience of the Revelation, and (2) the obligation to transmit its content. The former task, R. Baḥya posits, is more important, for "if one forgets the experience, he will end up denying the content."[55]

In connection with the obligation to transmit the Torah, Moses was instructed: "Thus shall you say to the house of Jacob and tell the children of Israel" (Exodus 19:3). The sages understand "the house of Jacob" as referring to the women and "the children of Israel" to the men.[56] Given the inclusion of both men and women in the transmission obligation, R. Ahron Soloveichik posits that the primary task of men is to pass on the content of the Revelation.[57]

Passing on the experience of Sinai translates concretely, according to R. Soloveichik, into the obligation to make the Revelation the motivational force in fulfilling the dictates of the Torah.[58] This understanding perforce involves the mother in the attitudinal realm of the child's development. By dint of the mother's own conduct, the child must be impressed with the centrality of the Torah in the Jew's life experience and with a sense of love and fear for the Almighty and for the Torah. Hence, the miẓvah to transmit the Torah to future generations also works to make marriage the ideal for women.

Parenting, to be discussed in chapter 5, is the fundamental building block of a society's moral climate. The challenge for government is to devise an incentive system which encourages parents on the margin to choose parenting over marketplace activities. Comparable worth subverts this objective. It does so by crowding women out of the very occupations which are best suited for the substitution at the margin between work and family demands.

Darkhei No'am

Both the intensity and the momentum of the comparable worth movement reflect a widespread social outrage against the wage treatment of women today. Does the principle of *darkhei no'am*, discussed in chapter 1, require that the legislative body of the Torah society accommodate the demands of this movement as a means of quieting dissension and ill-feeling? Analysis of the nature of the dissatisfaction behind the comparable worth movement indicates only a need to address the root cause of the dissension but not to follow the prescription of comparable worth.

The pay gap between men and women existed long before the comparable worth movement gained its current popularity. Coincidental with the movement's growth has been the dramatic increase in the rate of participation of women in the labor market. In 1950, 70 percent of American households were headed by men whose income was the sole source of family income. In 1984, less than 15 percent of families fit this traditional mold.[59] Some of the most strident advocacy of comparable worth comes from women who have adopted the singles lifestyle, either voluntarily or involuntarily, or who believe that it should be available as a viable option for women. Since financial independence and career fulfillment are made difficult by the relatively low wages of women in female-dominated occupations, the enthusiasm of this group for the comparable worth proposal is understandable.

Participation of women in the labor force on a full-time basis is, however, not the norm. In 1984, only about 46 percent of married women held down full-time jobs.[60] The motivation of most women for entering the labor force is merely to help out their families financially.[61] The current agitation for the comparable worth proposal is therefore symptomatic of a financial strain in the institution of marriage.

The *darkhei no'am* principle does not require the Jewish legislative body to meet the demands of every embittered group just for the sake of ending dissension. Rather, it merely requires the legislative body to address the root cause of the dissension and take remedial action. Since directly meeting the demands of comparable worth proponents would encourage a lifestyle antithetical to the Torah ideal and weaken the institution of marriage, rejection of the proposal is indicated. The underlying financial strain affecting the institution of marriage must, however, be addressed. Remedial action to strengthen the institution of marriage is indicated. The reader is referred to chapter 5 for a discussion of governmental measures to accomplish this.

In applying the *darkhei no'am* standard here, we should note that the comparable worth proposal is itself not free of the prospect of generating considerable social dissension.

Job evaluations often rest on controversial value judgments. Most basically, what are the relative weights which should be assigned to each of the job characteristics which comprise the comparable worth criterion?

Another issue is the problem of measuring the various dimensions of the job which comparable worth takes into account. For example, how should we define responsibility? Is it related to the number of people one supervises, the level of decision-making one holds within a firm, or the cost of misjudgment? An airline mechanic, for instance, may supervise few people but has a great deal of responsibility for people's lives. Is the mechanic's responsibility greater than that of top executives in the airline's office?[62]

Conclusion

Economic analysis, as we have seen, has much to contribute in the way of informed public debate regarding the issue of comparable worth. It points up the weakness of the equity argument for comparable worth, and in addition demonstrates that the very group the proposal is designed to help will fare worse. At the same time, the analysis indicates that the proposal would exert a negative impact on the institution of marriage and encourage lifestyles antithetical to Jewish values. All considerations therefore point to Halakhah's rejection of the idea of comparable worth.

• 4
Government Regulation of Advertising

MODERN ADVERTISING TYPICALLY avoids making direct and forthright claims. Instead, its claims are often implied in statements of opinion and, in addition, are subject to various interpretations. Consequently, any given advertising message could be regarded as useful, entertaining, and innocuous by one segment of the marketplace, but at the same time be viewed as misleading or deceptive by another group. The basic issue for government regulation of advertising is which consumer to protect. Should the law protect only reasonable, sensible, and intelligent consumers who conduct themselves carefully in the marketplace? Or must it also protect ignorant consumers who conduct themselves carelessly?

Our purpose here will be to present this issue from the standpoint of both American law and Halakhah. Various topics revolving around the issue will be discussed.

The Issue In American Law

Prior to 1914, misleading advertising claims in the United States were adjudicated by the judicial system under common law. The governing principle for these cases was the "reasonable man" standard. Accordingly, an advertiser could not be held liable for misrepresentation unless the court decided that a reasonable man would *rely* on the false or deceptive message. Under this standard, the person the courts protected was not the average or typical person, but rather an idealized person who always operated in the marketplace without the slightest negligence.

In 1914, the Federal Trade Commission (FTC) was established. This independent governmental agency was given the mandate to investigate "unfair" and "predatory" competitive practices, and to declare illegal all "unfair methods of competition and commerce." In 1938, its mandate expanded to include the mission of preventing false and misleading advertising.

The FTC in its early history, as Ivan Preston documents, broke away from common law precedent and adopted the "ignorant man" standard in protecting consumers against deceptive advertising. Preston cites several rulings that typify the agency's attitude during its early years.

In 1919, for instance, the FTC ordered a manufacturer to stop advertising that its automobile batteries would "last forever."[1] Since the same ad offered the customer, for the additional charge of 50 cents per month, the right to receive a replacement battery as soon as the purchased one wore out, no reasonable person would put stock in the claim that the battery "lasts forever." Nonetheless, the FTC viewed the replacement-service clause as confirming the deceptiveness of the "last forever" statement. The case indicated that the FTC felt that the law should protect even those consumers who conducted themselves carelessly in the marketplace.

The "ignorant man" standard reached an extreme when Clairol was forbidden to say that its dye would "color hair permanently." The FTC deemed that the public would take this as a claim that all the hair a person grew for the rest of her life would emerge in the Clairol color.[2]

Eventually, the standard applied by the FTC in these cases gave way to a narrower view of which consumer the agency should protect. The new attitude was articulated in the case of *Heinz W. Kirchner*.[3] The case concerned an inflatable device to help a person stay afloat and learn to swim. Called Swim-Ezy, it was worn under the swimming suit and was advertised as being invisible. It was not invisible, but the FTC found it to be "inconspicuous," and ruled that that was all the claim of invisibility would mean to the public. But what about those who might take the claim to mean that the device was "wholly invisible" or bodiless? The FTC made it clear that it no longer intended to protect people so ignorant.

> True—the Commission's responsibility is to prevent deception of the gullible and credulous, as well as the cautious and knowledgeable. . . . This principle loses its validity, however,

> if it is applied uncritically or pushed to an absurd extreme. An advertiser cannot be charged with liability in respect to every conceivable misconception, however outlandish, to which his representations might be subject among the foolish or feebleminded. . . . A representation does not become "false or deceptive" merely because it will be unreasonably misunderstood by an insignificant and unrepresentative segment of the class of persons to whom the representation is addressed.[4]

While the decision in *Heinz W. Kirchner* amounted to a repudiation of the "ignorant man" standard, it by no means returned us to the "reasonable man" standard of common law days. Rather, what emerged from this ruling was a "modified reasonable man standard." The new standard equated the reasonable person with the typical or average person as actually observed in the marketplace.[5]

The Issue In Jewish Law

Preliminary to the discussion of this issue, we note that misleading and deceptive advertising is prohibited in Halakhah under the interdict against creating a false impression (*geneivat da'at*).

The biblical source of the *geneivat da'at* interdict is disputed by talmudic decisors. R. Jonah b. Abraham Gerondi (Spain, ca. 1200–1264) places such conduct under the rubric of falsehood (*sheker*).[6] R. Yom Tov Ishbili (Seville, ca. 1250–1330), however, subsumes it under the Torah's admonition against theft (*lo tignovu*, Leviticus 19:11). What *lo tignovu* enjoins is both theft of property and the acquisition of something by means of deception.[7]

Bearing directly on the issue of deceptive advertising in Halakhah is the disclosure formula the rabbis of the Talmud devised to inform townspeople that the day's supply of meat was not kosher. A public announcement to this effect served a double purpose. Since it made it impossible for Gentile patrons to be duped into believing that the meat they were buying was kosher, it averted the possibility of the proprietors of kosher butcher shops violating the *geneivat da'at* interdict. It also alerted the Jews of the town not to purchase meat from a Gentile supplier on that day.

In respect to the exact formulation of the announcement, the following discussion takes place at Ḥullin 94a:

> What is the form of the proclamation? R. Isaac b. Joseph said, "Meat for the army has fallen into our hands" (*nafla bisra l'bnei ḥeila*). And why not proclaim, "Trefa meat for the army has fallen into our hands" (*nafla trefta l'bnei ḥeila*)? Then they would not buy it. Then are we not deceiving them? No. They are deceiving themselves. As in the following incident: Mar Zutra the son of R. Naḥman was once going from Sikara to Maḥoza, while Rava and R. Safra were going to Sikara; and they met on the way. Believing that they had come to meet him he said, "Why did the rabbis take the trouble to come so far [to meet me]?" R. Safra replied, "We did not know that the Master was coming; had we known of it, we should have put ourselves out more than this." Rava said to him, "Why did you say that to him? Now you have upset him." He replied, "But we would be deceiving him otherwise." "No. He would be deceiving himself."

The preceding passage presents several difficulties. First, given that an explicit announcement of the presence of nonkosher meat in the butcher shops repels Gentile customers, formulating the announcement in ambiguous terms should amount to a deliberate attempt at deception. Why, then, do we regard the purchase of nonkosher meat by Gentiles on the basis of the ambiguous announcement as constituting only self-deception on their part? Second, how can the Mar Zutra episode serve as support for the permissibility of making a calculated ambiguous announcement when the encounter between the rabbis and Mar Zutra was entirely fortuitous and the rabbis did nothing to create the false impression that they constituted a welcoming party for him?

In offering a solution to these difficulties we note, to begin with, that the Talmud does not say that the proclamation *nafal bisra l'bnei ḥeila* was implemented only after experience with the *nafal trefta* proclamation resulted in the loss of the Gentile trade. Switching of this sort, because it is calculated to "throw off" the Gentiles and restore the lost business, constitutes a *deliberate* attempt at deception. What the Talmud says is simply that the rabbis *theorized* that an *express* proclamation of trefa would repel the Gentile customers. Hence the *nafal trefta* proclamation was never used.

This leads to the proposition that *nafal bisra* entailed no *deliberate* attempt at deception. Since no announcement at all was made when the available supply consisted entirely of kosher meat, *nafal bisra* should clearly communicate the message that the meat for sale is not kosher. Both this proclamation and the *nafal trefta* proclamation communicate the same message, but with different promotional slants. *Nafal trefta* is decidedly negative, openly proclaiming that the meat is unfit for Jewish consumption, but available for sale to Gentiles. *Nafal bisra l'bnei ḥeila,* on the other hand, openly conveys only that Gentiles are the desired customer base of the product; the unfitness of the product for Jewish consumption is indicated only by means of reasonable implication.

The proposition that the difference between the two proclamations is merely a matter of promotional slant is supported by the comment of R. Solomon b. Isaac (Rashi; Troyes, 1040–1105) as to why Gentiles are repulsed by the *nafal trefta* proclamation: "It is a disgrace for them, since we do not want to eat it."[8] What makes nonkosher meat obnoxious to the Gentile is not the essentially value-free datum that Jews do not eat it, but rather the formal declaration that they do not desire to eat it. The following observation will clarify the point. There are two categories of nonkosher meat. One is meat derived from an animal which was not slaughtered in accordance with Jewish ritual law (*nebelah*). The second is meat derived from an organically defective animal (*trefa*). Since there is no qualitative difference between *nebelah* and kosher meat, the Gentile should rationally be indifferent between the two. Similarly, at fair market value, a Gentile should find no reason to reject *trefa*. If the Gentile finds nonkosher meat obnoxious, it is therefore not the product itself that repulses him, but the manner in which it is marketed. Expressly representing to him that the meat is *trefa* makes it a disgrace for him to purchase it, as the declaration openly proclaims that it is unfit for Jewish consumption, but suitable for Gentiles.

Thus, *nafal bisra* is not deceptive disclosure, but a creative way of marketing a product so that it becomes acceptable to Gentiles, whose sole reason for rejecting it would be the word *trefa* used in its promotion. Since no announcement whatsoever is made when the butcher shops are selling only kosher meat, *nafal bisra* should convey to a reasonable person that the meat is not kosher.

Recall that the Talmud characterizes those misled by *nafal bisra* as being guilty of self-deception. The result of the analysis in the preceding paragraphs shows that this applies only to the few who mistakenly think that the meat being offered for sale is kosher in the absence of an explicit specification to the contrary. But for the vast majority of patrons, no misunderstanding whatsoever takes place, for they correctly read into *nafal bisra l'bnei ḥeila* an implicit notification that nonkosher meat is being offered for sale.

Given the role the "reasonable man" principle plays in extricating *nafal bisra* from a deceptive characterization, the affinity of this case to the Mar Zutra incident is readily apparent. In the latter case, too, it is the "reasonable man" standard that frees the rabbis' conduct from the *geneivat da'at* interdict. If not for the judgment that a reasonable person would regard their encounter with Mar Zutra as clearly fortuitous, they would be obliged to correct Mar Zutra's mistaken belief that they constituted a welcoming party for him.

Further support for this thesis can be derived by comparing the text at hand with a point in *geneivat da'at* law expounded in the Jerusalem Talmud at Makkot 2:6. The case entails the following elements: A is well versed in one tractate of the Talmud, but the townspeople mistakenly think he is proficient in two tractates and accord him the honor due someone who is proficient in two tractates. The Jerusalem Talmud rules that A is obligated to disabuse the townspeople of their mistaken impression of him. This ruling apparently contradicts the rule, elucidated at Ḥullin 94a, that an individual is exempt from correcting a mistaken impression which is rooted in self-deception. Ready reconciliation of the two texts follows, however, from the "reasonable man" hypothesis. An individual need only be concerned about a mistaken impression held by a reasonable person. Since the various tractates of the Talmud, especially those in the same order,[9] are interconnected, complement each other, and overlap somewhat, proficiency in one tractate can easily be mistaken for proficiency in two tractates. Accordingly, a talmudic scholar must disabuse the townspeople of their inaccurate assessment of him. In sharp contrast, since a reasonable person would interpret Mar Zutra's encounter with Rava and R. Safra as nothing more than fortuitous, no corrective obligation devolved upon the rabbis to disabuse Mar Zutra of his error. In a similar vein, a reasonable person will take *nafal bisra* as constituting an implicit declaration that the meat at hand is not kosher. Accordingly, use of this formulation does not constitute deliberate deception.

In sum, claims of deception against a seller are evaluated on the basis of the "reasonable man" standard.

The Average or Idealized Man

What remains to be clarified is whether Halakhah regards the reasonable person as an average person or an "idealized" person.

Several cases relating to the law of debts bear directly on this issue.

Under certain conditions, if A acknowledges a debt to B, but does so outside a Bet Din (court of law),[10] the acknowledgment is not binding. Consider, for instance, the following case: B confronts A with a claim that he is due a sum of money. A acknowledges the debt in the presence of onlookers, but subsequently refuses to pay. The case moves on to the Bet Din, where A insists that his earlier acknowledgment of a debt obligation to B was merely a jest. It was his way of responding in kind to what he regarded as a ridiculous claim (*mashteh ani bakh*, "I was just jesting with you").

A's *mashteh ani bakh* defense will be accepted by the Bet Din.[11] Moreover, even when A does not make this defense explicitly, but merely denies that he ever admitted owing the money, the court will assume that something equivalent took place, since a person is not expected to remember words thrown out in a jocular way (*milta d'kedi lo dekhirei inshei*).[12]

However, where A enters a plea of *mashteh ani bakh,* whether explicit or implicit, the Bet Din will require him to affirm his defense by means of an oath (*shevuat hesset*).[13]

Mashteh ani bakh averts a court judgment against A only if he offers this defense himself. If A remains silent, the Bet Din will not deny B's claim by suggesting that the acknowledgment was made in jest and then turn to A for his confirmation.[14] Nevertheless, if A dies before the court proceeding begins, and B's claim is against A's estate, the Bet Din will entertain the possibility that the acknowledgment was made in jest and will require of A's heirs only that they take an oath that they did not receive instructions from A to make payment to B.[15]

The *mashteh ani bakh* defense has no standing when A not only acknowledged the debt but told the onlookers to serve as witnesses in the matter. *Attem edai* ("you are my witnesses") makes A's acknowledgment of the debt objectively evident. A subsequent plea that it should not have been taken seriously is rejected outright.[16] Moreover, if A remains silent, B's charge of *attem edai* to the onlookers may also work to vitiate A's *mashteh ani bakh* defense. This obtains when A initially acknowledges the debt in the face of B's claim and B then goes ahead and charges the onlookers with *attem edai*. However, if A was silent all along, his *mashteh ani bakh* defense remains intact.[17]

Another scenario involves the following elements: A volunteers to C in the presence of onlookers that he owes B, say, $1,000. A then asks the onlookers to serve as witnesses in the matter. On the basis of this admission, B enters a claim of $1,000 against A. Despite the fact that all the elements of an objectively evident admission of a debt of obligation are in place here, A may still have grounds to claim that the admission was not made in a serious vein. This occurs when A insists that he made the admission only so that the public would not hold him to be a wealthy man.[18] This explanation is accepted even when A was known at the time to be poor.[19] In the latter instance, A's motive would have been to make it appear that he was even poorer than people assumed.[20] According to many authorities, the Bet Din is required to suggest this line of defense to A if he does not himself bring it up.[21]

When the proceeding is against A's estate rather than against A, the court will entertain the possibility that the admission was bogus on the grounds discussed above. Accordingly, it will require that A's heirs only take an oath that A did not instruct them to make a payment to B.[22]

Underlying A's slippery defense is an implicit admission that he fell short of the highest ethical standards in his dealings with B. An ethically sensitive person is straightforward and does not employ ambiguity to further his cause. Confronted with an unfounded claim, he will not first acknowledge it and then say that he only meant to mock it; instead, he will respond to a baseless claim with a simple denial. Less ethical still is the practice of admitting to fictional debts so as not to be regarded as wealthy. If the intent is to create a false impression of poverty rather than to disabuse a false impression of wealth, the practice is clearly immoral. In the final analysis, A's explanation of his conduct is accepted because it comports well with the conduct of ordinary people,[23] and the court will not evaluate A's conduct as though he were a highly ethical person. Moreover, when B's claim is made against A's estate, the court itself will bring up the less than highly ethical defense of *mashteh ani bakh* because the conduct of the ordinary person must serve as the model in evaluating A's actions.

The court's attitude toward A's slippery defense translates into a guidepost telling B how to interpret A's actions. For the given circumstances, B should not have taken seriously A's admission or acknowledgment that he owed him money. Doing so would have been reasonable only if A were a highly ethical person. More realistically, B should decide what meaning to attach to A's actions on the basis of the behavior to be expected of the average person.

Thus, the Halakhah identifies the "reasonable man" as the man in the street rather than as a member of an idealized ethical elite.

The Rationale For The "Reasonable Man" Standard

Our discussion of the "reasonable man" standard indicates that when applied to mass media advertising, it serves to limit the disclosure and disabusing responsibility of the seller vis-à-vis his target audience. Provided that the message will not mislead a reasonable person, the seller need not be concerned about the likelihood that some people will be deceived by the ad. This point of leniency in *geneivat da'at* law may be derived from the judgment the rabbis made when they authorized the *nafal bisra* proclamation even though they realized that it would mislead some people. Because a reasonable person would take the declaration as an implicit announcement that the meat was not kosher, any erroneous impression on the part of the ignorant could be written off as self-deception.

Why the predictable deception of the ignorant is not regarded as deliberately deceptive conduct on the part of the seller is explained by the buyer's responsibility, imposed on him by the Halakhah, to educate himself in respect to market conditions. The following examples demonstrate this point.

1. Without explicitly informing customers of the practice, a grain distributor may mix together the grain he buys from the various farmers in the area.[24] Since it is generally understood in the marketplace that this is done, the distributor need not be concerned that a particular customer is unaware of the practice.[25]

2. Because it gives meat a deceptively fatty and succulent appearance, a butcher is prohibited from soaking meat in water.[26] Nevertheless, if this practice is common among butchers, the prohibition is suspended, as customers are expected to be aware of it and not be misled.[27]

3. The ethics of the price terms of a transaction concluded within the framework of a competitive norm is governed in Halakhah by the law of *ona'ah* (overreaching). The law of *ona'ah* prohibits an individual from knowingly concluding a transaction at a price which is more favorable to himself than the competitive norm.[28] What is objectionable on the basis of the *ona'ah* interdict is to prey on the opposing party's ignorance of market conditions in a commercial transaction. Hence an *ona'ah* claim is based on ignorance of the availability of a better market opportunity at

the time the disputed transaction took place.[29] Depending on how widely the price of the subject transaction departs from the competitive norm, the injured party may have recourse to void or adjust the transaction.[30] The Bet Din, however, will not order remedy in an *ona'ah* complaint if it assesses the price discrepancy involved as greater than the margin of error. Here, a claim by either the buyer or the seller that he was ignorant of a better market opportunity at the time the disputed transaction took place lacks credibility. In consequence, the Bet Din will treat the disputed sum as a voluntary gift.[31]

Thus, information-gathering is the buyer's responsibility to the same degree that the provision of information is the seller's responsibility. The seller is obliged to ensure that a reasonable person will not be misled by his representations. But the onus is on the buyer to educate himself to function in the marketplace as a reasonable person. If the buyer fails to operate in the marketplace as a reasonable person, and suffers some detriment on account of his misunderstandings, confusions, and misperceptions, the seller is not responsible.

In order to refine our formulation of Judaism's "reasonable man" standard, we must further elaborate in respect to (1) the extent of the seller's responsibility to disabuse his customers of possibly erroneous beliefs they may entertain regarding his product or service, and (2) the latitude the seller enjoys in deciding whether his message is free of deception as far as a reasonable person is concerned.

The Seller's Responsibility To Inform

Directly bearing on this issue is the rishonic dispute surrounding the wine barrel–hospitality case discussed at Ḥullin 94a. Here we are told that a host (A) should not delude his guest (B) into believing that he has acted toward him with magnanimous hospitality when in fact he has not done so. Opening a barrel of wine in honor of someone usually constitutes a gesture of magnanimous hospitality, as the wine remaining in the barrel may deteriorate as a result of its exposure to the air.[32] The magnanimity of the gesture is considerably reduced, however, when A happens to have sold the barrel of wine to a retailer just prior to the arrival of B.

What constitutes proper conduct for A in the latter circumstances is a matter of dispute between Rashi and Tosafot. In Rashi's view, A is prohibited from *telling* B that he is opening the barrel especially for him. Since B will reasonably assume that the barrel was not sold prior to his arrival, A's declaration will generate for himself an undeserved sense of indebtedness.[33] But if B is operating under that assumption he will just as assuredly be misled even if A says nothing while pouring out the wine for him. For this reason Tosafot disagree with Rashi, requiring A to disabuse B of his erroneous assumption and inform him that the barrel was sold prior to his arrival. Such disclosure will leave no doubt in B's mind that A's hospitality gesture entailed no particular expense.[34]

Rashi's position here is apparently at odds with the standard he himself sets for the sale of nonkosher meat to a Gentile. In the absence of the *nafla bisra* proclamation, a Jew may not sell nonkosher meat to a Gentile under the presumption that it is kosher (*be'ḥezkat kesheirah*).[35] Since the Gentile reasonably assumes that the meat is kosher, the butcher's silence dupes the customer into thinking he is buying kosher meat.

Applying this standard to the case at hand makes Rashi's view puzzling. To be sure, there is nothing inherent in A's opening of the barrel which directly communicates to B that he is the recipient of generous hospitality. But given the reasonableness of B's assumption that the barrel was not sold prior to his arrival, A's action generates a false impression of magnanimity. A should therefore be obliged to set B straight.

Perhaps the key to understanding Rashi's position is that the case at hand takes place in a social setting. Gestures of friendship, according to talmudic dictum, must be made openly and not in a manner which might result in the recipient's not connecting the friend with the gift: one who bestows a gift on a friend is obligated to inform him of it.[36] Underlying this rule of etiquette is the rabbis' conviction that open gestures of friendship promote pleasant and harmonious interpersonal relations.[37]

Let us assume that this rule of etiquette is operative for both parties in the wine barrel–hospitality case. Now, if A intends to bestow a generous gesture of hospitality on B, proper protocol requires him to forthrightly tell B that the barrel is being opened in his honor, rather than rely on B's reaching the same conclusion on his own based on the reasonable assumption that the barrel was not sold prior to his arrival. A's silence in the face of his having made an apparently magnanimous gesture should itself shake B's assumption that the opening of the barrel entailed considerable expense for A.

One could argue that if B is a reasonable person, he should interpret A's silence as a gracious way of telling him that no particular expense was involved in the hospitality gesture. Openly informing B runs the risk of offending him, as he might infer from the revelation that the barrel would certainly not have been opened for him if an expense had been involved. Depending upon A's exact use of words, his tone and voice inflection, B might find additional reason to take offense, concluding, for example, that A regards him as unworthy of a magnanimous gesture of hospitality. Hence, drawing attention to the lack of expense involved by a gracious silence represents the most diplomatic approach to an awkward situation. The situation is a good application of the talmudic dictum *milla be'sela mashtuka b'trein* ("a word is worth a sela, silence two selas"; Megillah 18a).

The foregoing discussion leads to an understanding of the dispute between Rashi and Tosafot. In Rashi's view, A is relieved only of a responsibility to clarify his intent. The silence with which he performs an apparently magnanimous gesture communicates to B that the gesture did not entail any particular expense. Given the awkwardness of the situation, silence is the most gracious way to making B understand this. Tosafot, on the other hand, regard A's silence as an inadequate means of undeceiving B of his erroneous impression. There are several reasons for this. One is that a false impression cannot be undone unless the force which attempts to remove it is at least as strong as the force which created it. Since the false impression was created by A's action, A's silence, notwithstanding its communicative power, cannot remove it. Only an explicit statement will accomplish this. Another reason is the consideration that the false impression here is not merely a conceptual error. It relates to personal worth, as it involves B's sense of A's regard for him. Since B wants to believe that A holds him in high regard, cognitive dissonance may set in and prevent him from recognizing the message inherent in A's silence.[38] Nothing less than an explicit statement is required here.

Some guidelines for the use of disclaimer clauses in modern advertising may be inferred from the preceding rationale of Tosafot's view. Unless the advertiser makes his disclaimer as bold and as prominent as the claim which precedes it, he has not met his responsibility. Once a false impression is created, it cannot be removed unless it is done by a force at least as strong as the force which created it.

The difficult nature of disclaimer clauses is fully recognized in American law. Illustrating this is the action the FTC took against the Thompson Medical Company in 1984. The FTC determined that the company had conveyed the false impression that its product, Aspercreme, was an aspirin rub when, in fact, the product had no aspirin content. Among other complaints, the FTC felt that the company's disclaimer, which appeared at the conclusion of its ads, was far too inadequate to counter the false impression conveyed by both the advertising copy and the name of the product.[39]

The dispute between Rashi and Tosafot repeats itself in connection with the Mar Zutra incident. Recall that Mar Zutra erroneously believed that the rabbis he met on the road constituted a welcoming party for him. As it turned out, R. Safra disabused Mar Zutra of his error. But Rava felt that silence would have been the proper course, as Mar Zutra was guilty only of self-deception. The rationale behind Rava's position, according to Tosafot, is simply that Mar Zutra should have realized that the rabbis he met were traveling in the opposite direction and his encounter with them was entirely fortuitous.

Rashi, however, interprets Rava's position differently: "Since we did not tell him that we came out in his honor [he is guilty of self-deception]." What Rashi implies here is that for the "reasonable man" (Mar Zutra), not telling him anything in these circumstances amounts to an implicit revelation to him that the encounter was nothing more than fortuitous. This is so because Mar Zutra's erroneous assessment resulted in his believing that the rabbis had conferred an extraordinary honor on him. Why? Mar Zutra had not provided the rabbis with advance knowledge of his trip, yet he imagined that they had gotten wind of it and set out to meet him. Moreover, even had he personally informed the rabbis of his arrival in advance, meeting them on the road would still have been a surprise, as he only expected to encounter them on the outskirts of the town. If the rabbis had really put themselves out for Mar Zutra, correct protocol would have dictated that they explicitly mention it to him. Doing so would be an expression of endearment and would strengthen the bond of affection their actions generated. Silence, on the other hand, works only to both dilute the impression inherent in their action and dissipate the bond of affection which would otherwise be generated. The tremendous gap between the rabbis' actions and words should have set Mar Zutra straight. If he persisted in his error, it is because he was not conducting himself in the manner of a reasonable person and hence was guilty of self-deception.

What follows from Rashi is that Rava's plea for silence was in fact a *plan* for disabusing Mar Zutra of his error. But such a responsibility certainly did not devolve upon the rabbis here, for it should have occurred to Mar Zutra that his encounter with them was entirely fortuitous. On this point Rashi is fully in agreement with Tosafot. Rashi's intent here is only to reinforce the judgment that Mar Zutra was guilty of self-deception because he should have taken the rabbis' silence as an implicit disabusing statement.

Note that Rava objected to R. Safra's conduct because it caused Mar Zutra distress. One can reasonably infer from this that Rava felt that his own proposed approach, calling for the rabbis to say nothing, would entail less anguish for Mar Zutra. Hence the Mar Zutra incident provides another example of the talmudic dictum *milla b'sela mashtuka b'trein.*

Tosafot reject Rashi's approach because in their view, silence, even in the context of a social setting, is not an adequate vehicle for dispelling illusions. If Mar Zutra was guilty of self-deception, the reason must be that it should have occurred to him that his encounter with the rabbis was nothing more than fortuitous.

Since it is etiquette which gives silence its communicative power, Rashi's rejection of silence as an informative technique in the sale of nonkosher meat when the *nafal bisra* proclamation was not made is readily understandable. Since silence does not dispel ambiguity in a commercial setting, Rashi would be in full agreement with Tosafot that in a commercial context, silence is not equivalent to an explicit statement. To illustrate, suppose that a manufacturer of sewing machines failed to disclose that model D lacked a design stitching capability. The manufacturer claims that the public should take the omission of disclosure as equivalent to an explicit statement that model D lacks this capability. But silence is not equivalent to an explicit statement. Accordingly, if the public generally expects the design stitching feature in a sewing machine, the only acceptable way to properly indicate that model D lacks this capability is to say so explicitly.

Thus all disputants agree that a seller can only satisfy his obligation by means of an explicit statement. Application of the "reasonable man" standard here, however, limits this responsibility. The seller need only be concerned with expectations held by a reasonable person that are material in making the purchasing decision at hand.

The Seller's Self-assessment—American Law

In this section, we compare American and Jewish law in respect to the latitude the advertiser enjoys in relying on his own judgment as to whether his commercial message has the capacity to deceive.

American law guarantees advertisers freedom of commercial speech.[40] A commercial message need not be pilot-tested to ensure that it is free of deceptiveness before it is released. Consumer and competitor complaints against commercial messages, however, are taken up by the FTC. If the FTC finds an ad deceptive, it has the authority to ban the ad and/or to order the advertiser to take corrective measures for the purpose of disabusing the public of the false impression conveyed by the ad. In making its findings, the FTC has the discretion to introduce extrinsic evidence, such as consumer surveys, but if it sees fit, it can base its decision entirely on its own judgment.[41]

Roger E. Schechter argues that in its adjudication of challenges against implied claims of commercial messages, the FTC should condemn an ad only if it puts a consequential number of consumers "at risk" of acting to their own detriment. Action, in turn, is induced by the ad's credibility and the ease with which consumers can independently verify the claims it makes.

Advertising media, ad content, and advertiser prominence all bear on credibility. Ads running in major national magazines probably have more credibility than those that appear in local newspapers. This may occur because consumers assume, at least subconsciously, that major magazine publishers attempt to screen advertisements for accuracy before allowing them to appear.

The nature of the product also influences ad credibility. Consumers probably assume that firms advertising medicinal products or other items that can have serious adverse physical effects are under special government scrutiny to be honest. While this is true to a certain extent, it is invalid in respect to such products as cosmetics, weight-loss preparations, and over-the-counter drugs.

Attributes of the person actually communicating the commercial message also affect an advertisement's credibility in the minds of consumers. Expert testimonials, for example, will enhance the credibility of the message.

In respect to verifiability, most products have three relevant traits: search, experience, and credence. Search traits are those that are apparent to a buyer before making the purchase. The price of an item, its color, and its other observable attributes are examples. Experience traits are those that manifest themselves only after purchase, including such factors as the taste of a toothpaste and the durability of a washing machine. Finally, credence traits are those that never manifest themselves to the buyer. Repair service is an example. Here, a buyer who has a product repaired will never learn whether certain specific repairs were actually necessary.

Advertising claims in respect to search traits can easily be verified by inspecting the item. The verifiability of claims in respect to the experience trait will depend on how frequently consumers purchase the item and how soon after purchase the trait manifests itself. Advertising which deals with credence traits is the most difficult to verify. Only external sources, such as a second opinion, can provide the requisite information. As a result, ads making claims about credence traits will be very difficult for all but the most diligent and aggressive consumers to verify.

Schechter uses a credibility-verifiability index to categorize ads along a continuum ranging from high- to low-influence ads: the combination of high credibility and difficult verifiability classifies the ad as having high influence; easy verifiability and high credibility classify the ad to be of moderate influence; difficult verifiability and ordinary credibility make for a moderate-influence ad; and finally, easy verifiability and ordinary credibility make the ad a low-influence one.

Categorizing ads along the high influence–low influence continuum leads Schechter to the following policy prescription for the FTC: (1) When a high-influence ad is challenged, the FTC may condemn the ad on the basis of its own interpretation of the implied claim. But the advertiser should be given the opportunity to prove that the FTC's interpretation is not representative of the target group which is exposed to the ad. An admissible rebuttal would require the advertiser to produce two methodologically valid consumer research studies showing that fewer than 5 percent of the representative sample interpreted the commercial in the challenged fashion. (2) When a low-influence ad is challenged, the FTC cannot ban it unless it demonstrates by means of two methodologically valid consumer research studies that more than 50 percent of the representative sample of the target group interprets the implied claim in the challenged fashion. (3) When a moderate-influence ad is challenged, the burden again is on the FTC to demonstrate that at least 25 percent of the representative sample of the target group interpreted the message in the challenged fashion.[42]

Self-Assessment and Halakhah

In secular society, a seller enjoys freedom to make the judgement that his representation is not misleading. This freedom is constrained only by the *practical* consideration of possible adverse reaction on the part of consumers and competitors. No such parallel freedom in commercial speech is found in Halakhah. Since misleading advertising violates the *geneivat da'at* interdict, the basic issue is whether the seller can *rely* on his own judgement that his message is not deceptive.

In the halakhic view, the judgment of sellers will be biased by the profit motive, and therefore self-assessments of whether a commercial representation is deceptive are regarded as basically unreliable. This contention is supported by the Halakhah's call for the appointment of public inspectors to ensure the honesty of commercial weights and measures.[43] R. Jeḥiel Michel Epstein (Belorussia, 1829–1908) explains that voluntary self-compliance is not relied upon to ensure the integrity of commercial weights and measures because of the unconscious distorting effect that the profit motive exerts on vendors. R. Epstein employs the same rationale to explain Maimonides' ruling[44] that in matters of kashrut one may only patronize a vendor who is known to be reliable.[45]

Another source for extrapolating the halakhic view on the reliability of self-assessment is the wine barrel–hospitality case referred to earlier. In this connection, the Talmud relates a hospitality incident involving R. Judah and Ulla. R. Judah opened a barrel of wine in honor of Ulla. The barrel had been sold before Ulla arrived. Two versions of the incident are recorded. In one, R. Judah told his guest about the sale. In the other, no such disclosure took place. The second version is defended by the Talmud on the grounds that Ulla was very dear to R. Judah, and consequently he would have extended him the hospitality gesture even if it entailed considerable expense.[46]

Curiously, the point of leniency in *geneivat da'at* law that emerges in the R. Judah–Ulla incident is conspicuously omitted by Maimonides and R. Jacob b. Asher (Germany, 1270–1343) in their treatments of the wine barrel–hospitality case. Noting the omission, R. Aryeh Judah b. Akiba (1759–1819) posits that the aforementioned codifiers regard the talmudic incident as lacking general applicability. Only a host like R. Judah, i.e., someone of exceptional moral character, is free of the obligation to correct his guest's false impression that he treated him with magnanimous hospitality. In the instance of someone like R. Judah, the host's self-assessment that he would confer generous hospitality on his guest even if it entailed a considerable expense is completely reliable. Such a self-assessment would not, however, free an individual of ordinary moral character from his obligation to make the disclosure. For an ordinary person, such a self-assessment amounts to self-delusion. Confronted with an actual opportunity to confer generous hospitality on a friend only at a considerable expense, the average person would find many convenient excuses not to do so. Since the point of leniency in *geneivat da'at* law that emerges from the R. Judah–Ulla incident does not have general applicability, Maimonides and R. Jacob b. Asher omit mentioning it.[47]

R. Aryeh Judah b. Akiba's conclusion regarding the unreliability of self-assessment apparently places him at odds with the responsa literature in respect to an issue dealing with the counteracting of unwarranted bias in the labor market. The specific issue involves the question of whether an individual is permitted to achieve a more youthful appearance by dying his beard to enhance his chances of securing employment. Addressing this question, R. Mosheh Mordecai Epstein (Hebron, 1866–1922) permits the conduct provided the employer's expectations with respect to performance will be met. Realizing that productivity could decline sharply with advancing age, R. Epstein points out that in the final analysis, the conduct's legitimacy rests on the honesty of the job seeker's self-assessment.[48] Advancing a similar analysis, R. Eliezer Meir Preil (1881–1934) arrives at the same conclusion.[49] R. Mosheh Feinstein (New York, 1895–1986) concurs with these rulings.[50]

If we distinguish between self-assessment cases relating to routine circumstances and those relating to extraordinary, hypothetical situations, we approach a reconciliation of the opinions. Self-assessment may very well be reliable when it relates to ordinary, predictable life situations. Even though productivity may drop off with advancing age, honest self-appraisal can indicate to the senior job seeker whether he can meet the employer's performance standards. The reliability of self-assessment in the realm of the hypothetical is another matter. Individuals of ordinary moral character cannot extrapolate with any degree of accuracy how they would react to a hypothetical situation requiring extraordinary effort on their part.

In the final analysis, the job seeker's self-assessment of his ability is reliable because he knows that it will be subject to objective verification. This is supported by the talmudic text at Ḥullin 94a, referred to earlier. Recall that Mar Zutra jumped to the conclusion that Rava and R. Safra, whom he met on his way to Maḥoza, were a welcoming party in his honor. Rava felt that Mar Zutra was guilty of self-deception and thus that there was no need to disabuse him of his error. Rava's confidence that his judgment was correct was rooted, as it appears to this writer, in the knowledge that Mar Zutra himself would soon come to the same conclusion. After all, Rava and R. Safra were traveling in the opposite direction of Mar Zutra. As soon as the three men parted company and went their separate ways, Mar Zutra would realize that Rava and R. Safra had not come as a welcoming party for him. The certainty that Mar Zutra's hindsight judgment would confirm his own *a priori* judgment gave Rava the confidence that his assessment was correct.

The selfsame feature of objective verifiability is what gave the rabbis the confidence that the marketplace would understand *nafal bisra* as an implicit declaration of *trefa*. If the rabbis were wrong, then the *nafal bisra* proclamation would greatly unsettle the marketplace. Sellers would think that they were representing their meat as nonkosher, but the Gentile clientele would take the representation to mean that the meat was kosher. This misunderstanding would manifest itself in a significant number of complaints of deception against the Jewish butchers. Any unsettling of the marketplace as a result of the proclamation of *nafal bisra* informs the rabbis that they erred in expecting the marketplace to read the meaning they intended into *nafal bisra*. This, in turn, will necessitate its replacement with a *nafal trefta* announcement.

What this implies for modern advertising is that a seller's judgment that his advertising copy will not deceive a reasonable person is generally unreliable. This leads to the proposition that in the Torah society, advertising copy must be pilot-tested before it is released. A scientifically designed pilot-test can ascertain the impressions the advertising message will have on the target group, as well as the inferences this group will draw from it.

Should the results fail to conform to actuality, revision of the ad would be in order.

Relaxation of the pilot-testing requirement would apply under certain conditions, as when the advertising claim is subject to independent verification by the consumer. Schechter's schema serves well to identify the factors which work to rid the seller of bias when relying on the accuracy of his own assessment. Specifically, if the seller's claim relates either to the search trait of a good or to the experience trait of an item which is subject to frequent repeat purchases, his self-interest militates against deceptive conduct. Since the seller's judgment that his message is free of deception is reliable in these cases, the pilot-testing requirement could be dispensed with.

Transparently False Advertising Claims

In American law, an explicitly false advertising claim is not legitimized by producing evidence that a reasonable person would readily recognize the falsity of the claim and hence not be deceived. To cite one example, this defense was rejected in the 1944 FTC action against Charles of the Ritz Distribution Corporation, a case involving explicitly false claims.[51] Charles of the Ritz falsely represented its product, Rejuvenescence, a skin cream, as having the property to restore youth or the appearance of youth to the skin, regardless of the condition of the skin or the age of the user. The corporation defended itself by maintaining that no reasonable person would take the claim seriously and hence no deception was involved. In rejecting this argument, the FTC reiterated a position taken previously by the circuit court that the Federal Trade Commission Act was not "made for the protection of experts, but for the public—that vast multiple which includes the ignorant, the unthinking and the credulous."[52]

The "reasonable man" defense does, however, find legitimacy in one category of cases involving explicitly false claims, the area of puffery.[53] Puffery refers to the favorable opinion a seller makes in representing his product or service.

Preston argues that the current legal approach to puffery is misguided. Statements of opinion or value often imply fact and thus should be considered as factual representations. To illustrate, a beer manufacturer's assertion that its product is "Milwaukee's finest" implies that standards of beer production and quality exist, on the basis of which the advertised beer is superior to competitors' beers. Given that no such quality standards exist, the manufacturer's assertion is misleading and deceptive.

Instead of approaching the issue of puffery by making semantic distinctions between fact and opinion, advertising messages should be examined on the basis of their behavioral/psychological impact. Whether the claim is fact, opinion, or value, the legal test should be whether the message deceives, i.e., creates untrue expectations which influence purchasers.[54]

Following Preston's line, Oliver suggests that whenever consumers overrate a product relative to its actual merits as a result of puffery, the advertising message should be regarded as deceptive.

The fact that consumers can recognize the exaggeration in an advertising message does not necessarily lead to the conclusion that the message does not have the capacity to deceive. To illustrate, if an advertiser states that detergent X gets clothes "cleaner than clean" or "whiter than white," this statement is likely to create an expectation that X cleans in some superior sense. If the appropriate discount is not made, the puffery will influence the consumer to regard the cleaning power of X more favorably than would be the case had the advertiser simply said "clean" or "white."

The deception inherent in puffery is often reinforced by the consumer's inability to disprove the advertiser's exaggerated claim. A case in point is the claim by a manufacturer of shock absorbers that his product gives the "most comfortable ride." Would the consumer be expected to buy three competing shock absorbers and interchange them on a weekly basis, for the purpose of testing the manufacturer's claim?[55]

Transparently False Claims In Jewish Law

From the standpoint of Halakhah, general recognition in the marketplace that a seller's explicit claim is false does not transform the representation into a truthful message. It remains false, albeit transparently false. Transparent falsity will not deceive a reasonable person, but it will dupe the ignorant and the credulous. Making a representation involving an explicitly false claim, even if the falsity is obvious to a reasonable person, is an act of deception perpetrated against the ignorant. The fact that the great majority of people exposed to the representation are not duped by it does not excuse the active deception perpetrated against the ignorant and credulous. In sharp contrast, when the seller's claim is rendered misleading only because ignorant people read an eccentric meaning into it, the claim retains its nondeceptive character and those who misread it are deceiving themselves.

Finally, even if the falsity of the explicit claim is universally recognized, and therefore the issue of deception does not arise, the use of transparent falseness has no place in the Torah society.

Standing at the basis of this proposition is the *imitatio Dei* role that Halakhah assigns to government. The relevant divine attributes here are *emet* (truth)[56] and *raḥum*[57].

In Jewish tradition, the ideal of *emet* is identified with the patriarch Jacob.[58] One way that Jacob manifested the character trait of *emet* was by deliberately exposing himself to a objectively verifiable standard. Illustrating this is the scheme for compensating himself that he proposed to Laban: All the spotted and mottled lambs would be removed from Laban's flock, leaving in Jacob's care only the single-colored lambs. Jacob's wage was to consist of the mottled and spotted goats born from the single-colored herd.[59] This compensation scheme would make any departure by Jacob from the stipulated conditions immediately evident to Laban. As Jacob put it: "Thus my honesty will tell, when you come to look into my wages with you: Any goat in my lot that is not speckled and spotted, any sheep that is not dark, you may consider to have been stolen" (Genesis 30:33).

For the advertising industry, the *emet* standard translates into a requirement to formulate claims in an objectively verifiable manner.

Raḥum is God's mercy in sparing a person misfortune which otherwise would befall him.[60] Man's perception of the *raḥum* element of God's mercy is heightened when the said misfortune is feared to be in the offing.

Carrying out the *emet* and *raḥum* aspects of its *imitatio Dei* mandate requires the government to set up an agency like the Federal Trade Commission to regulate advertising. Its function would be to foster integrity and a harmonious order in the marketplace. Defining the role of the agency in this fashion allows society as a collective to emulate God's attributes of *emet* and *raḥum*.

Without clearcut rules as guideposts for conduct in the marketplace, a wedge between expectations and actual experience is inevitably produced. Contentious relations along with cynicism and disappointment become the everyday experience of the marketplace. Adopting *raḥum* as its operational ideal requires the agency regulating advertising to formulate clearcut marketplace rules that give little room for subjective judgment and do not tolerate manipulation.

Taken together, the *emet* and *raḥum* ideals move the marketplace in the direction of objective standards and away from manipulation, with the result that order and harmony in interpersonal relations are promoted.

As should be clear by now, transparent lying as an advertising stratagem has no place in the Torah society. Such a practice totally detaches the seller's claims from any mooring in the world of objective verifiability and rests the legitimacy of his advertising method entirely on his own judgment that no one will be deceived. Subjectivism of the entirely reliable variety is but the first step on a slippery slope, culminating in the abandonment of objective verifiability in the marketplace.

On a more subtle level, transparent lying should be rejected as an advertising stratagem because it undermines the ideal of truth and integrity in the marketplace. If lying in any manner is permissible, subconsciously everyone becomes less committed to the truth.

The following text at Yevamot 63a makes this evident:

> Rav was constantly tormented by his wife. If he told her, "Prepare me lentils," she would prepare him small peas; [and if he asked for] small peas, she prepared him lentils. When his son Ḥiyya grew up, he gave her [his father's instructions] in reverse. "Your mother," Rav remarked to him, "has im-

proved!" "It was I," the other replied, "who reversed [your orders] to her." "This is what people say," the first said to him, "'Thine own off-spring teaches thee reason'; however, you must not continue to do so, for it is said, 'They have taught their tongue to speak lies, they weary themselves,' etc. (Jeremiah 9:4)."

Given the permissibility of altering the truth for the purpose of restoring domestic harmony,[61] Rav's objection to Ḥiyya's conduct is somewhat puzzling. According to R. Solomon Luria (Poland, 1510–1573), the key to understanding why Rav felt that his son's conduct was unacceptable is the fact that Ḥiyya's ploy entailed lying on a continuous basis. The ongoing repetition of a lie, even if the lie is permissible, corrupts character and accustoms one to lying.[62]

The lesson to be drawn from this text is that public policy should not sanction the use of transparent lying as an advertising ploy. Approving the use of lies on the theory that no one will be deceived by them tarnishes the ideal of truth by knocking it off its pedestal, thus dragging down the moral climate of society.

In respect to puffery, Halakhah would find no reason to treat it as a separate category. If a statement of opinion conveys an implied fact which is misleading, then the *geneivat da'at* interdict is violated. Thus, Halakhah's treatment of puffery conforms with Preston's and Oliver's critique of the current American legal approach to this issue.

• 5

Hakkarat Hatov and the Making of the Moral Personality

Carrying out its *imitatio Dei* role perforce involves the government in the moral sphere. Concretely, this mandate translates into a governmental obligation to assist people in their strivings for moral betterment. But the ideal for the individual striving for moral betterment is also encapsulated in *imitatio Dei* terms. Recall R. Soloveitchik's insight that for the individual, *imitatio Dei* does not simply demand specific conduct but sets a standard for character. What one must strive for is no less than to be worthy of being called by the names of God. For society, therefore, the ideal is to have the state's *imitatio Dei* mandate connect with the individual's strivings to be worthy to be called by the names of God. Assisting the individual in his spiritual strivings requires the state to involve itself in the realm of character development. Specifically, it must encourage in its citizens the character traits which foster the moral personality.

In this chapter we develop the thesis that in Judaism the key to the moral personality is the character trait of *hakkarat hatov* (gratitude). We then proceed to demonstrate that *hakkarat hatov* is a very delicate sensitivity. Recommendations for government policy with the aim of fostering and strengthening *hakkarat hatov* will be offered.

The Test Of Joseph's Piety

We begin with an analysis of Joseph's struggle in overcoming the wiles of Lady Potiphar.

> "He adamantly refused. He reasoned with his master's wife. `My master does not even know what I do in the house. He has entrusted me with everything he owns. No one in this house has more power than I have. He has not kept back anything at all from me, except for you, his wife. How could

I do such a great wrong? It would be a sin before God!'" (Genesis 39:8–9).

"The woman grabbed him by his cloak. 'Sleep with me!' she pleaded. He ran away from her, leaving his cloak in her hand, and fled outside" (Genesis 39:12).

At that moment, his father's image appeared to him through the window and said, "Joseph, your brothers will have their names inscribed upon the stones of the ephod [the high priest's sash] and yours amongst theirs. Is it your wish to have your name expunged from amongst theirs and be called an associate of harlots?" Immediately "his bow abode in strength" (Genesis 49:24). R. Johanan said in the name of R. Meir: [This means] that his passion was subdued.[1]

The preceding description of Joseph's struggle against sin makes it evident that his triumph in the test of piety was due to three independent moral forces: (1) the influence of his father, Jacob; (2) his attitude toward Potiphar; and (3) his sense of duty to God. We will take up each of these forces in turn, demonstrating that *hakkarat hatov* is the underlying factor which enabled Joseph to resist the wiles of Lady Potiphar.

The Influence of Jacob

Joseph triumphs in his trial of passion because he personalizes the moral dilemma. Specifically, Joseph equates succumbing to Lady Potiphar with being false to the moral principles his father taught him. If Joseph merely gave lip service to these teachings, what influence could they have had on him once he was no longer under his father's control? What influence could these teachings have had at the moment Joseph faced the seductive power of lust and at the same time was convinced that his father thought he was either dead or hopelessly missing? Overcoming a sin of passion by conjuring up an image of his father could only be efficacious under the assumption that Joseph cherished his father's moral teachings and harbored a deep sense of gratitude to him for them.[2] Hence for Joseph, *hakkarat hatov* was the link that transformed moral training into virtuous conduct.

In the Torah society, parents[3] and the school system[4] are assigned the function of moral education. Jacob's role in helping Joseph overcome his trial of passion serves as a model for effective moral training. Several implications and extensions of this model for parents and the school system will now be presented.

If the potential moral force of parents is to be realized, *hakkarat hatov* must take on a double role. It must, of course, be the child's response to the moral training provided by his parents; but to be effective moral educators, the parents themselves must be imbued with *hakkarat hatov*. Parents who lack *hakkarat hatov* will prove incapable of implanting this character trait in their children.

This proposition is illustrated by the lesson the Mekhilta derives from the spatial arrangement of the Decalogue on the two tablets of the Covenant (*shenei luḥot haberit*). The Decalogue was arranged on the two tables in two groups of five so that it would be read not only in the vertical order but also horizontally.[5]

This arrangement results in the pairing of "Honor your father and mother" with "Do not covet your neighbor's wife." Commenting on this linkage, the Mekhilta teaches that he who violates "Do not covet your neighbor's wife" will beget a son who will curse him and confer honor on someone else.[6]

Since coveting of all sorts is forbidden, the Mekhilta's dictum is generalizable to the stark assertion that coveting diminishes the potential for the parent to carry out his moral-educational role. The Mekhilta concentrates on coveting a neighbor's wife. Behavior of this sort on the part of the father manifests contempt for the mother of his children, who is the natural object of the child's love and *hakkarat hatov*. Someone who fundamentally violates *hakkarat hatov* cannot hope to implant even a modicum of this character trait in his child.

Ironically, everything the coveting father does for his child may be taken by the child as a quid pro quo gesture rather than as an expression of selfless love. With the motives of the coveting father always suspect, his moral teachings will never be taken seriously. Quid pro quo will quickly become the guiding principle for the child of a coveting father. With self-gratification directing the child's loyalties, it is not inconceivable that he will seek out an authority figure to replace his natural father, lavishing honor on the replacement father and at the same time cursing his natural father.

The flip side message of the Mekhilta's linkage of the two commandments is that a rarefied *hakkarat hatov* sensitivity tempers the coveting drive. We need not go far afield to find the rationalization for this. The more people appreciate what they already have, the less they will be driven to covet what is not theirs.

Let us take the lesson from the Mekhilta a bit further. In the teachings of R. Ahron Soloveichik (Chicago, 1918–), God bestowed two separate gifts upon humankind. One blessing is the gift of conquest, of power and of grasping (*kibbush*). The other is the gift of cultivation, of work and dedication and of reaching unto things and people (*ḥazakah*). While the *kibbush* mandate was given to the First Adam immediately following his creation, the *ḥazakah* mandate awaited his placement in the Garden of Eden. R. Soloveichik finds much significance in this. Humankind, he concludes, is capable of attaining great heights of progress with the gift of *kibbush*, but it cannot succeed in establishing a paradise on earth unless *kibbush* is coupled with the gift of *ḥazakah*.

The *kibbush* mandate, in our sages' view, was given to man, but not to woman. On the other hand, posits R. Soloveichik, *ḥazakah* is the mandate for woman. Its fulfillment is realized by means of reaching unto things and people, compassion, love, consideration, and guidance.[7]

Childrearing puts parents in contact with the multifaced needs and demands of their child. Hence parenthood is a fertile setting for the *ḥazakah* mandate. Dedicated parenting in the form of responding to the child's needs and demands in a sensitive, responsible, and supportive manner is fulfillment of *ḥazakah* on a high level.

To the extent that parents fail in the *ḥazakah* mandate, they will be rendered unfit for the moral-educational role. Moral preachments from ineffectual parents who frequently disappoint will likely be taken by the child as hypocritical ranting. Successful parenting, on the other hand, makes the child receptive to moral training. But if the ideal is for an individual to equate failing a test of piety with letting down his parents, then the childrearing and moral-educational roles of the parents must be fully integrated. Such integration makes moral training permeate every aspect of the life experience. In addition, it makes the gratitude parenthood compels inseparable from the gratitude their moral training elicits. This, in turn, works to *personalize* the moral dilemma. The converse of this proposition is that the more compartmentalized moral education is, the less it will elicit ethical conduct.

The selfsame assertion can be made in respect to education. Specifically, to be effective, moral education must permeate the entire curriculum, and character building must form a central goal of the educational enterprise. Assigning moral education this role catapults it from the periphery to being an integral part of the educational process. This, in turn, fosters a bonding between students and educators, which, in turn, works to *personalize* the moral dilemma.

Parenting and moral education naturally compel gratitude on the part of the recipient. But Halakhah does not leave the expression of gratitude to a matter of happenstance.

In respect to filial responsibility, Halakhah prescribes two specific duties for the child vis-à-vis his parents. These duties are *kibbud* (honor)[8] and *morah* (reverence).[9] *Kibbud* takes the form of acts of service, such as serving parents meals. *Morah*, on the other hand, denotes reverential conduct toward parents, such as not sitting in their place and not contradicting them.[10]

Similarly, Halakhah demands of the student special reverential behavior toward his religious (moral) teacher.[11]

Joseph's Attitude Toward Potiphar

A second moral force which enabled Joseph to resist Lady Potiphar was his attitude toward her husband. For Joseph, succumbing to Lady Potiphar amounted to betraying the trust of her husband, who was his master.

Logic does not compel that a test of piety be interpreted as a test of loyalty to Potiphar. Clearly, it was Joseph's revulsion at being an ingrate which pushed this equation on him. In other words, Joseph's deep sense of gratitude to Potiphar *personalized* his dilemma, tearing him between lust and loyalty.

What this points up is that *hakkarat hatov* is a desirable personality trait to deter unethical conduct. One who readily acknowledges and appreciates the advantages other people confer on him is less likely to be guilty of erroneously perceiving himself as a victim of exploitation. Hence, if one's personality is imbued with *hakkarat hatov*, this works to reduce misconduct which is rationalized as retaliation for exploitative conduct by others.

Another benefit proceeding from the *hakkarat hatov* personality is that expressions of gratitude promote a harmonious social order.

Gestures of friendship, according to talmudic dictum, must be made openly and not in a manner which might result in the recipient not connecting the friend with the gift.[12] Accordingly, someone who gives a gift of bread to a child not in the presence of his parents must take account of the fact that the child might consume the bread before the parents return, with the consequence that they may never come to know of the gift. To forestall this, the donor must rub traces of the bread's grain on the child's eyelid. When the parents notice the sign and ask the child about it, the child will tell them that so-and-so gave him a gift of bread and rubbed the grain on his eyelid as well. Putting the donor to all this extra trouble, according to R. Solomon b. Isaac (Rashi; Troyes, 1040–1105), is rooted in the conviction that open gestures of friendship promote pleasant and harmonious interpersonal relations.[13] Similarly, expressions of gratitude promote goodwill and build respect and trust in society.

Joseph's Sense of Duty to God

The third and final element summoned by Joseph in his trial of passion was the protest that the liaison violated God's moral code.

Submitting to God's moral code out of a sense of duty to Him, in the teaching of R. Baḥya b. Joseph ibn Pakudah (Spain, 11th cent.), is fundamentally rooted in an expression of *hakkarat hatov* to God.[14] One who is imbued with a refined sense of gratitude is led to imagine what life would be like, for instance, without the capacity to remember, or the ability to forget. The

Divine blessing inherent in each of our human faculties is therefore acutely appreciated.

Similarly, we take note that the elements in the physical world which we most desperately need for survival are available in relative abundance.[15] Air, which we cannot do without even for a short time, is ubiquitous. Water, which we can do without only for a short time, is in relative abundance. Food, which is vital, but less essential than water, is relatively more abundant than other products and services man desires. Because these circumstances work to enhance man's economic well-being, they are taken by the *hakkarat hatov* personality as reflecting God's kindness in sparing us from a desperate struggle just to survive. In regard to these benefits and the like, the fool is either blinded to their existence or takes them entirely for granted. The more refined one's *hakkarat hatov* sentiment, the more Divine blessings one will discover in his own life. This, in turn, drives man to serve God out of a sense of duty and debt. As a result, violating God's laws is regarded as acting in the manner of an ingrate.[16]

Since moral conduct impelled by a sense of duty to God does not entail personalizing the moral dilemma, the underlying *hakkarat hatov* motive represents a delicate sensitivity.

In the thinking of R. Aaron ha-Levi (Barcelona, 1235–1300), serving God out of a sense of *hakkarat hatov* is a sensitivity which is a by-product of filial *hakkarat hatov* for parents.

> A man should realize that his mother and father are the cause of his being in the world, and therefore it is truly proper that he render them all the honor and do them all the service he can. For they brought him into the world, and they labored greatly on his behalf during his childhood.
>
> Once a man has assimilated this trait, he will ascend by it to recognize the good done him by the Lord, who is the cause of his being and the cause of the existence of all his forefathers, reaching back to the First Adam. It was He who brought him into the world and provided for his needs all his life; who structured him and perfected his body; who gave him a soul and intelligence—for without the soul with which God graced us, man would be as the brute horse or mule. So a man ought

> to understand well how much effort is owed the service of the Lord.[17]

R. Aaron ha-Levi's theory catapults parenting into the basic building block in the formation of the moral personality. Dedicated parenting combined with moral training, as discussed previously, works to personalize the moral dilemma. But once the *hakkarat hatov* character trait develops, it is capable of widening and becoming sensitized to the debt owed the Almighty. This higher level of *hakkarat hatov*, in turn, works to impel virtuous conduct done simply out of a sense of duty to the Almighty. Hence parenting combined with moral training is capable of launching a hierarchy of successively progressive forms of virtuous conduct.

On the other hand, an individual's rejection of any sense of duty to God signalizes that his parents have failed. This assertion is explicitly made by the Talmud in connection with the following story:

> Our sages taught: It happened that Miriam the daughter of Bilgah became an apostate from the Jewish faith; and she went and married a military officer of the royal Greek rulers. When the Greeks entered the Sanctuary, she went and beat the altar with her sandal, exclaiming, "You wolf, wolf! You consume the property of the Jews, but you do not stand by them when they are sore-pressed!" When the sages learned of the matter, they sent and shut down its [the division of priests'] ring and blocked up its niche.[18]

Commenting on why Miriam's father, Bilgah (head of the division of priests), was punished for his daughter's apostasy, Abaya theorized, "Because people say, what a child speaks in the street it has heard either from its father or its mother." Accordingly, if Miriam displayed contempt for the altar, it must have been because she had been exposed to a disdainful attitude toward religion in her home.[19] Thus it was presumed that bad upbringing accounted for Miriam's apostasy.

Hakkarat Hatov as an Ethical Norm

Before we proceed to discuss some governmental policies that can foster the moral personality, we offer the following insights into the nature of *hakkarat hatov* as an ethical norm. These insights point to an assessment of *hakkarat hatov* as a delicate sensitivity. Since *hakkarat hatov* is the key to the moral personality, the significance of these findings is to bolster the case for government policies to foster the moral personality.

Our sages felt that it was not easy to develop *hakkarat hatov* as an ethical norm. This attitude can be drawn out by focusing on the miẓvah of honoring one's father and mother. *Hakkarat hatov* stands as the dominant rationale of this miẓvah; i.e., parenthood compels gratitude. Echoing this theme, R. Aaron ha-Levi writes:

> Among the bases of this miẓvah is the fact that it is proper that a man recognize and bestow kindness upon one who has done him good, and that he not be base, a dissimulator, and one who denies the good done him by another. For that is an evil trait, held most obnoxious both by God and man.
> A man should realize that his mother and father are the cause of his being in the world, and therefore it is truly proper that he render them all the honor and do them all the service he can. For they brought him into the world, and they labored greatly on his behalf during his childhood.[20]

Notwithstanding the compelling nature of the claim parenthood has on gratitude, our sages were well aware that man's devious side could adduce many arguments to deny this claim. Pulling together these specious arguments, R. Abraham Danzig (Prague, 1748–1820) railed:

> May the mouths speaking untruth be stopped. For they say that no gratitude is owed parents, for their immediate motive was self-gratification, and the child was merely created incidentally; that with the child born, the Lord made the nature of things such that they would raise him, as indeed all animals raise their young, without the young being grateful for this. . .

> For men who argue in this way show themselves to be, indeed, brutes, whom God denied reason and understanding. Concerning such opinion, our sages say, "Whoever is ungrateful toward his comrade will, in time, be ungrateful to God." For according to their thinking, they need not fear or honor God either, since we are His creations, and it is only proper that one be good and merciful to one's creatures. Doubtless those who say these things deny God in their hearts.[21]

Another insight Judaism offers in respect to the ethical norm of *hakkarat hatov* is that a shallow gratitude can dissipate and even turn into unwarranted hatred. Evincing this proposition is the midrashic exposition of the verse: "Then a new king arose over Egypt, who knew nothing about Joseph" (Exodus 1:8).

> He made himself a denier of the good he owed to Joseph and his people. He said, "These are not of Joseph's seed; they are like us," and also, "Joseph I know not." Did he not know Joseph? He can be compared, said R. Abin, to one who stoned a friend of the king, whereupon the king commanded, "Behead him, lest tomorrow he do the same to me." The Bible, therefore, wrote concerning him, as it were: Today he does not know Joseph. Tomorrow he will declare: I do not know the Lord. This teaches us that denial of the good one's fellow conferred on him is akin to denial of the existence of God.[22]

By appointing Joseph viceroy, Pharaoh spontaneously responded with a measure of *hakkarat hatov* toward him for interpreting his dream and proposing an economic plan which would avert disaster for Egypt.[23] In addition, Joseph was, at least initially, adored by the Egyptian masses.[24] His popularity spilled over to his family, as evidenced by Pharaoh's hospitable welcome of Jacob and his family upon their arrival in Egypt and by his generous offer to settle them in the land of Goshen, the most desirable part of Egypt.[25]

Astonishingly, when Joseph and his brothers died, all this Egyptian goodwill toward the Jewish people vanished. Not only did the goodwill dissipate, but it turned into hatred, culminating in a national policy of enslavement and genocide.[26] How did the

Egyptians justify this drastic change in attitude toward the Jewish people? R. Abin answers that as soon as an assimilationist trend became apparent among the Jews, the Egyptians began to feel that the Jewish immigrants were benefiting from their host country at least as much as they contributed to it. The Egyptian debt to the Jewish people was thereby cancelled, and Jewish indebtedness to the host country was, in the eyes of the Egyptian monarch, building up.

Pharaoh's changed attitude toward Joseph is, however, another matter. The enigma magnifies in light of the Torah's recording that Joseph's acts as viceroy enormously enriched Pharaoh's treasury.[27] Indeed, one school of thought has it that the "new king" referred to at Exodus 1:8 was a foreign invader;[28] an ethnocentric foreign invader would have no interest in recalling Joseph's contributions to Egypt. R. Abin, however, holds that the new king was "new" only in respect to his decrees;[29] he was neither a usurper of the throne nor an invader, but the natural heir of a particular dynasty.[30]

Distance from an event alters our perspective on it. At the time of the crisis, the Egyptian people regarded Joseph's policies as strokes of genius.[31] But respect for genius is not true *hakkarat hatov*. The 20 percent tax in kind on agricultural produce instituted for the purpose of public storage,[32] which culminated in the nationalization of the country's farmland,[33] fundamentally altered Egypt's economic structure. Instead of recognizing that their very survival was due to Joseph's prudent policies, survivors of the famine might very well have shifted focus to their landlessness and blamed it on Joseph. Viewing the 20 percent tax on their crops in the seven years of prosperity as amounting to nothing more than a vehicle for achieving forced private saving,[34] the argument for fixing blame could have run as follows: "Since the foodstuffs in the public granaries represent private savings, why were we made to exhaust our money, sell our cattle, and turn our land over to the state, all to obtain what is in any case our entitlement?"

What this argument conveniently ignores, however, is that left to its own devices the Egyptian economy would have produced a much lower output than was the case under Joseph's guidance. Without the tax, the superabundance would have engendered a tremendous loss in productivity due to a sharp increase in idleness and waste. More basically, the state-of-the-art technology could offer no means of storing grain without spoilage for the long period necessary to ensure economic viability.[35] Without an appreciation of the opportunity cost involved in pursuing alternative policies, the Divine wisdom inherent in Joseph's economic policies would not be perceived. Retrospective focus on only one component of these policies could easily lead an embittered soul to deny the enormous national debt owed Joseph and instead blame him for his own personal misfortune.

Standards For Hakkarat Hatov

Judaism's appreciation of the delicate nature of *hakkarat hatov* manifests itself in the extension of the *hakkarat hatov* obligation to surprising circumstances and also in the call for extraordinary measures to prevent the blunting and debasing of this ethical sensitivity.

Hakkarat hatov goes beyond an obligation to express gratitude to identifiable benefactors. This principle is derived from the conduct of the Patriarch Jacob:

> "And Jacob came in complete harmony to the city of Shechem . . . and encamped (*vayyiḥan*) before (*et pene*) the city" (Genesis 3:18). . . . Another interpretation: . . . he [Jacob] began to set up bazaars and sell cheaply. This teaches that a man must be grateful to a place whence he derives benefit.[36]

Connecting the word *vayyiḥan* to *ḥanan* (lit., "he conferred benefit"), the Midrash understands Jacob's gesture of gratitude as having gone beyond the conferring of benefits on specific people. Jacob understood that if Shechem generated a state or measure of satisfaction for him, then the totality of his benefit could not be accounted for by ascription to particular people. If a town generates a feeling of satisfaction, then it is the milieu or environment of the town that is responsible. The environment, in turn, is created by the interaction of the townspeople. The benefit taken as a whole is indeed greater than the sum of its parts.

Realizing that the essence of his benefit was the environment of the town, Jacob was moved to show his appreciation by doing something to enhance that which had generated the advantage for him.

Another dimension of Judaism's standard for the *hakkarat hatov* ethical norm is derived from Moses' conduct in implementing the first three of the series of ten plagues on the Egyptian people.

In connection with the first two plagues, the plague of blood and the plague of frogs, God commands Moses to instruct Aaron to smite the Nile with a rod as a means of initiating them.[37] R. Tanḥum comments on why God did not instruct Moses himself to smite the Nile.

> God said to Moses: "The water which protected you when you were cast into the Nile shall not be smitten by you." [38]

Similarly, to initiate the third plague, the plague of lice, God commands Moses to instruct Aaron to smite the earth.[39] R. Tanḥum explains:

> God said to Moses: "It is not proper that you should smite the earth which protected you when you killed the Egyptian."[40]

While one might argue that R. Tanḥum's dictum extends the obligation of *hakkarat hatov* to inanimate objects, we understand his teaching in a different vein. Since the river Nile and the Egyptian earth played such vital roles in rescuing Moses from a life-threatening contact with danger, these entities would naturally conjure up within him intense feelings of *hakkarat hatov*. Out of concern that smiting the very instruments of his salvation might blunt Moses' sensitivity to *hakkarat hatov*, the Divinely instructed task was given instead to Aaron. So precious is *hakkarat hatov*.

Government Subsidization Of The Family And Education

In the Torah society, parents and the school system are assigned the task of moral education. Therefore, in order to carry out its *imitatio Dei* mandate to assist man in his strivings for moral betterment, the state is required to put the family and the school system on a sound financial footing. Economic viability equips these institutions to carry out their mission of moral education with vigor and thoroughness. Issues relating to both the size and the form of this subsidy come to the fore. We will take up each in turn.

The Cost Disease of the Service Sector

In assessing the adequacy of the level of support provided, account must be taken of the phenomenon called the cost disease of the service sector. We will begin with a brief description of this phenomenon and its relevancy to the issue at hand.

The cost disease of the service sector refers to the phenomenon that the prices of services consistently rise faster than the general inflation rate. Consider these facts: From 1947 to 1986, the Consumer Price Index (CPI) in the United States increased at an average annual rate of about 4.2 percent per year compounded. Over this same time period, the corresponding rate of increase in the cost of hospital care, education per pupil, and a visit to a physician was 11.7 percent, 7.7 percent, and 5.5 percent respectively.

What accounts for this disparity is that productivity gains in manufacturing outpace productivity gains in the service sector. Productivity gains lag in the service sector because services by their very nature require direct contact between those who consume the service and those who provide it. Doctors, teachers, and librarians are all engaged in activities that require direct person-to-person contact. Moreover, since the quality of services will deteriorate if less time is provided per user, this makes labor-saving technologies difficult to introduce in the service sector.

Notwithstanding its lagging productivity gains, the competitive marketplace will force the service sector to raise wages at more or less the same rate as the manufacturing sector. If this were not so, the service sector would lose its labor force. Since costs are increasing faster in the service sector relative to the manufacturing sector, the profit motive will work to drive the service sector to cut corners in its employment of labor as a means of maintaining its profit margins. Hence, if the marketplace is left to its own devices, the quality of the output of the service sector is likely to deteriorate over time.

The cost disease of the service sector does not make deterioration of the quality of its output inevitable. To see why, we need only point out that the source of the problem is not declining productivity in the service sector, but rather, rising productivity in the manufacturing sector relative to the service sector.

Increasing productivity can never make a nation poor. We have a choice. More and better services over time can be obtained, but this will have to be at some sacrifice in the rate of growth of manufacturing. Government can influence the mix of output between services and manufacturing. Many vital services, such as education and health care, are subsidized by the public sector. To ensure that the quality of these services does not erode over time, the public sector must be committed to increase its support level per annum above the inflation rate.[41]

The Cost Disease of Moral Training

Let us now relate the cost disease of the service sector to the moral-educational sector. At once, it must be recognized that moral training is essentially a cottage industry. Its effectiveness is predicated upon *quality time*—personal contact between parents and children, and between teachers and students. Without this quality time the moral dilemma will not be personalized. Thus moral training is subject to a cost disease.

What the cost disease of moral training implies for government subsidization of the schooling system is clearcut. If the quality time (i.e., the personal contact between teachers and students) is not to deteriorate over time, the government must be prepared to increase its support level per annum over the inflation rate. Moreover, since moral education will be effective only if it is integrated into the entire curriculum, this subsidy must increase for the entire educational program.

As far as the parental institution is concerned, it is a vital service sector which operates outside the marketplace, and this fact must be recognized. Given the economic pressures to earn a livelihood and the tantalizing rewards of the marketplace, parents must be provided with appropriate incentives to take their parenting and moral-educational roles seriously. With the aim of putting the family on a sound economic footing, government subsidization of the basic needs of the family is required. Such programs as subsidized health care and generous tax deductions for dependents indexed to the CPI are indicated.

A more ambitious plan would be for government to set up an incentive system with the design to influence parents to choose at the margin more parenting and fewer marketplace activities.

With the aim of encouraging parents to personally involve themselves in parenting and in the moral-educational development of their children, the government could require employers to give parents of young children the option of working fewer hours with a commensurate reduction in pay. Currently, in Sweden, parents of children under eight may work a six-hour rather than an eight-hour day, with a commensurate pay reduction.[42] A possible extension of this idea in the Torah society might take the form of subsidizing parent-child learning groups in the study halls of yeshivot.

If society's commitment to the moral-training enterprises of family and schooling is anything less than vigorous, we may face the gloomy prospect that the rise in material well-being will take place at the expense of a deterioration in the moral climate.

Educational Vouchers and Moral Education

If government is to play a vital role in enabling moral educators to carry out their mission, attention must focus not only on the level of support but also on the form the subsidy takes. The form of the subsidy takes on particular importance because moral training is but one aspect of the broader religious-education mission that Halakhah imposes on parents and on the educational enterprise. It extends beyond moral education to include Torah study and training in religious rituals.[43]

One aspect of Judaism's social welfare program is its call for public support for the religious education of the indigent.[44] The paramount challenge for the public sector is how to provide its subsidy to the poor as part of a movement toward the overall goal of encouraging the educational enterprise to give proper emphasis to moral training.

One approach would be to provide public schools for those eligible for tuition-free education, while at the same time allowing private tuition-charging schools to operate. This model, which provides a close description of the educational landscape of the United States today, has long been attacked by economists as inefficient. The lack of tuition in the public schools makes captives of their clientele. The public school educational enterprise has no incentive either to exert its utmost to educate its clientele or to provide it with any choice, since withdrawal because of dissatisfaction is not a viable alternative.

A viable alternative to the model just described is offered by the voucher system.[45] Under this system, eligible households would receive a certificate, or voucher, which could be taken to any school that agreed to abide by the rules of the voucher system. The voucher schools, in turn, would redeem the vouchers for cash from state funds.

By subsidizing consumers rather than producers, the voucher system encourages the emergence of competing schools which would vie for the voucher certificates of the eligible households. This would promote diversity in the educational marketplace. Similarly, since the voucher system makes withdrawal upon dissatisfaction a distinct possibility, participating schools would be highly motivated to provide the best possible education for their pupils as well as to be highly responsive to parental input.

To strike a proper balance between professional expertise in the sphere of education and consumer sovereignty in the educational marketplace, voucher schools could be required to teach a common core curriculum and abide by certain regulations, such as maximum class size.

Another advantage of the voucher system would be to allow subsidized households willing to make an economic sacrifice for the religious education of their children to accomplish their objectives efficiently. By supplementing the value of the voucher with their own resources, the subsidized household would be able to gain entry into a school at which the cost of tuition exceeds the value of the voucher. Since the additional voluntary expenditures cannot be efficiently integrated with the cost of the subsidized education when the subsidy is provided in the form of public schooling, the marginal effectiveness of the supplementary spending must be more limited than under the voucher system.

The voucher certificate could very well prove a bonanza for moral education. One advantage is the parental input this system fosters. Compared to the alternative system, which makes the poor captives of a public school system, the voucher system more optimally promotes the desired partnership between parents and the educational enterprise in the moral development of the child.

Moreover, by injecting competitive forces into the educational enterprise, the voucher system offers the prospect of encouraging the development of innovative curriculum design in the area of moral education.[46]

Finally, the voucher system offers an optimal means of implementing other aspects of society's moral-education program. To illustrate, the encouragement of parent-child learning sessions as well as family-oriented educational programs could be promoted by offering voucher certificates to qualified households.

Government Policies to Strengthen Hakkarat Hatov

Government can play a constructive role in fostering the strengthening of the *hakkarat hatov* character trait by sponsoring research in such areas as moral-educational curriculum development, effective parenting, and personality development.

In addition, creative efforts must be directed toward legislating expressions of *hakkarat hatov*. Public recognition for outstanding humanitarian achievement and exemplary public service would be one aspect of this.

Similarly, as a measure of gratitude for the parenting and nurturing roles they once performed, senior citizens must be treated on the societal level with generosity and dignity. When issues like the mandatory retirement age, catastrophic health insurance, and changes in the indexing of social security benefits are being considered, the question of whether the proposed solution would advance or do violence to *hakkarat hatov* should be part of the analysis. Contemplated changes in society's treatment of veterans should also be put to the *hakkarat hatov* evaluative criterion.

In chapter 9 we develop the proposition that controlling inflation is a mandate for government in the Torah society. One basis for assigning government this role is the recognition that the adverse effects of inflation fall disproportionately on the elderly. In consequence, government failure to check inflation does violence to *hakkarat hatov.*

Finally, the legislative process should take into account the effect of alternative arrangements on avarice, the sentiment which stands diametrically opposite to *hakkarat hatov*. For example, deliberations on the desirability of allowing the introduction of new financial products or on the rules governing the hostile takeover process should consider whether doing so would have the effect of intensifying the climate of greed in society at large.

• 6
Trading on Superior and Insider Information

INTRODUCTION

VOLUNTARY EXCHANGE IS OFTEN predicated upon asymmetrical information on the part of the parties to the transaction. Without the informational advantage, the transaction would presumably have been concluded on terms less favorable to the party possessing the superior information.

Our purpose here will be to investigate the ethics of trading on superior information as treated in Jewish law.

Trading on superior information classifies itself into two categories of cases. In the first category the only moral issue involves the ethics of not sharing the superior information with one's opposite number. In the second category the moral dilemma expands because the trade entails misappropriation of the superior information and/or the violation of some other ethical norm. As a means of distinguishing the two kinds of cases, we refer to the former category as trading on superior information and the latter as trading on insider information.

We begin our investigation with the presentation of a category I case. The principles which will be brought to bear in analyzing this case include *umdana* (inferential fact determination) and the various halakhic injunctions which compel a disclosure obligation upon a market participant. Variants of category I cases will then be analyzed. We will then move to category II cases. Contrasts between Jewish and American law will be drawn. Finally, the implications of the insider-trading phenomenon for public policy in the Torah society will be discussed.

The Mineral Rights Case

The elements of the following case are drawn from the factual setting of a 1966 insider-trading case, *Securities and Exchange Commission* v. *Texas Gulf Sulphur Co.*[1]

Beginning in 1957 Texas Gulf Sulphur (TGS) conducted exploratory activities on its property located on the Canadian Shield in eastern Canada. After aerial geophysical surveys discovered numerous anomalies, it was decided that it would be very promising to conduct a diamond core drilling operation for further evaluation. Analysis of the core of the initial hole indicated a remarkable mineral ore strike. The discovery convinced TGS that it was desirable to acquire the mineral rights of the surrounding property owners. To facilitate these acquisitions, the president of TGS instructed the exploration group to keep the results of the drilling operation confidential and undisclosed even to the other officers, directors, and employees of TGS. In addition, the hole was concealed and a barren core was intentionally drilled off the anomaly. Having taken these measures, TGS proceeded with its land-acquisition program.

The government found nothing objectionable in the secrecy TGS employed in acquiring mineral rights to the surrounding properties. This was apparently common practice in the mining industry.[2] What the government did object to was the purchase of company stock by TGS officials prior to the public disclosure of the mineral strike.

At present our concern will be with the ethics of TGS's land-acquisition program. The ethics of the insider trading by TGS officials will be dealt with later.

Umdana

The validity of the contracts TGS negotiated with the owners of the surrounding land can be put to question on the basis of *umdana*. This principle retroactively voids a transaction when it is evident that if certain information had been known at the time of negotiation, the transaction would not have been entered into. Illustrating the principle is the following talmudic case, recorded at Ketubbot 97a. During a time of dearth in Nehardea, people sold their mansions in order to raise cash to buy grain. However, at the time the sales of the mansions were being effected, ships carrying grain were waiting in the bay for the high waters to subside. The arrival of new grain supplies would have depressed grain prices and obviated the need of the people to sell their mansions to raise cash. Had the Nehardeans only known of the impending arrival of the grain ships, they surely would not have sold their mansions. On the basis of *umdana,* R. Naḥman ruled that the sales of the mansions were retroactively void. Likewise, *umdana* should retroactively render null and void the TGS mineral rights contracts. Had the surrounding property owners only shared the secret of TGS's mineral strike, they certainly would not have agreed to the terms of the TGS offer.

Despite the affinity between the two cases, *umdana* cannot work to vitiate the TGS mineral rights contracts. We offer the following three rationales to support the above assertion:

1. According to R. Abraham David Wahrmann (Ukraine, ca. 1771–1840), *umdana,* as an independent legal principle, works to void a transaction only when the presumption leads to the assertion that had the plaintiff only been equipped with the informational advantage, he would have walked away from the transaction.

This requirement is satisfied in the talmudic case at Ketubbot 97a. Circumstances made it evident that the Nehardeans were interested in selling their mansions only as a means of raising cash to pay the soaring price of grain. Had the typical Nehardean only known that new grain supplies were on their way at the time he was negotiating the sale of his mansion, he surely would have walked away from the negotiations.[3]

This is not the case, however, in the mineral rights transaction. Here, *umdana* does no more than assert that had the surrounding property owners shared the secret of TGS's mineral strike, they would have managed to negotiate a higher price for their mineral rights. In the mineral rights case, *umdana* collapses the plaintiff's complaint into nothing more than a claim of overreaching (*ona'ah*). The merits of an *ona'ah* claim here will be discussed below.

2. As Tosafot points out, *umdana* is an ex ante rather than an ex post facto calculation. Dissatisfaction with the outcome of a transaction does not work to void it unless it is evident that the disaffected party would not have agreed to incur the risk of the unfavorable event.[4] To illustrate, suppose A buys an ox from B explicitly for the purpose of slaughtering it. Upon completion of the sale, A slaughters the ox and discovers that it is organically defective (*trefa*) and hence forbidden to consume. Halakhah rules that unless physical evidence can be found in the carcass which

indicates that the animal was already a *trefa* at the time the sale was completed, A has no recourse to cancel the transaction.[5] But why doesn't *umdana* work to cancel the transaction? Is it not self-evident that no one would purchase an ox for butchering if it turned out to be a *trefa*? The answer, posits Tosafot, is that it is equally self-evident that a vendee ex ante would incur the risk that the animal he is buying might turn out to be a *trefa*.

In the talmudic case, *umdana* works to produce an ex ante presumption that the Nehardeans would not have been interested in selling their mansions had they only known of the impending arrival of new grain supplies.[6] An ex ante case for *umdana* cannot be made in the mineral rights case, however. While it is self-evident on an ex post facto basis that the surrounding property owners would have held out for a higher price for their mineral rights had they only shared the secret of TGS's mineral strike, this proposition is certainly not evident on an ex ante basis, as the seller of a property right will assuredly incur the risk that the price of his asset might increase in value at some time after he sells it.

3. R. Moses Sofer (Hungary, 1762–1839), in his analysis of the parameters of *umdana*, distinguishes between instances where the *umdana* relates to the article of the transfer and instances where it relates to the circumstances of either the buyer or seller. Only in the latter category of cases, according to R. Sofer, does *umdana* work to vitiate a transaction. Once a transaction is completed, *umdana* rooted in the buyer's disappointment with his purchase cannot work to vitiate it. Doing so is tantamount to negating the concept of ownership transfer. Preserving the integrity of the concept of ownership transfer forces the attitude that once a symbolic act (*kinyan*) effects ownership transfer, what happens subsequently to the article of transfer is no longer the concern of the seller.[7]

Similarly, once a transaction is completed, *umdana* rooted in the seller's regret, on account of price appreciation, for having made the sale, cannot work to cancel the transaction. Doing so is tantamount to negating the concept of ownership transfer. In consequence, *umdana* is not operative in the mineral rights case. Since *umdana* relates, not to the circumstances of the buyer or seller, but rather to the value of the article of transfer, it cannot be invoked to vitiate the transaction.

Halakhah's Disclosure Obligation

We will now subject the mineral rights case to the disclosure obligation Halakhah imposes on market participants. This obligation proceeds from three different prohibitions. We will take up each in turn and relate it to the mineral rights case.

1. The law of *ona'ah*, as discussed in chapter 1, prohibits an individual from concluding a transaction at a price which is more favorable to himself than the competitive norm. On the basis of the *ona'ah* interdict, it is objectionable to prey on the opposing party's ignorance of market conditions in a commercial transaction.[8] But the prohibition of *ona'ah* does not impose a disclosure obligation for the case at hand. This interdict works only to modify or cancel a transaction when a better opportunity was available at the time the disputed transaction took place. Since the secret of the mineral ore discovery was by its very nature confidential, no better opportunity was available to the plaintiff at the time he transacted with TGS.

R. Abraham David Horowitz (Israel, contemp.) explicitly invokes the above proposition in the treatment of an insider-trading case. The elements of the case are as follows: A used his contacts with Israeli municipal officials to become privy to confidential information that the city government was planning a housing project in an area outside the city limits. Implementation of this plan would naturally work to enhance the value of the land in the target area. Sometime before the plan was made public, B, an owner of land in the target area, approached A and offered to sell his lot to him. At the negotiation A failed to disclose his secret information. The transaction was completed at the then-prevailing norm. When the housing plan became public, B sued A for price fraud. R. Horowitz advised A to placate B with a monetary settlement, but posited that the law of *ona'ah* did not require A to make the disclosure. Given the confidential nature of A's informational advantage, A's nondisclosure did not have the effect of depriving B of a higher price from another interested party. Had A not made the purchase, B would have sold his lot to someone else at the same price.[9]

Further support that the law of *ona'ah* does not compel the insider to disclose his confidential information can be derived from the rule which governs the rights of the Sanctuary to property which was dedicated to it. The rule states that the sale of such property must be conducted both in the locale (*mekomah*) where the dedication was made and in the time period (*u-be-sha'ato*) when the dedication was made (*ein le-hekdesh ela mekomah u-be-sha'ato*).[10] The *mekomah u-be-sha'ato* rule, according to Naḥmanides (Spain, 1194–1270)[11] and R. Yom Tov Ishbili (Seville, ca. 1250–1330),[12] applies not only to the Sanctuary but to monetary matters generally.

It follows from the *mekomah u-be-sha'ato* principle that a market participant has the right to withhold information germane to what the future price of the good he is trading in will be. Given that the current price reflects only information that is available in the marketplace, trading on nonpublic information amounts to trading with an inside track as to what the *future* price of the good will be. Disclosure of information relating to the future price of a good, however, does not fall within the ambit of the *ona'ah* prohibition.

2. The interdict of *geneivat da'at* prohibits an individual from securing an advantage or gain from his fellow by means of a false impression. By dint of this prohibition, the prospective buyer is entitled to forthright[13] disclosure of any defect[14] the article put up for sale may have.[15] This duty obtains even if the sale entails no element of *ona'ah*.[16] Failure to meet the disclosure obligation may allow the buyer to void the deal.[17]

Let us now relate the *geneivat da'at* interdict to the mineral rights case. TGS's offer to buy the mineral rights of a neighboring property owner's land without disclosing to him the secret of its mineral ore strike apparently amounts to "duping" him into selling his land below its true value. Such a characterization is, however, unwarranted. Characterizing TGS's silence as deceptive conduct is valid only if the property owner was entitled to the information he lacked at the time the transaction took place. Since TGS is the rightful owner of the mineral discovery, it is entitled to commercially exploit its property right in the discovery to the fullest extent possible. Requiring TGS to volunteer the information regarding the mineral strike amounts to a requirement for TGS to make a gift transfer to the owner of the neighboring property on the strength of his interest in selling his land. Such a requirement would not be a disclosure obligation, but a call for income redistribution.

The *geneivat da'at* interdict does become operative, however, in instructing TGS how to respond to direct questions by the owner of the neighboring property. Accordingly, suppose that in his negotiation with TGS, he shrewdly asks the company representative: "Do you have any information about natural resources such as gas, oil, and minerals, proposed legislation, nearby construction, or the like, such that if I shared your knowledge, I would be likely to increase my sale price by ten percent or more?" In response to these direct inquiries, TGS's options are limited to two courses of action. One alternative would be for TGS to refuse to answer, running the risk that the property owner will break off the negotiations. On the other hand, if TGS is determined to go forward with the purchase, the *geneivat da'at* interdict requires that it answer the questions in a forthright manner.

Elsewhere, we have developed the thesis that Halakhah permits diversionary tactics for the purpose of concealing entrepreneurial intent from one's opposite number in a negotiation. Identity disclosure provides a case in point: Tower, the head of a multibillion-dollar real estate development conglomerate, desires to build a Disneyland-like project in Seattle. Realizing that his open entry into the real estate market would have the effect of enormously bidding up the value of the parcels of land, Tower uses several of his less-known subsidiaries to negotiate the real estate deals. Alternatively, Tower creates a new corporation for the purpose of acquiring the desired parcels. With obscurity thereby achieved, Tower secures the desired parcels at relatively low prices. Since the use of one or the other of these ploys has merely enabled Tower to capture entirely for himself the market value of his entrepreneurial effort, his subterfuge for concealing his identity does not, in our view, violate *geneivat da'at* law.[18]

Extending the above principle to the case at hand allows TGS to make use of a subsidiary or a dummy corporation for the purpose of securing the mineral rights of the surrounding property owners. Since the ploy is designed to enable TGS to capture for itself the full value of its mineral discovery, the diversionary tactic cannot be characterized as wresting away a gain which is someone else's entitlement. To be sure, it is only permissible for TGS to distract its opposite number from investigating or inquiring who the actual purchaser is. Should the smokescreen fail, and the seller make a direct inquiry as to who the actual prospective buyer is, the negotiator must provide a forthright answer.

3. *Lifnei iver*, the prohibition of offering ill-suited advice, is derived from the biblical exhortation "Do not place a stumbling block before the blind [*lifnei iver lo titan mikh'shol*]" (Leviticus 19:14).[19] According to R. Mordecai Jacob Breisch (Israel, 1896–), it extends even to offering someone "passive" counsel which is ill-suited. Thus, if A fails to provide B with timely information that would enable him to avert a financial loss, A is in violation of the *lifnei iver* interdict.[20]

Consideration of the legal underpinning of the mineral rights case leads, however, to the proposition that the *lifnei iver* interdict is not an operative principle here. For purposes of exposition, let us for the moment remove TGS's informational advantage in its negotiation with a neighboring property owner. Given the uncertainty regarding the nature of the mineral deposits on the property, the sale is predicated on the basis of contrary attitudes toward risk and/or on opposing interpretations of available data.

The halakhic validity of such a transaction was addressed by R. Shmuel de Medina (Turkey, 1506–1589). Specifically, he dealt with the validity of an *ona'ah* claim on the part of the purchaser of a gold mine based on his disappointment with the mine's productivity. R. Shmuel de Medina ruled against the plaintiff. Both parties in a transaction of this kind are aware that a mine may prove very profitable but might also turn out to be a losing proposition, and therefore each firmly resolves at the outset to accept the outcome, whatever it may be.[21]

When a transaction is predicated upon contrary notions, the principles are adversaries and should bear no fiduciary duty to each other. An adversary relationship, of course, obtained in the TGS land-acquisition program. Hence *lifnei iver* would not impose on TGS an obligation to disclose its informational advantage.

A fiduciary element is introduced into the mineral rights case when the transaction is effected through a broker. Suppose TGS engages the services of a broker to make a bid on its behalf for the mineral rights of a neighboring property owner. The broker is not made privy to TGS's secret mineral discovery on its own property. On the basis of current market conditions, TGS is convinced that its offer is attractive and hence the broker will have no difficulty in convincing a client to take up the offer. Suppose the scenario proceeds in predictable fashion and the deal is consummated on the basis of the broker's advice. Since the advice is tendered in good faith, no infraction of *lifnei iver* is incurred by the broker. But in reality the advice is clearly ill-suited. TGS's scheme amounts, therefore, to a ploy designed to dupe the broker into becoming a conduit for ill-suited advice.

The indirect role TGS plays in proffering the ill-suited advice should not work as a mitigating factor here. Ordinarily, one is not regarded as "placing a stumbling block before a blind man" if a supervening event (*lifnei de-lifnei*) is required before the untoward outcome occurs.[22] But the *lifnei iver* interdict encompasses two components, (a) the prohibition of abetting a transgressor, and (b) the interdict against offering ill-suited advice.[23] It is only in reference to the former aspect, posits R. Ahron Soloveichik (Chicago, 1918–), that indirection works to remove the *lifnei iver* prohibition.

R. Soloveichik derives this rule from a distinction R. Isaiah b. Mali di Trani the Elder (Italy, ca. 1180–1260) draws between two talmudic cases. In the first, recorded at Avodah Zarah 14a, we are told that the type of incense used in idol worship may be sold to a non-Jew for the purpose of resale. Since the first purchaser resells the incense, and thus does not use it for idolatry, the second purchaser's use of it only constitutes *lifnei de-lifnei* from the standpoint of the original seller and thus does not entail an infraction of the law for him. In the second case, selling for the purpose of resale is not a mitigating factor because the item involved is a garment containing a concealed mixture of linen and wool (*sha'atnez*). Out of fear that the original purchaser may sell a garment containing concealed *sha'atnez* to a Jew, the Talmud prohibits the sale of such garments to a non-Jewish merchant.

The essential difference between the two cases, according to R. Trani the Elder, is that the concealed *sha'atnez* case entails a duping element while the incense case entails no misrepresentation.[24] Elaborating on the distinction, R. Soloveichik explains that the component of *lifnei iver* law prohibiting the abetting of a transgressor obtains only when the transgressor recognizes the prohibited nature of his deed. It is here that the *lifnei de-lifnei* leniency applies, as providing only an indirect opportunity to execute a prohibited action does not constitute encouragement of that action. If the transgressor does not recognize the forbidden nature of his conduct, the facilitator is guilty of duping him into forbidden conduct. Doing this falls into the rubric of the second aspect of the *lifnei iver* interdict, namely, the proffering of ill-suited advice.

It follows that the *lifnei de-lifnei* leniency is inoperative here. When the essence of the prohibition consists of the duping element, indirectness does not work to remove the "scheming" characteristic of the facilitator's action.[25]

While all this suggests that TGS is prohibited from enlisting the services of a broker to acquire the desired properties, the firm's conduct can be defended. First and foremost we must bear in mind that TGS had no obligation to share the secret of its mineral ore discovery. The introduction of the fiduciary element merely assures a prospective seller that TGS's offer is reasonable and fair on the basis of the information that has already been disseminated in the marketplace. Such advice is certainly prized by anyone who is concerned that his naivete and ignorance regarding current market conditions will draw him into a deal decidedly not in his best interests.

The broker's involvement in the transaction, providing he does not stray beyond the boundaries of legitimacy, does not put the seller at a greater disadvantage than would be the case had the principals transacted directly. To see this we need only focus on the operative disclaimer obligation for the broker in the case at hand. If the prevailing practice is for brokers to disclaim responsibility for their advice should it be rendered ill-suited on the basis of validation of currently available soft information or rumor, then the victim of a superior-information trade would have benefitted from the selfsame caveat. If disclaimers are customarily not made because the acceptance of risks is self-evident, the victim of the superior-information trade is exposed to no greater risk than other market participants. Finally, effecting a superior-information trade through a broker in no way precludes the prospective seller from seizing the initiative and questioning the broker regarding his knowledge of soft information and even rumor that would affect the price of the mineral rights. Once this inquiry is made, self-interest will dictate the prospective seller's next move. Hence the availability of nonpublic information does not affect the reliability and absoluteness of a broker's advice.

Cicero's Moral Dilemma

Another insider-trading case which entails no moral issue other than the ethics of trading on the superior information is a case presented by Cicero more than two thousand years ago. The essential elements of the case are the following: A merchant brings grain from Alexandria to Rhodes, where famine conditions prevail. While current market conditions allow the merchant to sell his grain at a very favorable price, he knows that several other ships laden with grain are on their way to Rhodes. If the Rhodians learn of the imminent arrival of the ships, the demand and hence the market price for the merchant's grain will fall. "Is he to report the fact to the Rhodians, or is he to keep his own counsel and sell his own stock at the highest market price?"[26]

What distinguishes Cicero's case from the mineral rights case is the property right in the informational advantage. In the mineral rights case, the insider created and developed the informational advantage and hence is its property owner. In Cicero's case, the informational advantage is the property of the public domain. Therefore, anyone who is aware of the information is free to exploit it. Since no better market opportunity was available to the Rhodian customers when they bought the grain from the Alexandrian merchant, the latter's informational advantage relates to the future price of grain rather than to current market conditions. Given that the Alexandrian merchant bears no responsibility to divulge his secret knowledge of the impending shipment, the ethics of exploiting the secret for commercial advantage parallels the analysis of the mineral rights case.

Secret Knowledge Regarding Someone Else's Property

In this variant, A has secret knowledge regarding the nature of B's property. A uses his informational advantage to acquire B's property at a price far below the true value of the property.

A basis for judging the ethics of this case is provided by an analysis of the following ruling by R. Eliezer b. Joel ha-Levi (Bonn, 1140–1225): A sold roofing material to B. Both parties were under the impression that the material involved was tin, and this was reflected in the price terms of the agreement. B then proceeded to sell the roofing material to C. Upon melting down the metal, C discovered that it was actually silver, with only the outer covering being tin. B then initiated an *ona'ah* claim against C. R. Eliezer b. Joel ha-Levi, ruling against B, averred that C was under no obligation to make any adjustment to B. Since B was unaware of the silver component of the material, he never acquired title to it when he bought the material from A. Given that B has no property right in the silver, C bears no responsibility to B on account of the windfall.[27]

R. Mordecai b. Abraham Jaffe (Prague, ca. 1535–1612) extends R. Eliezer's ruling to the instance where identification of the true nature of the article can be determined by outward inspection, without melting down the article or breaking it up.[28]

A caveat is noted by R. Jaffe. Dismissal of the *ona'ah* claim obtains only if B acquired the article by means of a sales transaction. The *ona'ah* claim is valid, however, in the event B acquired the article either by means of inheritance or as a gift.[29]

R. Jaffe's ruling provides a setting for permissible trading on superior information: Browsing at the display counter of the Yahalom jewelry store, Mirma finds an item to his fancy. Pointing to the item of interest, Mirma motions Yahalom to remove the item for his inspection. Upon removing the item, Yahalom comments that the piece of jewelry is a cubic zirconium tennis bracelet. Mirma's expertise in diamonds, however, makes him strongly suspect that the piece of jewelry is, in fact, a diamond bracelet.

While Yahalom's attention is temporarily diverted in answering the inquiries of a different customer, Mirma takes a quick glance at the item through a special optical instrument, confirming his suspicion that the piece of jewelry is, in fact, a diamond bracelet. With the aim of discovering the extent of the property right Yahalom has in the bracelet, Mirma quickly ascertains that Yahalom does not carry a line of diamond bracelets. A mixup of the store's inventory, therefore, could not account for Yahalom's mistake. Further prodding by Mirma fills in the last critical fact, namely, that Yahalom purchased the bracelet from a particular wholesaler.

What Mirma's probing has accomplished is to establish that Yahalom's property right in the diamond bracelet is deficient. Specifically, it consists of no more than the dollar value of a cubic zirconium bracelet. Armed with the secret of Yahalom's deficient property right in the bracelet, Mirma may conclude the deal at the cubic zirconium price.

We should note that Yahalom bears no responsibility to disclose the information which will reveal his deficient property rights in the bracelet. If Mirma is unable to elicit this information, the mistaken characterization of the bracelet must be ascribed to inventory mixup. Without certainty that he is dealing with the element of deficient property ownership, silence in the face of the mistaken characterization amounts to allowing Yahalom to sell him X when he requested Y.[30] Such conduct violates the *geneivat da'at* interdict. A transaction concluded in this manner amounts to an agreement concluded in error (*mekakh ta'ut*).

A variation of the above case occurs when Mirma specifically asks to be shown a cubic zirconium bracelet but is mistakenly shown a diamond bracelet. Irrespective of whether Yahalom's property right in the diamond bracelet is deficient, the clear intent of the parties was to complete a transaction vis-à-vis a cubic zirconium bracelet. Mirma's acceptance of the diamond bracelet for the quoted price amounts to accepting X when he requested Y. Probing to find out if Yahalom has deficient property rights in the bracelet is here not a legitimate pursuit. Concluding the deal on the basis of the mistaken premise amounts therefore to a *mekakh ta'ut*.

Rothschild's London Exchange Coup

In this concluding example of a category I case involving trading on superior information, we describe conduct which straddles the boundary of permissibility. Here are the elements of the case: On June 19, 1815, Napoleon went down to defeat in the battle of Waterloo at the hands of Lord Wellington. The Rothschild network of couriers, which was in all respects a private news-gathering agency, brought news of the British victory to Nathan Rothschild in London many hours before anyone else in the city learned the news. For days the London Exchange had strained its ears. If Napoleon won, English consols were bound to drop. If he lost, the enemy empire would shatter and consols rise. Equipped with the scoop about the British victory, Nathan Rothschild entered the trading pit in the London Exchange. His name was already such that a single substantial move on his part sufficed to bear or bull an issue. Instead of sinking his worth in consols, as another man in his position would surely have done, Rothschild sold consols. Rothschild's substantial trade triggered panic selling of British consols. After the consols had plummeted in value, Rothschild proceeded to buy a giant parcel of consols "for a song." News soon reached the London Exchange of Wellington's victory. British consols soared in price. Rothschild then sold his consols and made a fortune.[31]

One salient point in evaluating the ethics of Rothschild's conduct is the consideration that the informational advantage here was the product of Rothschild's investment in a private news-gathering agency. To be sure, Rothschild cannot be said to have had a property right in the news of Wellington's victory, as the news was the property of the public domain. But did Rothschild enjoy a right to protect his investment against free-riding?

For argument's sake, let us assume that Rothschild would have suffered no loss if his trade had been copied by other investors. Hence, concealing the news of Wellington's victory by selling consols effectively denied fellow investors the opportunity to profit from the news, while all along entailing no loss for Rothschild. Such conduct should be prohibited by dint of the interdict not to act in the manner of the inhabitants of Sodom. This interdict is violated when A refuses to allow B to infringe upon his right even though such infringement generates no loss for him and at the same time affords B the opportunity to secure a benefit or avoid a loss.[32]

Rothschild's conduct can, however, be defended on the basis of the comment by R. Mordecai b. Hillel (Germany, 1240–1298) et al. on the following talmudic dictum pertaining to squatters: Unless the apartment involved was up for rent, Halakhah denies the landlord's claim for rent against the squatter.[33] Commenting on this law, R. Mordecai b. Hillel et al. posit that while the rent claim for having occupied the apartment is denied, the landlord is within his rights to deny the squatter's request to live in the apartment gratis. Since the landlord could theoretically rent the apartment, notwithstanding that at present he opts not to, denying the squatter's request to live in the apartment gratis is legitimate.[34]

Application of R. Mordecai b. Hillel's ruling to the case at hand frees the Rothschild trade of a Sodomitic element. Given the commercial value of Rothschild's superior information, it is legitimate for him to protect his investment against free-riding.

The assumption that free-riding entails no loss for Rothschild is in all probability invalid. Investment profits depend critically upon timing. What profit Rothschild will actually realize from the scoop depends upon the price at which he sells the consols. To gain maximal advantage from the commercial value of his superior information, he would have to sell the consols at a price which at the very least reflects the British victory at Waterloo. The longer Rothschild can manage to keep his scoop a secret, the more likely the actual news of Wellington's victory will result in a run-up in the price of British consols. Since the news of the victory is a surprise event for the marketplace, the price of consols at that time provides a gauge of the value of consols which factors in the British victory. But if Rothschild's superior information leaks, then the firm news of the British victory will, in all probability, not cause any run-up in the price of consols, as this information will have already been discounted by the market. Hence, investor copying of the Rothschild trade may effectively deprive the financier of the advantage of a surprise event, which would be very helpful in deciding the timing of the sale of his consols. Without this edge, Rothschild suffers the prospect that a wave of sudden selling may depress the price of consols before he gets around to liquidating his own position.

Proceeding from the right to protect an investment from free-riding is the right to employ diversionary tactics for the purpose of keeping the public off balance in respect to the informational advantage. Selling consols on the knowledge of Wellington's victory is a diversionary tactic which is at once costly and daring. Several scenarios are possible. In one scenario, Rothschild's substantial selling does not trigger panic selling and the tactic manages only to throw the public off in regard to Wellington's victory. By shortening the time span between his own entry as a buyer of consols and the arrival of the report of Wellington's victory, Rothschild increases the probability that the actual report will be a surprise event. Should the tactic trigger panic selling, as circumstances proved to be the case, Rothschild would be conferred with the additional bonanza of the opportunity to purchase a huge parcel of consols "for a song."

Characterizing the selling of consols on the knowledge of Wellington's victory as sending a "false signal" to the market is valid only on the assumption that traders have a legitimate right to share gratis in Rothschild's superior information. Since Halakhah recognizes no such right, Rothschild cannot be said to be guilty of *geneivat da'at* conduct.

In the context of the modern investment stratagem of arbitrage, Rothschild's conduct can be defended on even more fundamental grounds. Arbitrage entails the purchase and sale of the same or related commodity in order to profit from price discrepancies. To illustrate, suppose the current price of gold and silver are $375 and $5 an ounce respectively. This represents a 75:1 spread in the price ratio. A expects this spread to narrow considerably. Speculating on his intuition, he purchases 100 contracts of silver in the London Metals Exchange. Later that same day, A sells short 100 contracts of gold on the New York Commodity Exchange. To be sure, the prices of precious metals, including gold and silver, usually rise and fall in tandem. But if the spread between the prices of gold and silver narrows, as A expects, the strategy will pay off in a net profit regardless of the direction taken by the price of precious metals. Two scenarios are possible: If the prices of gold and silver rise, the profit generated by the liquidation of the long position on silver will more than offset the loss incurred on the closing out of the short position on gold. If, on the other hand, the prices of gold and silver fall, the profit earned on the liquidation of the short position on gold will more than offset the loss incurred in closing out the long position on silver.

The prevalence of arbitrage activity puts in question the reasonableness of inferring a trader's opinion of price direction on the basis of a particular trade he makes. Any such inference is entirely at the risk of the one who makes it.

Trading On Insider Information

We begin our discussion of insider trading with a brief overview of legislation against this practice in the United States. We will then proceed to present a number of landmark court decisions in this area. These cases will be evaluated from a halakhic standpoint.

The Securities Exchange Act of 1934

Congress enacted the Securities Exchange Act of 1934 in response to certain unethical trading practices which had contributed to the stock market crash of 1929. The act was designed primarily as a mechanism to regulate sales and purchases of securities, and to protect investors against manipulation and deception in the stock market.

Under section 10(b), the Securities and Exchange Commission was vested with general regulatory powers over securities transactions. The SEC gained express authority to prescribe rules necessary and appropriate in the public interest to prohibit any manipulative or deceptive device utilized by any person in relation to securities transactions.

In 1942, the SEC utilized the rule-making power granted by section 10(b) to promulgate rule 10b-5. This rule proscribed any person from making "affirmative misrepresentations, half-truths or omissions in connection with a purchase or sale of securities."[35]

SEC v. Texas Gulf Sulphur Co.

Texas Gulf Sulphur (TGS), as will be recalled from the previous section, made a significant mineral discovery on property it owned near Timmins, Ontario, and ceased drilling for several months so that it could acquire land around the site. During this period, company officers, employees, and tippees purchased stock in the open market without disclosing the potentially significant discovery to the investing public. After rumors of the discovery were given prominent attention in the press, TGS issued a press release stating that the rumors were exaggerated. Over the next four days, company officers, employees, and tippees made further purchases of stock before TGS finally disclosed to the investing public that the company had in fact made a significant mineral discovery.[36]

In *SEC* v. *Texas Gulf Sulphur* (1968), the court found the TGS officials guilty of violating rule 10b-5. Ruling against defendants, the court interpreted the rule as requiring anyone in possession of material insider information to either disclose it or abstain from trading in the securities concerned. The rule, according to the court, is based in principle on the justifiable expectation of the securities marketplace that all investors trading on impersonal exchanges should have equal access to material information.[37]

In evaluating this case from the standpoint of Halakhah, the equal-access doctrine would not provide a basis for finding against the defendants. A market participant, as the previous section demonstrated, does not have a legitimate claim to access to all the information his opposite number has.

What becomes salient from a halakhic standpoint, in evaluating the conduct of the defendants, is the identification of the property right in the informational advantage.

Standing as the most basic issue here is whether TGS has a property right in the report of the mineral find, separate and distinct from its property right in the mineral discovery itself. The discovery was brought to light, of course, by the labor services of both TGS employees and outside consultants. But the output we are dealing with here is *information*, which is something intangible. In Halakhah a property right can be acquired only in something which is tangible (*davor she-yesh bo mammash*).[38] In this regard tangibility is defined as something which has height, width, and depth.[39]

The tangibility condition can, however, be met here by means of appropriate contract design. Instead of a quid pro quo arrangement, calling for the employee to confer title to specific information to TGS in exchange for compensation, the contract would call for the employee to commit himself to engage in specific tasks for TGS, including the production and provision of reports. The very same approach was proposed by R. David b. Solomon ibn Abi Zimra (Safed, 1479–1573) in finding the legal underpinning of an agreement between a householder and a dyer. Instead of viewing the agreement as calling for the dyer to confer the householder with title to the dye, this decisor understood the obligation of the dyer to consist of a *commitment* to dye the householder's garment. Since a personal commitment is bound up in the physical being of the obligator, the tangibility requirement is met.[40]

Another saving factor here is the recognition Halakhah gives to prevailing business practice in respect to the nature of property rights which can be acquired. If prevailing business practice gives recognition to the acquisition of something which is intangible, Halakhah too would find recognition of the practice.[41]

Applying the above approaches to the case at hand provides a ready legal underpinning for TGS's acquisition of the mineral ore reports. But what principle prohibits the employee from divulging the information to anyone other than the employer? Confidentiality here, as it appears to this writer, proceeds from the very nature of the labor agreement. Once a labor agreement is struck, the output of the worker is automatically the legal property of the employer. This principle is expressed in the form of the talmudic dictum: *yad po'el ke-yad ba'al ha-bayit*, "the hand of the worker is like the hand of the employer" (Bava Meẓia 10a). In a market economy, *yad po'el* translates, in this writer's opinion, into the worker's obligation to hand over the entire *value* of his output to his employer. Given that the *value* of the mineral report to TGS is considerably diminished if its confidentiality is breached, *yad po'el* prohibits the employee from divulging its contents to anyone but his employer in the proper chain of command.

The confidentiality requirement implicit in a labor contract where the obligation of the worker consists of providing information can be reinforced by the insertion of an explicit secrecy clause. Since intangibility is not a legal impediment when it comes to making a personal commitment operative, the secrecy clause is halakhically binding. The confidentiality objective can also be explicitly achieved by means of binding the employee by an oath of secrecy.

Given the pivotal role knowledge of the report plays in TGS's negotiations with its neighboring property owner, the informational advantage is a commodity having market value.

Adding substantially to this value is the protection secular law affords the mineral ore reports as a trade secret.[42]

At this juncture we should take note that Halakhah does not recognize corporations as legal personalities separate and distinct from their owners.[43] To be sure, halakhic nonrecognition of this legal fiction does not impede the creation of a business entity akin to the corporation in the Torah society. By means of advance stipulation, members of a partnership can both limit their liability in dealing with outsiders and make themselves residual claimants in respect to the assets of their business entity.[44] What the nonrecognition of the legal fiction does here, in the case at hand, is to assign the property right in the mineral ore report to the shareholders on a pro-rated basis.

Given the proprietary interest the shareholders have in the mineral ore report, trading on the nonpublic knowledge of this report amounts to exploiting another's property for commercial gain. The propriety of calling for the disgorgement of a defendant's gain follows from an analysis of R. Yose's dictum, recorded at Mishnah Bava Meẓia 3:2.

> [If] one rents a cow from another and lends it to someone else, and it dies naturally, the renter must swear that it died naturally, and the borrower must pay the renter. Said R. Yose: How does that person do business with another's cow? Rather, the cow should be returned to the owner.

In the view of the first opinion expressed, when the animal dies, the renter becomes exempt from paying and acquires the animal.

Since the renter is not liable for accidents, he takes the oath merely to placate the owner. Therefore, the borrower—who is responsible for accidents—must pay the renter.[45] R. Yose, however, regards the renter who lends out the deposit as an agent of the owner. Therefore, the payment for the cow should be given to the owner, not the renter.[46]

While talmudic decisors follow R. Yose's line,[47] authorities are in disagreement regarding the conditions necessary to trigger the prohibition of doing business with someone else's property.

The majority position in this matter is to call for disgorgement whenever A makes commercial use of B's property while having no right to make use of it. The circumstance that B suffers no loss thereby is not a saving factor according to this school of thought.

Exemplifying this point of view are the following two rulings of R. Solomon b. Abraham Adret (Spain, ca. 1235–1310):

A rents B's field to C without having any authority to do so. Given that the property in question has not been up for rental, B suffers no loss thereby. Nonetheless, it would be unconscionable for A to keep the rent, as this would amount to doing business with another's property. R. Adret, however, hedges on a definitive ruling regarding the disposition of the rent B received. It might be appropriate, he points out, to return the rent to C on the grounds that B suffers no loss.[48] In another application of R. Yose's dictum, R. Adret ruled that if A builds up B's ruin and rents it to C, A must surrender the rent to B. Since the ruin is not rentable without A's improvements, this too is a case where A's commercialization of B's property entails no loss for B.[49]

A final example of a ruling which follows the above line is the subletting case that came before R. Joseph Ḥabiba (Spain, late 14th–early 15th cent.): A rents an apartment from B and then sublets it at a higher rent to C. In respect to the disposition of the rent differential, R. Ḥabiba finds the critical factor to be whether A was within his rights to sublet the apartment. If A's subletting was legal, then he bears no responsibility to surrender the differential to B. B's unjust-enrichment claim against A is dismissed on the grounds that A's gain causes B no harm (*zeh nehene ve-ze lo ḥaser*). The circumstance that B suffers no loss as a result of A's subletting activity, however, is not a saving factor when A did not have permission to sublet the apartment to C, as would be the case when C's household was larger than B's. Here, A must surrender the rent differential to B on the grounds that it is unconscionable to do business with someone else's asset.[50]

The aforementioned rulings are in apparent opposition to the principle, alluded to earlier, that A cannot be made to pay for a benefit he derives from B's property when the latter suffers no loss thereby. What, then, is the basis for calling for disgorgement of A's profits? Addressing himself to this dilemma, R. Ya'akov Yesha'yahu Bloi (Israel, b. 1929) suggests that commercialization amounts to a clearcut manifestation of ownership. Since such conduct would presumably be regarded as obnoxious by the owner of the property, we must treat A's conduct as if it had been forbidden by the owner in advance.[51]

A minority interpretation of R. Yose's dictum is expressed by R. Ephraim b. Aaron Navon (Constantinople, 1677–1735). Disgorgement, in R. Navon's view, is called for only when the following two conditions obtain: (1) the defendant's commercialization of the plaintiff's property was unauthorized; (2) the plaintiff suffers a loss in conjunction with the unauthorized use of his property. Understanding this to be the position of R. Ḥabiba, R. Navon insists that the subletting case speaks of the instance where A rents an apartment from B below its market value and then goes ahead and sublets it to C at a higher price. Here, A bears a responsibility to surrender the differential to B in the event the subletting was not legal. If A was, however, within his rights to sublet the apartment to C, Halakhah does not compel him to surrender the differential to B, despite the loss B suffers in conjunction with A's commercial activity.[52]

The TGS Insider-Trading Case and R. Yose's Dictum

Consideration of the circumstances of the TGS insider-trading suit makes for a case for disgorgement of the defendant's profits on the basis of R. Yose's dictum.

Most basic in building this case is the demonstration made above that the informational advantage is the property right of the TGS shareholders.

Another critical element in making the case for disgorgement is a prohibition for the insiders to trade on the secret information in the context of an impersonal stock exchange. This prohibition, as it appears to this writer, stems from several considerations.

One basis for the prohibition is the insider's labor contract with TGS. Fulfillment of the employee's end of the labor contract, as discussed above, disallows him from divulging the mineral ore report to anyone but his superior, in the usual chain of command. This secrecy requirement, as discussed above, can be reinforced by either explicitly inserting a confidentiality clause in the labor contract or subjecting the firm's employees and consultants to a secrecy oath. While trading on the insider information does not, in and of itself, breach the confidentiality requirements, it carries with it the danger of destroying the secret. Through price movement and traders' talk, the insider trading works to tip potential real estate sellers to the existence of a valuable find in their land for which they should significantly raise their selling price. As a result, the insider trading may set into motion a scenario which eventuates in compromising TGS's negotiating position.

Another basis for the prohibition of trading on the insider information is the fiduciary element inherent in the employee role. Entering into a labor contract should subject the employee to the *lifnei iver* interdict. Insider trading by an employee of TGS amounts to an offer to buy the holdings of TGS shareholders when the insider knows that the shares will be worth much more once the news of the mineral find is made public. Hence, the action of the insider constitutes ill-suited advice.

A saving factor here is that the buy offer is made on the impersonal stock exchange, whose operation depends on the participation of specialists. Because of the participation of specialists, the stock exchange is not a continuous auction market. Specialists maintain inventories in certain stocks, much like dealers in used cars, rare coins, and art. If a public investor wants to buy, the specialist sells at his "ask" price quotations; if a public investor wants to sell, the specialist buys at his "bid" price quotation, which is lower than his ask price.

In addition, a specialist frequently trades not for his own account but on behalf of some public customer who has entered a limit order to buy or sell at a certain price. Finally, floor brokers with public orders to "buy at the market" sometimes trade with each other around the specialist's booth rather than with the specialist himself. This phenomenon is known as "trading in the crowd."[53]

As the preceding description indicates, the insider trade either preempts a trade which would have in any case occurred or induces a trade which would not have otherwise occurred. Preemption is a possibility because at the same time that the insider makes his bid to purchase shares in TGS, other players, including specialists, are doing likewise. But we must consider the possibility that the direct or indirect changes in the intermediary's inventory brought on by the insider trade may have precipitated a different pattern of price quotations. The new pattern of quotations may either induce new transactions or deter ones that would otherwise have occurred. For example, if an insider trade increases a specialist's inventory, the latter may react by lowering his price quotation in order to both encourage purchases from him and deter sales to him. If, on the other hand, an insider trade decreases the specialist's inventory, the specialist may react by increasing his prices in order to both encourage sales to him and deter purchases from him.[54]

This analysis has much relevance for the *lifnei iver* interdict. *Lifnei iver* is violated only if the facilitator's action will almost certainly lead to an untoward consequence.[55] Given the possibility that the insider trade merely preempts a trade which would have occurred in any case, the fiduciary insider trader in the impersonal stock exchange should be free of the *lifnei iver* interdict. Recall, however, R. Soloveichik's proposition that the *lifnei de-lifnei* caveat does not apply to the prohibition of proffering ill-suited advice. Following this line, the absence of the near-certainty element should not constitute a mitigating factor. Notwithstanding that the party in privity with the insider trader might have conducted the same transaction with some outsider, the trade violates for him his position of trust.

The TGS fiduciary insider, in R. Navon's minority position, would not be called to return his profits unless an additional condition is met. This condition is the demonstration that the party in privity with the insider trader incurs a loss as a result of the transaction. A close reading of R. Navon's position reveals that satisfaction of the loss condition does not require that the loss involved be of the nature that the defendant is legally responsible for it, but only that the plaintiff incurs a loss in conjunction with B's use of his property.[56]

Evidence of this proceeds from R. Navon's interpretation of R. Ḥabiba's subletting case. Understanding the subletting case as expressing his interpretation of R. Yose's dictum, R. Navon, as will be recalled, insists that the case speaks of the circumstance where B rents an apartment from A below its market value and then sublets it to C at a higher price. The plaintiff's loss—the rent differential—is not a loss in the sense that B is legally responsible for it. Moreover, the loss is not an actual loss but only a forgone earning or opportunity cost.

The type of loss the party in privity with the insider trader suffers is akin to A's loss in the subletting case. With the loss condition met, a case for disgorgement of the insider trader's profits can be made even according to R. Navon's understanding of R. Yose's dictum.

Chiarella v. *United States*

Reflecting the Supreme Court's current theory of insider-trading liability is its 1980 decision in *Chiarella* v. *United States*.[57] The defendant in the action, Chiarella, was a "mark-up" man for a financial printer, Pandick Press. Clients of Pandick Press were corporations involved in acquiring target companies through mergers and takeovers. Because of the need for secrecy involved in such acquisitions, names were omitted from the documents until the final printing. However, Chiarella was able to deduce the names of the target corporations and used the information to purchase stocks in the targets prior to the takeover announcements. Once the announcements of the takeovers were made, he sold the stock at a substantial profit.[58]

The government brought a criminal action against Chiarella, and the district court found that he had violated Section 10(b) of the 1934 Securities and Exchange Act and SEC rule 10b-5. The Second Circuit Court of Appeals affirmed the conviction.[59]

On appeal, the Supreme Court reversed the conviction. Holding that mere possession of material nonpublic information does not give rise to a duty to disclose before trading, the court explicitly rejected the "parity of information" theory espoused in *SEC* v. *Texas Gulf Sulphur Co* . According to the *Chiarella* majority, in order for a duty to disclose to be present, there must exist a relationship of trust and confidence between parties to a transaction. Since Chiarella was not an agent, a fiduciary, or one in whom the sellers had placed their trust and confidence at the time of the transaction, he was under no obligation to disclose his knowledge of the impending takeover prior to the transactions. Hence his trading activities were held not to be in violation of the securities fraud law.[60]

The *Chiarella* court's rejection of the parity of information theory is, as the previous discussion indicated, in accord with Halakhah. Its overturn of Chiarella's conviction, however, is at odds with R. Yose's dictum. Analysis of the details of the case readily points to the presence of all the elements needed to trigger a disgorgement requirement for Chiarella: The information Chiarella made use of to trade on was the property right of the acquiring companies which hired Pandick Press. Chiarella had no right to trade on the confidential information, as such conduct directly violated his terms of employment with Pandick Press. Trading on the confidential information carries with it the danger of alerting the marketplace to the identity of the target company. Any subsequent run-up in the price of the target company's shares resulting from the leak increases for the acquiring companies the cost of achieving control of the target. Thus Chiarella's trading entails a possible loss for the acquiring companies. Moreover, Chiarella's breach of confidentiality inflicts damage in the form of reputational harm to his employer, Pandick Press.

It follows from this analysis that Halakhah, far from exonerating Chiarella, would treat him very harshly. By dint of R. Yose's dictum, Chiarella would be required to give up the profits he earned on the insider trading and hand them over to the acquiring companies.

Moreover, Pandick Press may have a legitimate damage suit against Chiarella. Relevant in assessing this claim is the following case dealt with by R. Solomon Leib Tabak (Hungary, 1832–1908): While employed by A, B picks up A's trade secret. B reveals the trade secret to C. Equipped with the trade secret, C goes into competition with A. A sues B for loss in earnings resulting from C's competition. In his evaluation of the claim, R. Tabak lays down the principle that an employee is responsible for causing his employer a loss in earnings even when the link between the worker's action and the damage is indirect (*gerama*). For B to be held liable, however, the following conditions must be met: (1) the confidentiality clause must be stipulated before A gives the trade secret to B; (2) it must be evident that A relies on B not to reveal the secret, as would be the case when it is known that another party is in readiness to use the trade secret in competition with A; (3) the monetary loss relates directly to the job B was hired for.[61]

Let us apply R. Tabak's criteria to the case at hand. The confidentiality condition is easily met, as Chiarella's contract prohibited him from trading on insider information. Since the viability of a financial printer hinges on the confidentiality element, it is evident that Pandick Press relied on Chiarella to maintain secrecy. Satisfaction of the third condition obtains when the acquiring companies sue Pandick Press to recover fees and/or cancel outstanding contracts with it on account of Chiarella's insider trading.

We should note that R. Tabak's criteria pertain only in respect to the issue of employee responsibility for the monetary loss he indirectly causes his employer. Irrespective of whether each and every element of R. Tabak's liability criterion obtains, an employee is prohibited from taking action which might even indirectly cause the employer a monetary loss.[62]

Dirks v. *Securities and Exchange Commission*

The case of *Dirks* v. SEC[63] entails issues essentially different than those raised thus far in our exploration of category II cases. The background and details of the case follow.

Dirks was an investment analyst and officer of Delafield Childs, Inc., a registered broker dealer specializing in providing financial analysis of insurance company securities to institutional investors. Secrist, a former officer of Equity Funding Corporation of America (EFCA), an insurance holding company, contacted Dirks and informed him that EFCA's assets were vastly overstated as a result of massive fraud within the corporation. Secrist told

Dirks that EFCA was selling partnerships in nonexistent real estate and creating fictitious insurance policies and records.

Dirks conducted a program of extensive research and investigation in response to Secrist's accusations. Dirks's efforts finally paid off when he managed to coax some former company officials to admit to doctoring the company's insurance records or to having been aware of such improprieties.

Although Dirks did not personally trade on the information he developed, he passed on the damaging facts to both his own clients and other investors. These tippees profited handsomely from the revelations. Specifically, owners of large blocks of EFCA stock sold in advance of the precipitous price drop brought on by public disclosure of the fraud. Other traders "sold short" or purchased "put" options in order to further profit from the knowledge of the debacle at EFCA.[64]

Invoking the parity of information doctrine, the SEC censured Dirks for selectively disclosing the insider information he had obtained about EFCA.[65] On the basis of this doctrine, any person who knows or should know that the information he possesses is insider information is bound either to publicly disclose that information or to abstain both from personally trading on it and from tipping others.[66]

On appeal, the Supreme Court overturned the SEC's censure of Dirks. In rejecting the SEC's judgment, the court insisted that the disclosure-or-abstain rule cannot be invoked when its operation would exert an inhibiting influence on the role of market analysts. Holding Dirks culpable for his behavior would discourage other analysts from conducting similar investigations in the future. One way to encourage investigations to ferret out fraud is to afford Dirks and others like him a property right in their disclosures, thereby permitting them to reap the profits of their labor.[67]

Of the three court cases discussed thus far, the sharpest difference between American and Jewish law occurs in the *Dirks* case.

One fundamental issue the *Dirks* case raises is the proper course of conduct A should pursue when he observes B engaged in wrongful conduct which is harmful to C. Two conflicting duties come into play here. On the one hand, A's failure to warn B of the harm may be a violation of the biblical injunction "Do not stand idly by the blood of your neighbor" (*lo ta'amod al dam rei'kha*; Leviticus 19:16). While the verse prohibits a bystander from remaining idle in a life-threatening situation, the Mekhilta extends the interdict to a prohibition against withholding testimony in a monetary matter. Basing himself on the Mekhilta, R. Israel Meir ha-Kohen Kagan (Radun, 1838—1933) understands the monetary application of the *lo ta'amod* interdict in broad terms: A's failure to supply B with timely information that would avert a financial loss for B is a violation of the *lo ta'amod* interdict.[68]

A's report to C regarding B's wrongdoing may, on the other hand, run afoul of the biblical interdict against talebearing.[69] Two varieties of talebearing have been identified by the sages. If C is merely a third party in respect to a true but damaging report, then A's talebearing is called *lashon ha-ra*. Should C be the victim or intended victim of B's wrongdoing, then A's talebearing is called *rekhilut*. Depending upon the circumstances, talebearing may involve the violation of a total of thirty-one pentateuchal positive commandments and prohibitions.[70]

In his classic *Ḥafeẓ Ḥayyim*, R. Israel Meir ha-Kohen Kagan outlines a resolution of the above conflicting considerations: *Lo ta'amod* suspends the prohibition against talebearing only when certain very stringent procedures and conditions are met. What follows is an overview of these procedures and conditions:

1. Impetuous action must be avoided. Before taking action A must be certain that B's conduct is wrongful. Should B's conduct be subject to favorable interpretation, he must be given the benefit of the doubt.

2. Certainty that B's conduct entails wrongdoing which is injurious to C does not allow A to immediately disclose the information to C. Rather, the first step for A is to confront B directly with the accusation. A's objective should be to pressure B to confess the wrongdoing to the injured party (C).

3. Informing C of B's wrongdoing becomes a possible option only when the direct approach to B proves futile.

4. In informing on B, A's objective should be for C to summon B to a Bet Din (Jewish court) which will determine the disposition of the case.

5. Since A is bound by the objective of introducing a Bet Din into the process, he is disallowed from making the disclosure if an assessment on his part concludes that C will not elicit the help of a Bet Din and take punitive action against B on his own. The prohibition against disclosure is compelling when C will have nothing more to rely on than A's testimony against B. Here, since a Bet Din will not impose a judgment in a monetary matter on the basis of the testimony of a single witness, A's *rekhilut* will cause B to suffer consequences in excess of what Torah law calls for. But suppose A intends to corroborate his accusation with B's testimony. In this instance, *rekhilut* presents evidence which a Bet Din would act upon. Nonetheless, given the difficulty of predicting the exact judgment the Bet Din would arrive at, legitimacy would not be given to *rekhilut* when A estimates that C would take action against B without the instruction of a Bet Din. In any case, cautions R. Kagan, it is prohibited to accept as truth accusations made outside the Bet Din. Consequently, making accusations against B to an individual (C) who will not introduce the Bet Din into the process amounts to abetting a transgression.

6. In making his report A must not exaggerate the extent of the misconduct he observed.

7. Should B's misconduct be known to A only at second hand, R. Kagan is unresolved as to whether A may make the disclosure to C. In any event, A may not here present his report as fact, but may merely disclose what he has heard and advise C to investigate on the basis of the information. Should A fear that despite these qualifications C would regard the report as undisputed fact, he may not make the disclosure, as B might here be treated more harshly than warranted.

8. A must be reasonably certain that his disclosure will be acted upon. Lacking this confidence, A should not divulge the damaging information. Making a disclosure which stands to be ignored can easily lead to a train of events wherein C will at some later point be convinced of B's misconduct and in the process of reproving him for it, express regret for ignoring A's report. Telling B that A spoke ill of him violates for C the *rekhilut* interdict. Consequently, if A assesses that his report will

in all likelihood be ignored, he should not make it, as doing so makes him responsible for C's *rekhilut*.

9. Though obligated to make the damaging disclosure even when his motives are selfish, A should force himself, as much as possible, to act with purity of motive so as to avoid possible infringement of *rekhilut*. In the absence of purity of motive, it is very difficult to avoid distortion and exaggeration of the misconduct and to avoid miscalculation regarding the ramifications of the disclosure.

10. With the aim of pressuring B to confess his guilt and/or make amends to C, A is permitted, under certain conditions, to divulge the damaging report against B to third parties. Hence *lo ta'amod* suspends the interdict against spreading evil reports (*lashon ha-ra*), albeit subject to the same restrictions that govern suspension of the *rekhilut* interdict.

11. Disparaging reports should not, however, be made to people of immoral character. Feeling no sense of outrage at the misconduct, they will neither work constructively to pressure the offender to make amends nor take action to prevent future harm. Hence, no useful purpose is served by the disclosure.[71]

Let us now apply R. Kagan's criterion to the *Dirks* case. For purposes of exposition, we assume that the Torah society would create an agency akin to the SEC for the purpose of regulating financial markets in accordance with Halakhah. Accordingly, we shall regard the SEC as the Bet Din of the financial markets.

We should note at the outset that the widespread fraud at EFCA signifies that the company's shares are being traded on the premise of vastly overstated assets. As a result, exposure of the scandal at EFCA prevents the investing public from being defrauded.

In pursuing the objective of exposing fraud at EFCA, Secrist may have acted properly up to the point of contact with Dirks. Proper handling of the scandal would have required Secrist, in his initial step, to directly confront the wrongdoers. In the event confrontation fails to make the wrongdoers come forward and confess their guilt, Secrist's next step would be to present his allegations to the top management of EFCA. Should management prove unwilling to investigate his charges, Secrist would be obligated to present his allegations directly to the SEC. Enlisting the aid of an influential individual, such as Dirks, who was a respected analyst, for the purposes of pressuring the authorities to take his charges seriously would also have been legitimate.

Secrist, however, had quite a different motive for involving Dirks. He disclosed the damaging information to Dirks in the hope that the latter would disseminate it to his clients, who, in turn, would unload their holdings of EFCA shares on the market. The precipitous price decline of EFCA shares that would accompany the substantial selling would, in turn, put pressure on the SEC to launch an investigation into the affairs of EFCA.[72] Alerting the authorities to the scandal in this manner effectively protects a select group of shareholders from loss at the expense of the investing public. Since it is the avoidance of loss for the investing public which legitimizes Secrist's revelations, sharing the information with someone who will inevitably disclose the information on a selective basis violates *rekhilut*.

We now turn to Dirks's conduct. From the standpoint of Halakhah, the only legitimate role for him is to exert pressure on EFCA's management and/or on the SEC to investigate the allegations. Since the entire investing public is entitled to the damaging information, disclosing it exclusively to his clients amounts to advising them to defraud the investing public. Such conduct by Dirks violates both the *rekhilut* and the *lifnei iver* prohibitions.

Because selective disclosure here entails the violation of several biblical prohibitions, Halakhah, in opposition to the *Dirks* court, would not afford Dirks a property right in his discovery. But suppose Dirks acts properly and hands over the information he developed to the SEC. Is Dirks entitled to any compensation for his efforts?

Most relevant here is the consideration that it is *lo ta'amod* which both legitimizes Dirks's investigation and compels him to turn over the information he develops to the SEC. *Lo ta'amod,* in its most basic form, entails the rescuing of human life. The actual act of rescue, being the fulfillment of a religious duty, warrants no monetary compensation.[73] Nonetheless, if in order to accomplish the rescue, the rescuer either incurs expenditures[74] or abandons his gainful employment, the rescued party must compensate him for his efforts.[75]

While Dirks's information effectively rescues the investing public from financial disaster, the actual beneficiaries of his efforts cannot be identified. In consequence, a case for compensating Dirks for the information he developed cannot be made. Mandating such compensation by means of legislation is, however, within the purview of legislative action in the Torah society.

Tippee Liability and American Law

The *Dirks* court enunciated the parameters for tippee liability in insider-trading cases. In setting forth its criterion in this manner, the court affirmed the principle that mere possession of nonpublic material information does not give rise to a duty to disclose or abstain. This duty can be created only by a fiduciary relationship. Accordingly, a duty to disclose or abstain for a noninsider can only come about by way of inheriting this duty from the insider. The tippee does not inherit the duty to disclose or abstain from the insider unless a two-pronged test is met. First, it must be determined that the tipper has breached a fiduciary duty by improperly disclosing the nonpublic information to the tippee. Whether or not disclosure is a breach of duty depends upon the tipper's purpose in making the disclosure. If it personally benefits the tipper, either directly or indirectly, the disclosure is improper. Examples of direct or indirect personal benefits include financial gain, reputational gain that will translate into future earnings, and the dissemination of confidential information to a trading relative or friend as a gift. Tippee liability, however, is not established by merely showing the tipper's breach of duty. The second prong of the test requires that the tippee either knew or should have known that there had been a breach.[76]

The test for determining tippee liability was applied in the case of *Securities and Exchange Commission* v. *Switzer*.[77] In this case, University of Oklahoma football coach Barry Switzer overheard, while sunbathing at a secondary school track meet, a conversation between G. Platt, the president of Texas International Co. (TIC) and his wife, which divulged material, nonpublic information relating to a major forthcoming event at TIC. In the overheard conversation, Platt revealed to his wife that TIC was planning to liquidate its subsidiary, Phoenix. The disclosure included the planned date of the public announcement.This information was likely to affect the investment decision of a reasonably prudent investor because the pro-rata value of Phoenix assets could reasonably be expected to exceed the market price of its stock at the time of the public announcement. Switzer and some of his friends bought shares in the company based on what he had overheard.[78]

The *Switzer* court applied the two-pronged *Dirks* test to determine whether a tippee acquires a fiduciary duty. Specifically, the court required a showing, first, that an insider had breached a fiduciary duty to the shareholders by disclosing insider information, and second, that the tippee knew or should have known that there had been a breach. The court found that Platt had not breached a fiduciary duty, and therefore Switzer had not acquired or assumed a fiduciary duty. It determined that Platt had no intention of communicating the information to Switzer, and that Switzer had inadvertently overheard the conversation. Because Switzer did not acquire a fiduciary duty, any information he passed to other defendants did not constitute insider trading.[79]

Furthermore, the court stated that even if the plaintiff (the SEC) had satisfied the first prong of the *Dirks* test, it failed to satisfy the second prong. Specifically, the court found that the "defendants did not know nor did they have reason to know, that the information disseminated by a corporate insider was for an improper purpose."[80]

Tippee Liability and Jewish Law

Several variants of tippee involvement in insider-trading cases can be identified. In one class of cases, analogous to the TGS insider-trading case, the informational advantage is the property of the shareholders. Trading on the information, as discussed earlier, amounts to "doing business with someone else's asset." Given the above rationale, disgorgement should be called for whether the trader was an insider or a tippee outsider. Being unaware that the information was confidential should not be an extenuating factor, as the tippee had no right to trade on the information.

Taking advantage of an insider's offer to sell material nonpublic information entails the additional violation for the tippee of "abetting" a transgressor, which is an aspect of the *lifnei iver* interdict.

Another type of insider trading falls into the category of cases analogous to *Dirks*. The salient feature here is that the informational advantage is not a property right but rather consists of an accusation of fraud. For expositional convenience, our analysis of the halakhic perspective of this strain of tippee liability in insider-trading cases will refer to the *Dirks* case, discussed above.

Given that an accusation of fraud made outside the Bet Din amounts to *lashon ha-ra*, Dirks and his tippees are prohibited from accepting the allegations as fact or even as possibly true. Acting upon Secrist's information by selling Equity Funding stock short or buying put options on the company's stock manifests on the part of the tippees a conviction that the price of EFCA shares will decline and hence amounts to giving credence or plausibility to the *lashon ha-ra*.

While it is forbidden to give credence to *lashon ha-ra*, an individual is, nevertheless, permitted to be cautious on the basis of what he has heard and take action to avoid damage or financial loss. The legitimacy of adopting a guarded policy in respect to *lashon ha-ra*, however, should not work to permit the tippee to unload his portfolio of EFCA shares. Such conduct would be analogous to selling merchandise which one suspects might be defective. A sale of this kind exploits the ignorance of one's opposite number and is therefore prohibited.

Since public disclosure of the *lashon ha-ra* is not an option open to the tippee shareholder, the tippee will effectively be stuck with his EFCA holdings. While Equity Funding is under official investigation, trading in its shares would be suspended. If the charges proved true, liquidation of the company would be ordered. If the charges, on the other hand, turned out not to be substantiated, trading in the shares would resume.

Final judgment regarding the ethics for the tippee in selling off his EFCA shares must, however, take into account the degree to which the *lashon ha-ra* has permeated the investment community. As a preliminary matter, we note that every transaction in the secondary financial markets is predicated on the basis of contrary expectations. Accordingly, a participant in these markets may be fully expected to realize that an exchange of information with his opposite number may well make him change his mind about going through with the transaction.

From the contrary-expectation feature of the secondary financial markets it follows that once the rumor of fraud at EFCA becomes accessible to the financial community, the burden of both discovering and interpreting the import of the information should fall on the buyer. Selling EFCA shares under these conditions, therefore, cannot be said to amount to exploiting the ignorance of an unsuspecting public.

What, however, is the criterion which decides when information passes from the category of being confidential to the category of being accessible to the investing public? Two factors are crucial here.

1. The tippee's source should be someone whose information is second-hand. Obtaining the information from someone who has no direct knowledge of the fraud indicates that broadcasting of the rumor is beyond the stage of selective and controlled dissemination and has entered the phase of being circulated in a spontaneous and uncontrolled manner.

2. A price decline in EFCA shares occurs either just prior to or subsequent to the tippee's exposure to the rumor. In the absence of other developments, the tippee should have the right to ascribe the drop in price to the rumor of fraudulent practices at EFCA. Selling off EFCA shares in this investment climate cannot be characterized as exploiting an unsuspecting investment public. Quite to the contrary, the burden of discovering the rumor should fall squarely on the prospective buyer of EFCA stock.

When both of these mitigating factors combine together, a strong case can be made for allowing the tippee to unload his holdings of EFCA shares.

Insider Trading And Public Policy

We now turn to the issue of insider trading and public policy. The economic literature has produced several arguments in favor of legalizing insider trading. We will critically evaluate them from the standpoint of Halakhah.

Price-Efficiency Effects of Insider Trading

The price efficiency argument for legalizing insider trading stresses the importance to the economy of directing financial capital to those places where society values it most. Stock prices are considered to be at their true values when they reflect as accurately as possible the prospects of the corporate issuers. If a firm's value is under-represented by its share price because, for example, the firm has strategic reasons for not divulging information about a valuable discovery, a marketing strategy, or an expansion or acquisition plan, then it will be more costly than it would otherwise be for that firm to raise capital in the equity market. The firm, therefore, will not engage in the optimal amount of investing, and resources will not flow to those uses which society values most highly.

Advocates of legalizing insider trading believe that trading on insider information moves share prices toward their true value more quickly than if insider trading were banned.[81]

The thesis that insider trading promotes efficiency in the capital markets faces several difficulties, however.

One difficulty is that illegal insider trading has not been shown empirically to have any significant effect on share prices. A recent study examined increases in stock prices of target firms in 172 successful tender offers over a three-week period before their announcement. The study found that by one day prior to the announcement, the average stock had appreciated to 38.8 percent of its price one day after the tender offer was announced. It was shown, however, that a significant portion of the run-up could be explained by three legally available influences on pre-bid trading—media speculation, the bidder's foothold acquisition in the target, and whether the bid was friendly or hostile. Thus, a large portion of the run-up could be explained by factors other than illegal insider trading.[82]

Another criticism of the price-efficiency rationale for insider trading is that permitting insider trading may delay or distort the transmission of valuable information to the market. This would occur if insiders at lower echelons of management concealed information from their superiors in order to avoid the danger of an early price run-up which would diminish their gains and leave them with too little time to arrange financing of their trades. It might also occur if members of the firm deliberately released false information in order to take advantage of profits available from resulting price swings.

Finally, legalizing insider trading is not the most efficient means of promoting correct pricing in the capital markets. The latter goal could be achieved instantaneously by adopting a disclosure rule requiring full disclosure by the company of material non-public information. There will, of course, be situations in which immediate full disclosure is undesirable, as, for example, in the TGS case discussed above. In these instances, however, there is no reason to believe that insider trading leads to an optimal price-adjustment path for company shares.[83]

Transaction Costs

Another consideration in evaluating the thesis that insider trading promotes efficiency in the capital markets is an analysis of the transaction costs which arise from insider trading. A rule permitting insider trading can be expected to put into motion two opposing forces affecting transaction costs.

On the debit side, it can be expected to cause an adverse selection problem for the specialist. By maintaining an inventory of various stocks, the specialist, as will be recalled, provides continuous trading opportunities for investors. In a legal environment which permits insider trading, the specialist faces the risk that his opposite number may be an insider. Given the increased risk factor, the specialist can be expected to reduce his bid price and/or increase his ask price. Thus a rule permitting insider trading would increase the spread between his bid and ask prices. The result for firms is that the cost of using the market for financing rises, thereby altering the proportions of the funds they choose to derive from debt and equity.

Counteracting somewhat this negative effect on transaction costs is that a rule permitting insider trading reduces duplicative information gathering in the marketplace. This follows from the proposition that the presence of insiders in the market exerts a disincentive for outsiders to engage in information gathering. Since insiders can capture gains from changes in market value associated with new information before outsiders, outsiders will be discouraged from engaging in information gathering. Thus insider trading reduces the overall amount of money that society spends to achieve an adjustment in share prices because it reduces the cost to society of duplicative information gathering by outsiders.[84]

Efficient Managerial Incentives

Another facet of the economic case for legalizing insider trading is the thesis that insider trading is an indispensable method of compensating entrepreneurs. The attractiveness of this compensation scheme is that it allows managers to profit from their efforts on behalf of the firm without having to negotiate with owners. When managers believe their entrepreneurial activities will enhance the value of the firm, they can invest in the company's shares at their discretion. Having acquired an interest in the future course of the share price, managers will concentrate their efforts on behalf of the company to ensure that their programs will succeed and the resulting enhanced performance be disclosed.[85]

One major objection to this compensation scheme is the fact that insider trading does not reward efficient management as such. Rather, it rewards the *possession* of confidential information, whether favorable or unfavorable to the corporation's prospects.

Moreover, such a plan gives insiders as much of an incentive to destroy a company as to revolutionize it, or to reduce earnings as to increase them. One can imagine cases where managers would have an incentive to take steps to accelerate the demise of their firm. Managers would have an incentive to manipulate the disclosure of information about the firm in a manner calculated to produce sharp, if temporary, spurts in the price of the firm's stock. Their energies would be deflected from managing the firm so as to maximize its present worth to managing publicity about the firm so as to maximize the volatility of its stock.[86]

It is inconsistent to claim that such market forces as concern for one's reputation are sufficient to deter insiders from exploiting bad news, and at the same time deny to such factors the power to motivate good entrepreneurial performance.[87]

Insider Trading And Jewish Law

We have demonstrated that certain instances of insider trading entail infringement of the prohibition against talebearing. Insider trading may also entail the breach of a confidence. For these variations of insider-trading cases, legislation to permit the practice cannot be considered. Given that such legislation comes into conflict with ritual law, it enjoys no halakhic sanction.[88]

Suppose, however, that the insider trade infringes only on Halakhah's prohibition against "doing business with someone else's asset." Here, the effect of legislation permitting the practice would merely be to alter the distribution of property rights. If such legislation stands to improve the efficiency of the capital markets, a halakhic basis for consideration of it would have been demonstrated. But the economic case for deregulating insider trading, as discussed earlier, is far from convincing.

Moreover, Halakhah would oppose the legalization of insider trading on moral grounds. One ideal for the Torah society, as will be recalled, is the creation of a legal environment which encourages *imitatio Dei* conduct. Adopting a legal rule which would lead to an increase in conflict-of-interest problems does violence to this ideal. By opening the door for the introduction of compensation schemes which allow employees to trade on insider information, deregulation does just this. Whether or not such a scheme works in the long run to increase society's wealth is irrelevant as far as Halakhah is concerned. What is morally unacceptable, as discussed above, is that such a scheme creates opportunities for managers to profit from their own sloth, ineptness, and/or destructive behavior. This drives a wedge between the interests of the managers and the interests of the shareholders.

Easterbrook's analysis of the adverse-selection problem sheds light on why conflict of interest will become widespread under a rule permitting insider trading. Let us suppose that firm A allows its executives to engage in insider trading but firm B contractually forbids such conduct. Given the absence of government involvement in the enforcement against insider trading, B will find it very costly to enforce its prohibition. Most importantly, it will be very costly to detect an insider's trades because he can hide his trading activity. Specifically, the insider can buy stock in street names or through nominees; he can route orders through a chain of brokers to make tracing difficult; the list of evasive devices is long.

About the only thing a firm can do by itself to reduce the cost of enforcing compliance with a no-trading pledge is to prohibit all ownership of stock by its employees. This drastic response could not interdict managers from passing tips to friends and family or trading secretly through nominees. If a ban were enforceable, however, it could have costs far exceeding those of insider trading, as stock ownership is very useful in aligning managers' incentives with those of other shareholders.

Whenever a firm writes a contract that it does not plan to enforce or cannot enforce, it will face a serious problem of adverse selection. Accordingly, dishonest executives will find employment with B especially attractive. Since they will get their salaries and also be able to engage in insider trading, they will be overcompensated. To avoid overcompensating the dishonest executives, B will be forced to reduce salaries across the board. As a result, the honest executives—those who do not trade on insider information—will be underpaid and will leave. To increase the quality of its managers, B will have no recourse but to rescind its "voluntary prohibition" of insider trading.[89]

The foregoing discussion demonstrates that in the Torah society a case cannot be made for the government to suspend the prohibitions involved in insider trading.

Left to its own devices, the private sector, as indicated, would be bedeviled with difficulties in enforcing the insider-trading prohibitions. Thus, in a Torah society the government's mission to suffuse the legal environment with *imitatio Dei* conduct requires that it play a vigorous role in enforcing the ban on insider trading.

In an effort to rectify the ineffectiveness of the enforcement remedies available to the SEC for insider-trading violations, Congress enacted the Insider Trading Sanctions Act of 1984 (ITSA). Congress designed the ITSA to impose a severe monetary civil penalty as the primary means of deterring future violations of insider trading. Under this legislation, the SEC has the authority to seek, and the courts have the power to impose, up to a maximum penalty of treble damages on insider-trading violations subject to the act.[90]

In 1988, Congress passed the Insider Trading and Securities Fraud Enforcement Act (ITSFEA). This act significantly increased the maximum criminal penalties for insider-trading offenses.[91] One provision of ITSFEA empowered the SEC to award bounty payments to persons who furnish information leading to the imposition of civil penalties for insider trading. Without being subject to judicial review, the SEC was empowered with broad discretion concerning these bounty payments.[92]

These recent congressional enactments in the area of insider trading, as the thrust of the preceding discussion indicates, would be very much applauded by Halakhah.

• 7
Resale Price Maintenance

IN THIS CHAPTER OUR TASK will be to explore the issue of resale price maintenance from the standpoint of both economic theory and Halakhah. The practice will be identified, along with the various economic theories which have been advanced to rationalize it. Finally, we will argue that prohibiting this practice creates settings for veiled or hidden misconduct in the marketplace. Therefore, from the standpoint of Halakhah, adopting a per se legality approach toward resale price maintenance agreements is indicated.

Resale Price Maintenance

Resale price maintenance refers to a contractual agreement between the seller and reseller of a good to fix the price the reseller charges. In the United States this practice is prohibited as a violation of the antitrust laws. Merely suggesting retail prices, of course, is not illegal. Under the Colgate doctrine, a manufacturer may simply refuse to sell to retailers who do not charge its suggested price. Such a refusal, if not accompanied by coercion, is not illegal, because sellers generally have freedom of contract to deal with whomever they choose.

In 1937 the Miller-Tydings Act allowed states to pass so-called fair trade laws that permitted the manufacturers of branded items to set resale prices. This law was repealed in 1975.[1]

Notwithstanding the current per se illegality for resale price maintenance, antitrust scholars are in broad disagreement over the proper legal treatment of resale price maintenance.[2]

The Rationale

A long-standing puzzle to economists is why manufacturers prefer resale price maintenance. Such arrangements apparently run counter to their own self-interest. Since a higher resale price reduces the demand for the manufacturer's good and hence its sales revenues, one might expect the manufacturer always to encourage, rather than restrict, competition among its dealers in order to minimize the retail price of its product.

The Retail Cartel Model

One rationale for resale price maintenance offered in the economic literature is the retail cartel model. In this model resale price maintenance is viewed as a collusive tactic used by retailers to drive up the price of a particular product. Resale price maintenance comes into play because each dealer is worried that the others will "cheat," i.e., that other dealers will reduce the price in order to make additional sales at the expense of those adhering to the fixed price. To this end, the dealers conscript the manufacturers to help them out. The manufacturers set a fixed resale price and penalize dealers that sell at a lower price.[3]

The retail cartel model, as Easterbrook points out, suffers from manifold difficulties. Most basically, for the model to be plausible the industry must be one in which the dealers can form a cartel. But retail markets have free entry. The atomistic nature of the retail market makes it almost impossible to sustain a cartel with or without the aid of manufacturers.

Secondly, why would manufacturers go along with this arrangement? A manufacturer that helps dealers form a cartel is doing itself in. It will sell less, and dealers will get the monopoly profits.

Moreover, for the retailers' cartel to be effective, all manufacturers must join in and agree to resale price maintenance. If there are holdouts, noncooperating dealers can sell the holdouts' product for less. That would destroy the cartel. Yet why would all manufacturers want to go along? It pays for one or more to hold out. Dealers could conscript all manufacturers only when the conditions of a manufacturers' cartel existed.

Finally, there is the problem of verification. Why are manufacturers any better at policing than dealers? The cheating dealer cannot attract extra business without advertising its lower prices. Once it does, its fellow conspirators learn it is cheating in the same way manufacturers do. They could enforce the deal themselves. The extra enforcement from the cutoff by the manufacturer may be too late, or too little.[4]

All of these considerations make the retail cartel model for resale price maintenance highly implausible. As Easterbrook sums up:

If we see many dealers and many manufacturers we can exclude the cartel possibility. And if we see some manufacturers using restricted dealing while others do not, or if we see substantial differentiated products, we can exclude the cartel hypothesis no matter how many or few dealers and manufacturers there are.[5]

The Manufacturers' Cartel Model

In a variant of the model just discussed, resale price maintenance is viewed as symptomatic of a price-fixing agreement among manufacturers in a particular industry. In order for a price-fixing agreement to work, it must be accompanied by an agreement to restrict supply. Specifically, each member of the cartel must be assigned a quota. If this is not done, supply may exceed demand at the official price set by the cartel, with the result that market forces render the agreement meaningless. But each member of the cartel has a strong incentive to cheat on the agreement. Each firm would like to enjoy the benefit of the cartel (a higher price) without paying the price (holding down output). If only one firm expands output, price will not fall appreciably, but the additional sales at the official cartel price add significantly to the firm's profit. It is thus in each firm's self-interest to violate the cartel agreement to restrict output. Here is where resale price maintenance comes into play. Let a member of the cartel try to increase output by giving retailers secret price concessions. Since the retailers are unable openly to reduce the price at which they can sell the product to final consumers, they manifestly are deprived of the most powerful instrument to increase sales to customers. Therefore, a manufacturer who would induce retailers to increase their purchases from him by offering them lower prices loses profits to no avail.[6]

As a rationale for resale price maintenance, the manufacturers' cartel model lacks widespread applicability. It describes a rare phenomenon. To be successful, a manufacturers' cartel would have to encompass practically the whole industry. Since real-world firms differ in size, cost conditions, and other respects, agreement will not come easily, and when it does come, it will reflect some sort of compromise among divergent views. As happens with any compromise, some firms will be unhappy with the outcome, and they are all the more likely to refuse to join the cartel, or to join, but violate the cartel policy and expand output. Relatedly, the profits of the cartel are likely to encourage new entry, but new entry will work to destabilize the cartel.

Moreover, resale price maintenance alone will not be sufficient to inhibit individual members of the cartel from expanding supply by offering secret deals to distributors. Special terms of sale which have the effect of price concessions must also be outlawed. These terms of trade may include favorable credit terms, free delivery service, less than the prevailing price on a tied article, and the like.

To be successful, therefore, a cartel must be able to induce its members to both hold down output and restrict entry into the markets. These tasks are very formidable to accomplish, and history is strewn with examples of cartels that flourished for a short time only to disintegrate because of internal and external pressures.

The Telser Model

A rationale for resale price maintenance which enjoys wide support in the economic literature is the Telser special-service model. This rationale explains why an *individual* manufacturer might prefer resale price maintenance. In Telser's model, retailers are the least-cost means of delivering valuable information regarding a manufacturer's product to potential buyers. Yet, even though consumers value this information more than the cost of providing it, a suboptimal flow of information will be supplied without resale price maintenance. This outcome occurs because retailers cannot charge for the information they supply. Thus, nothing prevents a consumer from engaging in free-riding in the form of eliciting product information from a full-support retailer but making his purchases from a discounter who supplies no information. If a sufficient number of consumers engage in free-riding, the full-service sellers may decide that the cost of providing these services exceeds the profits made from the sales of the good and decide to either stop carrying the product or cease providing services. The result is that product information is supplied at suboptimal levels, if at all.[7]

Telser's special-service rationale for resale price maintenance is, as Posner points out, entirely consistent with effective competition at the manufacturer level. This is so because product differentiation among competing manufacturers makes presale services for the different brands of the same product noninterchangeable. To illustrate, Fords and Chevrolets may be good substitutes for one another, yet have sufficiently different design and performance characteristics so that a demonstration ride or other presale service offered by a Ford dealer may not be an adequate substitute for presale services offered by a Chevrolet dealer. Hence a particular manufacturer cannot effectively free-ride off the dealer services offered by dealers of a rival manufacturer.[8]

Resale price maintenance can be a solution to the free-rider problem. By requiring all sellers to charge the same price, the manufacturer can remove the incentive for consumers to obtain services from one seller while buying the product itself from another. Furthermore, by preventing resellers from competing with one another on price, a manufacturer may be able to encourage a higher level of nonprice competition.[9]

While acknowledging the hypothetical possibility of free-riding, some antitrust scholars deny that it is a real phenomenon. One has gone so far as to say, "I understand the theoretical appeal of that argument. As a practical matter, however, the `free rider' might be characterized as the Loch Ness Monster of Antitrust—everyone's heard of it, but except for an occasional shadowy outline, nobody's ever seen it."[10]

Disputing this school of thought, Kelly makes use of the case-study method to demonstrate that the free-rider phenomenon exists in the real world and significantly reduces consumer welfare. These case studies document free-riding of retail services in the automobile, wall-covering, and personal computer industries.[11]

For the purpose of demonstrating that the free-rider phenomenon entails violation of various aspects of Jewish business law, we will draw upon Kelly's case study in the personal computer industry. Kelly's data for this case study originate from an antitrust suit against Apple Computer, Inc.

Apple distributed its personal computers through a network of independent dealers that numbered approximately 1,000 by 1981. The company believed that its success depended upon educating its potential customers about the benefits they might derive from a computer. This educational task was carried out by the independent Apple dealers, who would assess the needs of prospective customers, put together a combination of hardware and software that met these needs, provide hands-on instruction, and finally, assist the purchaser when he had a problem after the sale.

Convinced that mail order sales did not meet its support criteria, Apple sent its dealers a modification of their dealer agreements which called for them to agree in writing not to engage in mail order sales as a condition of remaining an Apple dealer. Apple subsequently began monitoring their compliance with the ban on mail order sales, and terminated eight of the dealers. Subsequently, six current or former Apple dealers brought a suit against Apple, alleging that the company was attempting to fix Apple prices. The legal action was decided in favor of Apple.

In the course of the court proceedings, the plaintiffs conceded that they had engaged in free-riding. Most of their mail order customers had shopped at other dealerships before contacting them, and they routinely sent any mail order customers who sought information to other dealers rather than attempt to instruct them or provide support over the telephone or through the mail.[12]

Free–Riding In Jewish Law

We now turn to an analysis of the free-rider conduct in the Apple Computer Company distribution chain from the perspective of Jewish law.

Directing information-seeking customers to full-support dealers represents a violation of Jewish business ethics by the mail order dealer. The prohibition of this conduct is derived from the talmudic dictum recorded at Bava Batra 21b as understood by R. Meir b. Samuel (Ramerupt, ca. 1060–ca. 1155).

> Fishing nets must be kept away from a fish the full length of the fish's swim. And how much is this? Rabbah son of R. Huna [d. 322] says: A parasang.

R. Meir explains that the dictum refers to the circumstance where A, in order to increase his catch, casts a net containing a dead fish into the sea. Since A's doing so is based upon the notion that clusters of other fish will be attracted to the vicinity of the dead fish, B may not cast his net in the same area. Interloping action of this sort is regarded as a form of robbery: Since it is A's initiative which attracts the swarm of fish, B's interloping action would effectively appropriate his toil and effort for the purpose of commercial advantage.[13] R. Meir b. Samuel's criterion for unfair competition finds substantial support in the rabbinic literature.[14]

Proceeding from the above line is the prohibition against the mail order dealer directing his information-seeking customers to full-service dealers. Such action constitutes appropriating someone else's toil and effort for commercial gain.

Ona'at Devarim

The free-rider conduct in the Apple distribution chain may also run afoul of Judaism's prohibition against causing someone needless mental anguish (*ona'at devarim*).[15] In a commercial setting, as cited in the Mishnah at Bava Meẓia 4:10, *ona'at devarim* occurs when an individual prices an article he has no intention of buying. What is objectionable here, according to R. Menaḥem b. Solomon Meiri (Perpignan, ca. 1249–1306), is that pricing an article creates an anticipation on the part of the seller that he will make a sale. This anticipation is dashed when the inquirer decides not to pursue the matter further.[16] While a prospective buyer need not concern himself with the disappointment a vendor may experience should his price inquiry not culminate in his making a purchase, pricing an article he has no intention of buying causes the vendor needless distress and is hence prohibited.[17]

A clearcut application of the *ona'at devarim* interdict is provided by the free-rider behavior of consumers in the computer market. Consumers who make inquiries at the full-support dealers but plan all along to make their purchases at the discount mail order store violate the *ona'at devarim* interdict. Since the consumer elicits the expertise of the salesperson at the full-support store with a closed mind in respect to making a purchase there, the disappointment the salesperson experiences when the inquiry does not culminate in a sale is fully the responsibility of the insincere consumer.

By dint of the biblical verse "and do not place a stumbling block before the blind" (*lifnei iver lo titein mikh'shol*; Leviticus 19:14), it is prohibited to aid in the commission of a transgression.[18] Given that the above-described free-rider conduct by a consumer violates the *ona'at devarim* interdict, a dealer who directs a customer to engage in such conduct is in violation of the *lifnei iver* interdict.

Deterring Fraud

A limitation of the Telser theory, according to Springer and Frech, is that it can only be applied to search goods, such as stereo equipment, personal computers, and furniture. But the theory cannot readily account for the purely vertical resale price maintenance of many relatively simple, repeat-purchase items involved in recent Federal Trade Commission complaints, among them Florsheim shoes, London Fog raincoats, Levi-Strauss jeans, and Pendleton shirts.

Extending Telser's theory, Springer and Frech offer the hypothesis that resale price maintenance is the manufacturer's means of making the consumer aware of relative differences in quality among the various models of his product. In a legal environment that prohibits resale price maintenance, the manufacturer's desire to signal relative quality differences by relative price differences can be thwarted by the misleading markups of independent retailers. Resale price maintenance represents an effective counterstrategy because under resale price maintenance, the store pursuing the misleading markup strategy must remove the preticketed price and substitute its own. Manufacturers can and do make this a costly and laborious process by appending tamper-resistant price labels, thereby deterring misleading markups. In a word, resale price maintenance can deter retailer free-riding on manufacturer brand-name capital.

Springer and Frech present an empirical test of their hypothesis. The data they used originated from an antitrust suit against a famous shirtmaker. Because the research was done while the case was still in litigation, the government did not allow the authors to identify the shirtmaker. The company in question produced four basic models of its shirts. Although all of the maker's shirts were of exceptional quality, one of the four (hereinafter referred to as model D) was inferior to the others in the basic series. While model D is almost indistinguishable in the store, the coarseness of its weave renders it relatively uncomfortable in actual use.

Before the manufacturer signed a consent agreement to discontinue all preticketing and suggested prices for several years, its policy included a call for retailers to maintain a $1 spread between the lower-quality model D and its other basic shirts, models A, B, and C. Two field surveys, conducted after the consent decree was signed, provide direct evidence in support of the misleading-markup model. In one survey, fully eighteen of twenty-one stores were charging identical prices for model D despite its lower quality, lower wholesale price, and history of lower preticketed resale prices. In the second survey, eight of the twelve stores sampled charged identical prices for all models, regardless of quality.

Another empirical finding of the researchers was that free pricing led to higher retail markups, rather than the lower ones envisioned in most of the literature.[19]

Misleading Markups

The misleading-markup practice described by Springer and Frech violates Judaism's prohibition against creating a false impression (*geneivat da'at*).[20] Since inferior model D was almost indistinguishable in the store from the other models, mixing it together and pricing it the same as the other models dupes the consumer into believing its quality is the same as that of the other models. An analogous case in Jewish law is the prohibition against a vendor mixing small quantities of inferior produce with a higher-grade variety. Since the difference in quality is not outwardly distinguishable, the practice is regarded as a ruse to dupe the consumer into believing that the entire display is of equally high quality.[21]

Retail Price Maintenance in the Torah Society

In extrapolating the treatment of resale price maintenance from a halakhic perspective, a distinction must be drawn between isolated and industrywide cases. In the instance when resale price maintenance is practiced by one or several manufacturers of a particular industry, the Telser special-services rationale for resale price maintenance is compelling. For this variant of resale price maintenance, the manufacturers' cartel model is inapplicable, and the retail cartel model is extremely unconvincing. Since making resale price maintenance illegal produces an economic environment which invites free-rider conduct, the *imitatio Dei* imperative requires the Torah society to take action for the purpose of eliminating the setting for this objectionable conduct. Allowing resale price maintenance accomplishes this.

In the industrywide case, resale price maintenance may be symptomatic of a cartel arrangement. But Halakhah does not object per se to restraint of trade. It is subject to regulation in Halakhah only under very limited circumstances. One such circumstance is a price-fixing agreement among vendors of essential foodstuffs that has the effect of circumventing Halakhah's one-sixth profit rate constraint for this sector. Another instance is a restraint of trade agreement which threatens firms excluded from the agreement with ruination. We have discussed these restraint of trade issues elsewhere.[22] In any case, the objectionable forms of restraint of trade are sufficiently recognizable so as not to disturb the basic case for resale price maintenance.

Implementation of resale price maintenance will, of course, be at the expense of those consumers who are knowledgeable and prefer the product to be sold without frills at a lower price. But, as Easterbrook has pointed out, if the no-frills demand is significant enough, the profit motive will ensure that firms emerge to cater to this segment of the marketplace. Providing a case in point is the computer industry. Apple Computer, as discussed earlier, caters to the customer who wants to be educated in respect to the hardware-software combination that will best serve his needs. Commodore, on the other hand, caters to the consumer who is already knowledgeable and knows exactly what he wants. This consumer is searching for a no-frills outlet at a bargain price. Restricted dealing thus may increase the number of ways manufacturers can compete to provide what some segment of the population wants to buy. The more ways there are to slice up the product-service continuum, the more likely any one customer's wants will be satisfied.[23]

• 8
Unauthorized Copying and Dubbing

THE ISSUE OF UNAUTHORIZED copying and dubbing comprises the subject of this chapter. We will begin by delineating the manner in which American law and Halakhah separately approach this phenomenon. Our survey will make it apparent that the current legal environment affords the unauthorized copier many opportunities for invisible misconduct. With the aim of eliminating the invisible misconduct settings while preserving the halakhic notion of what constitutes the proper distribution of property rights here, we go on to suggest directions for legislative reform in this area.

Unauthorized Copying And The American Legal System

In the United States, common law protects the owner of an intellectual work from unauthorized use as soon as it is created. After publication, however, only copyrighted works are protected. If a work is published without observing the strict formal requirements of copyright law, including the notice of copyright, both common law and statutory copyright protection are permanently lost and the work is thrown into the public domain.

Under American law, protection of a copyrighted work extends for a period of twenty-eight years, subject to renewal upon application for another twenty-eight-year period. When the copyright expires, all exclusive rights end, and the work enters the public domain.[1]

In order both to promote the progress of science and the useful arts and to support the public's right of access to a work, American copyright law does not confer an absolute monopoly right to the owner of an intellectual work.[2]

Limitations on the rights of the owners of intellectual property find expression in the judicially established "fair use" doctrine. Incorporated into the 1976 Copyright Act,[3] this criterion determines whether a particular unauthorized use is "fair" on the basis of the following four factors: (1) the purpose and character of the use, including whether it is of a commercial nature or is for nonprofit educational purposes; (2) the nature of the copyrighted work; (3) the amount and substantiality of the portion used in relation to the copyrighted work as a whole; and (4) the effect of the use upon the potential market for or value of the copyrighted work.[4]

Invoking the fair use doctrine, the court in *Williams and Wilkins* v. *United States* (1975) validated a limited photocopying right for a user of a copyrighted work. In the case, the defendant libraries, the National Library of Medicine (NLM) and the National Institute of Health (NIH), supplied single photocopies of individual articles contained in the plaintiff's four medical journals, upon request, to their own research employees and to private scientists, scholars, researchers, and other libraries. The photocopying practices were instituted for the primary purpose of gaining easier access to scientific materials. Requesting parties were not charged for the copies. Under this photocopying system, several million pages of copyrighted periodicals were copied per year. Though requests were generally limited to a single copy of one article of no more than forty or fifty pages from a given journal, some exceptions were made so long as the reproduction consisted of less than half of a journal.

In upholding the medical libraries' photocopying practices, the courts regarded their use as fair since it promoted the advancement of science. In addition, the court stressed the nonprofit nature of the institutions and the personal nature of the use by the libraries' patrons. Finally, in the court's judgment, the plaintiff had failed to prove actual damages. In fact, the plaintiff's subscription sales were shown to have steadily increased over the time interval encompassing the complaint.[5]

While the 1976 Copyright Act incorporated the fair use doctrine, it placed some restrictions on library photocopying. Specifically, reproduction is disallowed when the purpose of the user is direct or indirect commercial advantage. Additionally, the law provided that photocopying by libraries is a noninfringing use only as long as it is not systematic and does not constitute "a substitute for purchase or subscription."[6]

The Copyright Act failed to precisely formulate what constituted "excessive" photocopying. That task fell to the newly founded National Commission on New Technological Uses of Copyrighted Works (CONTU).[7] Guidelines interpreting this provision were adopted by CONTU after "lengthy consultations" with author-publisher groups and the library community. Generally speaking, the guidelines provide that a library requesting photocopies of articles from periodicals through interlibrary loan may receive five photocopies within one year from a single periodical to which it does not subscribe. The filled request of a sixth copy from the same periodical within one calendar year constitutes an infringement.

The Copyright Act provides that reproduction of published works to replace copies that are damaged, deteriorating, lost, or stolen is permitted if the library, after a reasonable effort, determines that an unused replacement cannot be obtained at a fair price. Similarly, out-of-print works may be reproduced in their entirety at the request of the user provided that it is established that a copy cannot be obtained at a fair price. All permissible library duplication is subject to the requirement of copyright notice.[8]

During the course of the legislative hearings conducted in connection with the 1976 Copyright Act, educational groups proposed a specific blanket exemption, granting teachers and professors free use of copyrighted materials "for educational and scholarly purposes." Refusing to go this far, Congress, instead, urged the various interested parties to meet in an effort to devise a set of minimum standards for educational fair use. An ad hoc committee made up of representatives of professional organizations was formed and guidelines were formulated. Under the guidelines, a single copy of a chapter from a book or of an article from a periodical or newspaper may be made for a teacher's own use in "scholarly research or . . . in teaching or preparation to teach a class."

The guidelines established three basic criteria for multiple classroom copies, which "in any event" may not exceed one copy per pupil per course. Copying must meet four tests: (1) brevity, (2) spontaneity, (3) cumulative effect, and (4) inclusion in each copy of a copyright notice.

Brevity limits the amount of work that may be copied. Very short works may be copied in their entirety. Longer works may only be excerpted, with excerpts limited to 1,000 words, or 10 percent of the work, whichever is less, although at least 500 words may always be copied. The spontaneity condition requires that the decision to use the work and its actual use must be so close in time that it would be unreasonable to require the teacher to request permission from the copyright holder. Finally, the cumulative-effect test is designed to prevent teachers from circumventing the rules by multiple use. Accordingly, multiple copying is limited to no more than nine instances for one course during one class term. Selections from any one author must be limited to one short poem, article, or story, or two excerpts per term. Finally, no more than three selections from any collective work are allowed in any one school term.

The guidelines conclude with general prohibitions against (1) copying which is used to create, replace, or substitute for anthologies or compilations; (2) copying from "consumable" works, such as workbooks, exercises, and test booklets; and (3) copying which substitutes for the purchase of books or periodicals. Furthermore, the guidelines stipulate that copying may not be directed by higher authority, nor shall it be "repeated with respect to the same item by the same teacher from term to term." Finally, students may not be charged for the copied materials beyond the photocopying costs.[9]

In March 1991, the U.S. District Court in Manhattan ruled that businesses that commercially copy professors' collections of articles and excerpts without first obtaining permission violate the Copyright Act.[10]

Unauthorized Audio Recording

Under the 1971 Sound Recording Amendment to the 1909 Copyright Act, the unauthorized reproduction and commercial distribution of records and tapes became illegal.[11] Home recording from broadcasts or from tapes or records, however, is not prohibited by law, provided the recording is done for private use with no purpose of capitalizing on it commercially. Hence home audio recording is excluded from liability for copyright infringement.[12]

Unauthorized Copying And Halakhah

In secular law, as discussed above, unauthorized copying is treated under the rubric of copyright infringement. The halakhic parallel to copyright law takes the form of a medieval rabbinic edict (ca. 1550) prohibiting the publication of a religious work while copies of an earlier printing by another publisher were still available for sale.[13] In the spirit of this ordinance, it became customary for prospective authors of religious works to secure from a rabbinic authority a formal ban on the publication of the same work by others for a specified period of time. The text of the ban was usually published in the preface of the work. Once conferred, the ban was effective not only within the jurisdiction of the issuing authority, but upon all of Israel.

Since the purpose of the original edict was to promote the widest possible dissemination of Torah works, posits R. Mosheh Sofer (Hungary, 1762–1839), the ban does not extend beyond the sale of the earlier printing. Extension of the ban beyond this period would merely serve to create a commercial property right for the publisher of the previous printing, a windfall unintended by the edict. However, notwithstanding its lack of force, a ban extending beyond the sale of the previous printing remains operative within the jurisdiction of the issuing authority.

Promoting the social interest by means of conferring monopoly privileges apparently runs counter to an ancient ordinance promulgated by Ezra (5th cent. B.C.E.). To afford Jewish women with easy access to beautification aids, Ezra allowed itinerant cosmetics salesman to peddle their wares from door to door, despite the competition this would create for local storekeepers. Apparently Ezra saw the encouragement of free entry as a more important social interest than the protection of local tradesmen.

Defending the protectionist approach for the case at hand, R. Sofer posits that sufficient economic incentive would be lacking to motivate investors to undertake the publication of religious works without the expectation of monopoly status. Without this privilege, entrepreneurs would direct their investments elsewhere. In sharp contrast, local stores, which carry, besides cosmetics, a whole line of other products, would not be likely to close down on account of the competition of cosmetics peddlers.[14]

The rabbinic edict described above bears only a faint resemblance to modern copyright laws: (1) coverage included only religious works; (2) no provision for a fair use exemption was made; and (3) applications were processed through the rabbinical courts rather than through governmental agencies.

Expanding the edict that protected religious works into a full-fledged copyright law is, however, well within the purview of communal legislation in the Torah society.[15] One caveat should be noted. Copyright protection in a Torah society can never be as comprehensive as it is under American law, which constitutionally guarantees freedom of speech. The halakhic prohibition against *inciting* the evil inclination[16] makes the reading of erotic works a forbidden activity.[17] Relatedly, in the Torah society it would be prohibited to either create, publish, or study works espousing heretical ideas.[18] Forbidden works, naturally, do not qualify for copyright protection. Extending copyright protection to them would amount to no less than encouraging their dissemination and therefore would constitute a violation of the *lifnei iver* interdict by the public sector. Moreover, given the duty of the public sector to assist man in his battle against the evil inclination, taking action which fosters the incitement of the evil inclination would amount to gross dereliction of its *imitatio Dei* duty.

A much broader view of copyright protection in the Torah society is advanced by R. Joseph Saul ha-Levi Nathanson (Poland, 1810–1875). In the opinion of this decisor, the owner of an intellectual property is inherently entitled to an exclusive publication right in his work for an unlimited period of time. Securing a ban against potential encroachers is unnecessary. Such a ban, if secured, would only be for the purpose of notifying the public that the author has no objection to the reissuing of his work at the expiration date.[19]

An exclusive unlimited publication right for the author of a religious work is, however, denied by R. Yiẓḥak Yehudah Schmelkes (Galicia, 1828–1906). To be sure, the author of a religious work enjoys the right to preserve for himself the miẓvah to disseminate his work as well as the right to realize a return on the toil and effort expended on it. But once the original edition has run out, the author may not restrain others from reissuing the work.[20] In a later responsum, dealing with the same issue, R. Schmelkes refrains from definitively denying the author of a religious work an unlimited right of republication. Instead, he surmises that this right might very well be valid either by dint of some Torah law or by dint of custom.[21] In any case, if secular law confers an unlimited republication right on the owner of intellectual property, this right becomes valid for the author of a religious work as well, the operative principle here being *dina de-malkhuta dina* ("the law of the land is law"). Notwithstanding that the Jewish court does not generally follow secular law when it is in conflict with Halakhah, the secular copyright law is fully operative here because it promotes a valid public policy.[22]

Unauthorized Photocopying

R. Sofer's analysis of an 1820 infringement case involving the Rödelheim Maḥzor (High Holy Day prayer book) bears directly on the treatment of unauthorized photocopying in Jewish law. Wolf Heidenheim, the publisher of the maḥzor, had secured a rabbinical ban against republication by other persons for a period of twenty-five years. Shortly afterward, a publisher in Dyhernfürth proceeded to issue the Rödelheim Maḥzor. Rabbis took opposing views, but the majority upheld Heidenheim's right to the protection of his work.

After defending Heidenheim on the basis of the rabbinical notices against republication printed in the maḥzor, R. Sofer found an even more basic reason to restrain the publisher in Dyhernfürth. Heidenheim had not reprinted an extant edition of the maḥzor from the public domain; rather, he had produced an improved edition of the maḥzor, complete with revisions, annotations, and a German translation of the Hebrew text. Since the Rödelheim Maḥzor entailed considerable innovation on the part of Heidenheim, it reissuance by the firm in Dyhernfürth amounted to no less than appropriating someone else's toil and effort for the purpose of commercial advantage.

R. Sofer found the action of the second publisher analogous to the understanding of the talmudic dictum recorded at Bava Batra 21b expounded by R. Meir b. Samuel (Ramerupt, ca 1060–ca. 1155):

Fishing nets must be kept away from a fish the full length of the fish's swim. And how much is this? Rabbah son of R.Huna [d. 322] says: a parasang.

As explained in an earlier chapter, R. Meir understands the dictum as referring to a situation where A, in hopes of attracting large numbers of fish to the vicinity, casts a net containing a dead fish. B may not cast his net in the same vicinity because interloping action of this sort is regarded as a form of robbery. Since it is A's initiative which attracts the swarms of fish, B's interloping action effectively appropriates A's toil and effort for the purpose of commercial advantage.[23] Likewise, R. Sofer posits, the publisher in Dyhernfürth must be prevented from reaping commercial advantage from the reissuing of the Rödelheim Maḥzor. The second publisher's action amounts to appropriation of Heidenheim's toil and effort for commercial gain.[24]

A logical extension of R. Sofer's restraining order in the Rödelheim Maḥzor case, according to R. Yaakov Yesha'yahu Bloi (Israel, b. 1929), is the prohibition against unauthorized photocopying and home recording for the purpose of resale. Such action amounts to the appropriation of someone else's toil and effort for the purpose of commercial advantage. R. Bloi calls this action unlawful encroachment (*hassagat gevul*).

Commercial gain is understood by R. Bloi in the sense of quid pro quo. Since it is irrelevant whether the motive of the one who makes the copy available is the receipt of money or the expectation of reciprocation of goodwill, copying a work for a friend falls under the rubric of commercial gain.

Likewise, undeserved goodwill is secured by a school when it photocopies portions of various books for classroom use. Since the students realize the benefit of the educational matter without having to purchase the work, the goodwill the school secures thereby amounts to a misappropriation of someone else's toil and effort. Accordingly, in opposition to R. Shmuel ha-Levi Wasner (Israel, b. 1913), R. Bloi disallows a teacher from photocopying selections from various works for classroom distribution.[25]

The minimum educational fair use guidelines, as will be recalled, disallow the practice of multiple copying for classroom use when its purpose is to create, replace, or substitute anthologies or compilations. Accordingly, for copyrighted works, the practice described in R. Wasner's responsum may very well run afoul of American copyright law.

The unlawful-encroachment principle is also invoked by R. Ḥayyim David ha-Levi (Israel, contemp) in his ruling against the school practice of purchasing a single copy of a children's workbook and photocopying it for class distribution.[26]

Multiple copying of consumable works for classroom use, as will be recalled, violates the minimum educational fair use standard for copyrighted works in the United States.

In his treatment of the consumable-works case, R. Ḥayyim David ha-Levi also invokes the ruinous-impact rationale for prohibiting the practice. If every school adopted the policy of photocopying consumable materials for classroom use, argues R. Ḥayyim David ha-Levi, a ruinous impact would surely be inflicted on the author and publisher of the work.

With the aim of averting such loss for the owner of a work, R. Ḥayyim David ha-Levi prohibits the practice of dubbing a purchased cassette for a friend. If this practice were given legitimacy, he argues, its frequency would undoubtedly make it impossible for the owner of the work to recover even his costs.

On the basis of this criterion, the only copying practice which R. Ḥayyim David ha-Levi finds legitimate is the photocopying of several pages from a book. Photocopying of this sort will certainly not correspond to a lost sale for the owner of the work. By the same logic, the area of permissibility, according to R. Ḥayyim ha-Levi, might extend to the taping of a single song from a multisong cassette; but here again with the proviso that the recording is made only for personal use.[27]

While this argument is compelling in the case of unauthorized copying of consumable educational materials, it has much less force in relation to the unauthorized copying of prerecorded cassettes. Indicative of this is the testimony offered in the 1985 congressional hearings by the groups that opposed a bill calling for the imposition of royalty fees on blank tapes and recording equipment. In opposition to the bill, it was pointed out that record companies use poor-quality tapes, recorded at high speeds, and with shorter playing times, for the distribution of prerecorded music on cassettes. Because of the inferior sound and tape quality of prerecorded cassettes, consumers prefer to make their own cassettes of albums they have purchased. Since portability is the main reason for home audio recording, many consumers buy both the music record and blank tapes to make their own cassettes rather than buy the industry's inferior cassette offerings.[28]

Whether or not a universalized practice of unauthorized copying would exert a ruinous impact on the owner of the work is, in the final analysis, a matter of empirical finding. The answer to this question may very well depend upon many factors, such as the nature of the work, the medium involved, and the size of the audience the work is expected to appeal to.

Unauthorized Copying For Personal Use: A Halakhic Perspective

In his treatment of unauthorized copying in Jewish law, R. Zalman Nehemia Goldberg (Israel, contemp.) posits that Halakhah confers a property owner with the prerogative to exclude from the sale of his work the right to copy it. R. Goldberg extrapolates this principle from R. Meir's dictum that anyone who disregards an owner's stipulation is treated as a robber.[29] R. Meir's dictum, according to the Talmud, underlies the following mishnaic teaching:

> If one hires an ass to drive it on the mountain[top], but drives it on the plain, or to drive it on the plain but drives it on the mountain, even if both are ten miles, and it perishes, he is liable [for damages].[30]

R. Meir's dictum also supplies the rationale behind his own teaching:

> If one gives a *dinar* to a poor man to buy a shirt, he may not buy a cloak therewith; to buy a cloak, he must not buy a shirt, because he disregards the owner's desire.[31]

One possible approach in understanding why R. Meir regards the lessee and the poor man in the above cases as robbers for disregarding their respective instructions is to read a conditional clause into the charges given them. R. Goldberg rejects this approach, as a conditional clause is generally effective only if the consequences of alternative actions are made explicit. This is called the *tenai kaful*, or double condition, requirement. In the charity case cited above, for example, the recipient is branded a thief for spending the money on something other than a shirt only if the donor stipulated that expenditures on anything else would be regarded as misappropriation.[32]

To be sure, the *tenai kaful* condition is in some instances dropped. This occurs when the intent of the stipulator is objectively evident. Illustrating this point is the following real estate transaction: A sells his land to B. In the course of the negotiation, A mentions to B that he is selling his land because he plans to settle in Ereẓ Israel. Should A cancel his plans to settle in Ereẓ Israel, the sales transaction with B becomes void. Notwithstanding the absence of the *tenai kaful* condition, it is objectively evident that A intended to sell his land only in the eventuality that he would emigrate.[33]

In the case at hand, without a *tenai kaful*, we may not presume that the stipulator desires that one who ignores his stipulations should be regarded as guilty of misappropriation. All this leads R. Goldberg to propose that the rationale behind R. Meir's principle is that we read into the language of the stipulation a reserve-clause intent. Accordingly, if A gives alms to B to buy a shirt, A's intent is to withhold title to his money unless B uses it in the manner stipulated. B's use of the money for anything other than the purchase of the shirt is therefore regarded as misappropriation.

The novelty in R. Meir's teaching is that validity is given to a reserve clause even when it both lacks concreteness and has no monetary value from the standpoint of the alienator. This is the case here, as the reserve clause takes the form of preventing the acquirer from using what he purchased in a particular manner.

R. Meir's position is, however, a minority view. In both the charity case and the animal-for-hire case, the sages, R. Meir's disputants, do not regard departure from the given instruction as constituting robbery. They would not even regard such conduct as unethical unless the alienator couched his restrictive-use clause in the form of a prohibition. Putting the restrictive-use clause in the form of an explicit reserve clause, however, does make violation of the clause a matter of misappropriation, even according to the sages.

Therefore, if A sells his work to B but explicitly excludes from the sale the right to copy the work, the reserve clause is fully valid. Violation of the clause by B is regarded as misappropriation (*gezel*).[34]

R. Goldberg's dictum finds precedent in the rulings of R. Joseph Saul ha-Levi Nathanson. In the opinion of this decisor, as will be recalled, the owner of an intellectual work has the right to prohibit the republication of his work for an indefinite time period. Similarly, R. Nathanson prohibits the practice of reverse engineering for the purpose of producing a replica of someone else's invention.[35] What follows is the right of an author to prohibit the photocopying of his work, even if the copy is made from a purchased original and is done for personal use.

Rejecting R. Goldberg's reserve-clause interpretation of R. Meir's dictum, R. Naftali Bar-Ilan understands the restrictive-use instruction cases in terms of the principles which govern conditional stipulations. While the *tenai kaful* condition is lacking, circumstances make the intent of the stipulator objectively evident. Consequently, violation of the restrictive-use demand amounts to misappropriation. In the sages' view, however, the restrictive-use demand does not work to limit the acquirer in the use of the article, as the *tenai kaful* conditions are not met.

While Jewish contract law fully recognizes the validity of a reserve clause, this type of clause, points out R. Bar-Ilan, is not valid when the right withheld is intangible in nature (*davar sh-ein bo mammash*). Accordingly, if the seller of a work stipulates that he is not including the right to copy his work in the sale, the reserve clause is invalid. Since the transaction remains intact despite the inclusion of a nonvalid reserve clause, copying the work presents no moral dilemma for the buyer.

R. Bar-Ilan then turns his attention to the issue of whether the seller of a work can prohibit copying the work by means of a stipulation. Resolution of this issue hinges on an understanding of the following distinction that R. Joseph Caro draws between a gift and a sales transaction: If A confers B with a gift of a parcel of land, and stipulates that the gift is predicated on the condition that no lien attach itself to the land, the stipulation is fully valid. Consequently, B's creditor (C) has no right to collect his debt from the gift property. In contrast, if A sells a parcel of land to B, with the stipulation that the sale is predicated on the condition that no lien attach itself to the land, C has the right to collect his debt from the land.[36] Addressing himself to this distinction, R. Joshua ha-Kohen Falk (Poland, 1555–1614) explains that in the gift case, we may presume that the donor desires to confer the gift to B only under the condition that it should not be taken away from him by a creditor. Consequently, C's seizure of the land amounts to collecting the debt from A's property and is therefore disallowed. In the sale case, however, we may presume that it makes no difference to A whether he sells his field to B or C. Given this indifference, we cannot read into A's condition a desire to cancel the sale in the event the condition is violated. C's collection of his debt from the property B bought from A is hence valid.[37]

Applying R. Falk's rationale to the case at hand effectively frustrates A from attaching a no-copying clause to the sale of his work. Since presumably A is not prepared to cancel the sale of his work if his stipulation is not met, the condition cannot constrain the buyer from copying the work.[38]

The Nehene Principle

Aside from the issue of theft and the ethics of violating a stipulation by the seller, copying an original of a work which is available for sale deprives the owner of the work of the revenue he would otherwise have earned from the sale of another original. Given this loss, R. Goldberg obligates the one who copies the work to compensate the owner with the value of his benefit. The talmudic principle which is invoked here is that if B derives a benefit from A, and A incurs a loss in the process, B must compensate A for the value of the benefit (*zeh nehene ve-ze ḥaser-ḥayyav*).

The applicability of this principle to the case at hand, R. Goldberg points out, is not clearcut. All the talmudic cases relating to the *nehene* principle involve instances where B derives a benefit from A's property. In the case at hand, B dubs or photocopies a purchased original of A's work. Rather than benefiting from A's property, B merely derives a benefit from A's expenditure.

Extension of the *nehene* principle to the latter instance is, however, made by R. Ezekiel b. Judah ha-Levi Landau (Prague, 1713–1793). In a responsum he dealt with the following case:[39] A commissioned B to print Mishnayot for him with his own commentary to appear on the bottom of each page. Instead of conforming to the prevailing practice of destroying the typeforms as the work progressed, B destroyed only the typeforms of A's commentary, while preserving the typeforms of the text of the Mishnayot. This allowed B to use the typeforms twice; once to complete the job for A and a second time to publish his own edition of the Mishnayot. A protested that B had benefited from his expenditure and should therefore be made to compensate him for the value of the benefit.

R. Landau sympathized with A's complaint. While A had no proprietary right in the typeforms, B nevertheless benefited from A's outlay. *Nehene,* however, is not a sufficient condition to impose liability on B, for it must be demonstrated that B's benefit entails a loss for A. Once the loss condition is met, B incurs liability for the full value of his benefit even if A's loss amounts to only a fraction of the value of the benefit. Since B's edition of the Mishnayot would surely diminish the market for A's work, the loss condition, in R. Landau's judgment, was met in the typeforms case. Accordingly, R. Landau ordered B to compensate A in the amount of the value of his benefit.[40]

Agreeing that the *nehene* principle is operative in the unauthorized-copying case, R. Bar-Ilan proposes the following self-assessment procedure as a means of ascertaining whether the loss condition is met: If A assesses that had the possibility to copy B's work not been open to him he would have purchased the original, then he must compensate B for the value of his benefit. In the event B's work is out of print, copying the work does not result in any loss for B. Consequently, A may copy the work with no compensation responsibility to B. Nonetheless, in the event the work is subsequently reissued, B may become liable, at that time, for his previous action of copying A's out-of-print work. This occurs when honest self-assessment tells B that had he not already copied A's work when it was out of print, he would now certainly be interested in purchasing an original of the newly reissued work.[41]

In opposition to the rabbinical views which prohibit unauthorized copying for purely personal use, R. Yaakov Yeshayahu Bloi finds no moral issue regarding this practice. The *nehene* principle, in R. Bloi's view, cannot be invoked as a rationale for imposing compensation responsibility on the copier. Without any constraining conditions set by the seller, the sale confers the buyer with *all possible personal uses* of the work, including a lending right and a copying right. Notwithstanding that the latter two rights diminish the sales prospects for the owner of the work, in the absence of stipulation to the contrary, they remain intact. In a similar vein, subsequent to the sale of his work, the seller has a right to reissue it, even though such action increases the relative supply of the work and hence diminishes the value of the originals of the previous edition.[42]

R. Bloi's position may be supported by the consideration that the applicability of the *nehene* principle rests on the ruling of R. Landau in the typeforms case. R. Israel Joshua Trunk (Poland 1820–1893), however, disputes the ruling. Standing at the basis of his objections is the observation that the author has no property right in the typeforms. Given this fact, the printer's use of the typeforms to produce his own work amounts to nothing more than benefiting from the use of his own property.[43]

While the *nehene* principle does not call for compensation responsibility in cases of unauthorized copying for personal use, the seller's stipulation is fully effective if he expressly prohibits such use.[44] In respect to this point, R. Bloi is in agreement with R. Goldberg.

A Comparison with American Law

Our survey of the American law and halakhic treatments of unauthorized copying indicates two major differences in approach. First, American law protects a published work from infringement only if it is copyrighted. An uncopyrighted published work, however, is regarded as part of the public domain and thus is unprotected. In sharp contrast, Halakhah, in a wide variety of cases, entitles the owner of intellectual property to protection against infringement even if he did not secure a prohibition against such action through copyright or by means of rabbinical ban.

Second, American law does not confer the copyright holder with absolute protection against unauthorized copying. With the aim of both promoting science and the useful arts and allowing for the free flow of information, the fair use doctrine confers users of copyrighted works with a limited right to engage in unauthorized copying. The fair use doctrine clashes, however, with the halakhic principles which protect the owner of a work from unauthorized copying.

Multiple copying of educational materials for classroom distribution provides a case in point. Provided the minimum guidelines, discussed earlier, are satisfied, the fair use criterion is met. Satisfaction of the halakhic standard, however, is another matter. Unauthorized copying of a work for a purpose that is not purely personal, as will be recalled, is, in R. Bloi's view, prohibited. Such action amounts to appropriating someone else's "toil and effort" for the purpose of securing a quid pro quo anticipated advantage. On the basis of the *nehene* principle, legitimacy would not be given to this practice unless the teacher ascertained that neither the school nor the students' parents were interested in purchasing the educational materials in question. However, given the fact that a declaration of nonpurchasing intent will trigger the photocopying option, the authenticity of such a declaration may well be questioned.

Another illustration of the divergence between Halakhah and secular law may be seen in the following scenario relating to cassette copying: A and B share in the expense of acquiring a collection of records. A agrees to make cassette copies for B from his records, and B agrees to do the same for A. In American law, this arrangement would be looked upon innocently. Despite the underlying quid pro quo element, the absence of any blatant commercialization makes the agreement fall into the category of fair use. From a halakhic standpoint, however, the arrangement is objectionable on several counts. Since it effectively deprives the artist and/or record company of revenues they would otherwise earn from additional record sales, A and B owe compensation for the value of the benefits received to the owners of the property rights to the records. Moreover, given the quid pro quo element of the agreement, the arrangement violates R. Bloi's unfair-encroachment criterion. Finally, this arrangement may run afoul of R. Ḥayyim David ha-Levi's ruinous-competition criterion. This occurs when an assessment is made that if such a practice was universalized it would culminate in a state of affairs wherein the proprietors would not even recover their costs.

Our comparison of Halakhah and American law in regard to the issue of unauthorized copying has found that Halakhah goes beyond American law in protecting the property owner against infringement. The practical significance of the relative stringency of Halakhah here is to subject the Jew to a standard which is stricter than the code of conduct expected of one who is bound by American law.

Unauthorized Copying And Veiled Misconduct

The current legal treatment of unauthorized copying provides no mechanism for the detection of instances of infringement on the part of users. Moreover, in the framework of a legal environment which affords opportunities for hidden misconduct, the *nehene* principle works to induce the user even more in the direction of unjust enrichment. This bias follows from the "self-assessment" aspect of the *nehene* rationale.

The halakhic case for viewing self-assessment as essentially unreliable was made earlier in chapter 4. Latitude for relaxing this negative attitude toward self-assessment, as will be recalled, obtains only when the self-assessment is subject to objective verification. Insofar as both the current halakhic and legal environments afford the unauthorized copier opportunities for veiled misconduct, self-assessment cannot be used as the means for legitimizing questionable actions. It follows that we must regard as unreliable the copier's self-assessment that had the opportunity to copy the work not been available to him, he would not be interested in buying the work.

The unreliability of self-assessment is explicitly invoked by R. Ḥayyim David ha-Levi in his analysis of the ethics of dubbing a purchased cassette for a friend. He prohibits this action on the grounds that if it was universalized it surely would result in financial ruin for the performing artist. One should not make light of this concern by claiming that in the absence of the dubbing opportunity, the original would not be purchased. Such a self-assessment, warns R. Ḥayyim David ha-Levi, is merely a convenient rationalization for questionable conduct and therefore should not be relied upon.[45]

Inaccurate self-assessment may work to undermine the requirement for ruinous competition in these cases in yet another way. Specifically, the unauthorized copier may come to believe that the producers of the work fully anticipate unauthorized copying and price the work with the aim of achieving an adequate return even under the worst-scenario assumption of widespread unauthorized copying.

Carried to the extreme, self-assessment produces the assertion that unauthorized copying ultimately benefits the creator of the work. It was precisely this type of argument that representatives of the recording-equipment industry used in the 1986 Senate hearings in connection with the legislative proposal to tax blank tapes. Basing itself on studies, the industry claimed that for the majority of home tapers, audio recording is a stimulus to future purchases of prerecorded music. According to the study, 55 percent of home music tapers reported that they often or sometimes bought a record after taping all or part of it. Sixty-four percent of those questioned said that borrowing or taping a record enabled them to discover a performer or composer they liked and, hence, led them to purchase a prerecorded copy of that artist's work. Moreover, tapers were "not only more likely than nontapers to be current buyers of records and prerecorded tapes, but on the average, tapers spend more money on prerecorded music than do nontapers."[46]

At the same hearings, however, the Recording Association of America (RIAA) contended, also based on a study, that sales of prerecorded music might be approximately 25 percent greater without home taping.[47]

The conflicting contentions in this matter make it halakhically invalid to view unauthorized copying as an investment expenditure made on behalf of the owner of the work with the latter's implied consent. Notwithstanding its weakness, the argument that the owner of a work actually gains from unauthorized copying might be invoked by the copier to convince himself that his actions are not harmful to the owner.

The Copyright Clearance Center

At hearings prior to the enactment of the 1976 copyright revision law, Congress urged the formation of an organization which would deal with the problem of unauthorized copying. Toward this end the Copyright Clearance Center (CCC) was established in 1977. Its purpose was to provide an efficient means of conveying permissions and collecting requisite fees for photocopying which does not fall into the category of fair use. Operationally, publishers register titles with the CCC. Lists of these titles, along with copyright payment schedules, are sent to user organizations. User organizations voluntarily register with the CCC and report on their photocopying practices, making the appropriate payments. Another plan offered by the CCC is called the Annual Authorization Service. It calls for user organizations to pay an annual fee for a license to photocopy from participating titles.[48] This program expanded in 1991 to include an Academic Permissions Service which set license fees for the making of photocopy anthologies for sale and/or distribution to the academic community.[49]

From the standpoint of Jewish law, the CCC approach is decidedly suboptional. Most basically, it fails to recognize the futility of setting out to curb hidden misconduct by means of a self-enforcement mechanism. Moreover, since registration and reporting by user organizations are voluntary and self-policing, the approach fails to address the problems of unauthorized copying by nonregistered users and underreporting by registered users.

Finally, given the fact that registered users constitute a minority of total users,[50] the clearinghouse approach might very well work to bias participant users in the direction of underreporting. Aware that most users escape making any payment whatsoever for their photocopying activities, registered users may cease to regard payments to the CCC as quid pro quo fees and instead might come to see them as gifts or subsidies to the owners of intellectual property. If this attitude prevailed, the tendency toward underreporting could become very substantial.

A Halakhic Approach To Unauthorized Copying

From the standpoint of promoting Torah values, the legal treatment of unauthorized copying should reflect the dual objective of eliminating unjust enrichment on the part of users and minimizing the opportunity for them to engage in veiled misconduct. We will argue that the imposition of a surcharge on reprography equipment can accomplish these two objectives.

We begin our argument with the basic fact that unauthorized copying cannot take place without the use of reprography equipment. The unauthorized copying of cassettes, for instance, must make use of blank tapes and audio recording equipment. Similarly, unauthorized photocopying must make use of photocopying machines.

In certain instances, a frequent unauthorized copying intent can be identified at the point of purchase of reprography equipment. Falling into this category is the purchase of a dual cassette recorder. Characterized by the recording industry as a "copyright killer machine,"[51] its feature of two cassette wells makes it almost certain that infringement will be involved in its use. Similarly, use of photocopying machines by libraries and by copying shops serving universities will undoubtedly involve a considerable amount of unauthorized copying.

Less frequently, unauthorized copying can be expected to emanate from photocopying machines which are purchased by business firms, nonprofit organizations, and householders. Finally, in certain instances, infringement is a case-by-case matter, depending upon the use the reprography equipment is put to. Fitting into this latter category are blank cassette tapes. While the use of blank tapes may certainly entail infringement, many noninfringing uses may be identified. Included in this latter category are students who tape classes with an instructor's permission, businessmen and legislators who tape meetings, musicians who tape their own original music, and persons who correspond via cassettes.

With the aim of eliminating both unjust enrichment and settings for hidden misconduct, the government could tax reprography equipment. Several tax rates could be established depending upon the expected frequency of unauthorized copying. The tax revenues would, in turn, be allocated among publishers on the basis of their respective sales revenues. Publisher revenues would, in turn, be distributed to authors and artists on the basis of the sales revenues from their respective works.

In recognition that certain uses of reprography equipment entail no infringement whatsoever, appropriate exemption provisions would be a desirable feature of the tax system described above. Specifically, upon documentation, certain purchases would be exempt from the tax. The purchase of blank cassette tape by a speech therapist provides a case in point.

The tax approach to unauthorized copying finds precedent in the royalty scheme on blank tapes adopted by a number of European countries.[52]

In the area of unauthorized photocopying, Professor Albert P. Blaustein proposed a royalty plan in testimony at the 1973 hearings of the Senate Subcommittee on Patents, Trademarks and Copyrights. In the Blaustein proposal, all noncommercial photocopying, with the exception of consumables, would be regarded as fair use. Authors would, however, be entitled to royalties for the unauthorized photocopying of their works. As a means of collecting these royalties, Blaustein suggested that a 10 percent surcharge be added to the selling price or rental price of all photocopying machines. A quasi-governmental clearinghouse would be established to administer the royalty plan.

Under the Blaustein plan, royalties would be distributed by dividing all copyrighted books, periodicals, and other publications into five groups based on the extent to which they are usually photocopied. Those in the "most frequently copied" category would divide 50 percent of all royalties collected, while the fifth category (including such works as novels) might receive as little as 2 percent of the royalties.[53]

Unauthorized Copying and Price Discrimination

In assessing the adequacy of the expected revenue yield in compensating authors and artists, Liebowitz's work on price discrimination should be taken into account.

The substitution of copying for purchase has generally been viewed as decreasing the potential appropriability of copyright owners. Liebowitz attacks this conventional wisdom by pointing out that direct payment need not be made to sellers of products in order for them to appropriate revenues from users. He illustrates the concept of indirect appropriation with the used car market. New cars bought by car-rental companies are almost always resold before their useful lives expire. The price a rental company is willing to pay for a car depends not only on its value as a vehicle that can be rented but also on its resale value when the company is finished renting it. When the company buys new cars, it includes the expected discounted value of the car's resale price in the price it is willing to pay. The purchaser of the used car from the rental company does not pay anything directly to the manufacturer, but the manufacturer received indirect payment when it sold the new car in anticipation of this later resale. Thus, direct payment is not essential in order for the car manufacturer to appropriate revenues from future users of its used products over the useful lives of these products.

Analogously, publishers can indirectly appropriate revenues from users who are not original purchasers. To accomplish this, it is only necessary for the publisher to engage in price discrimination among purchasers of originals, charging a higher price for those originals that would be used to make many copies. Scholarly journals which are subscribed to by both individuals and libraries provide a case in point. Most journals sent to individuals are photocopied only infrequently, as they are intended primarily for the private use of the subscriber. Journals sent to libraries, on the other hand, are much more frequently photocopied, since their function is to assist researchers.

A library's willingness to pay for journals should increase when photocopying is done on the premises because the availability of photocopying causes a library's users to value the library's journal holdings more highly. The library's funding, in turn, is almost certainly related in some manner to the tastes and values of library users. As long as libraries pay subscription prices related to the valuation of journals by library users, publishers need not be harmed by the photocopying done in libraries; this, of course, implies price discrimination if publishers are also to sell to individuals.

In order for publishers to price-discriminate successfully, they must be able to prevent library subscribers from disguising themselves as individual subscribers. Under present institutional arrangements, this objective can readily be achieved. One factor working to facilitate this objective is that libraries do not usually buy their journals directly from publishers, but instead through middlemen. These agencies can be charged the higher discriminatory price, since they are very easy to identify. Secondly, publishers could imprint some sort of mark in institutional subscriptions to enhance detection.

These theoretical considerations lead Liebowitz to offer the hypothesis that, over time, the phenomenon of photocopying would have the effect of increasing the price paid by libraries for journals relative to the price paid by individuals. An examination of the pricing policies of economics journal publishers for the years 1959 and 1983 provides support for this hypothesis. In 1959, the year the Xerox 914 was introduced, only three out of the thirty-eight journals then in existence (or 8 percent) price-discriminated between institutions and individuals. In 1983, fifty-nine out of eighty journals (74 percent) charged higher prices to libraries. (The 1983 price differential, averaged over all journals in the sample, was about two-thirds of the individual price.)[54]

Studies have uncovered the very same pattern of subscription-rate discrimination in respect to journals in many other disciplines.[55]

Liebowitz's work has much relevancy for our proposal to tax reprography equipment in a legal environment which declares all noncommercial copying of intellectual property fair use. Since price discrimination, in certain instances, effectively allows intellectual property owners to indirectly charge those who copy their works, the phenomenon calls for, other things being equal, a downward adjustment of the tax structure which is designed to achieve fair compensation for the owners of intellectual property.

• 9
Full Employment and Stabilization Policy

SINCE THE ENACTMENT OF the landmark Employment Act of 1946, the United States government has committed itself to the responsibility of adopting policies that will foster the attainment of full employment and price stability. The Humphrey–Hawkins Act of 1978 put these goals into quantitative form by setting a 4 percent unemployment rate and a 3 percent inflation rate as the nation's economic objectives.

Our purpose here is to demonstrate that in the Torah society full employment and price stability are mandated goals for the public sector. In the policies of a biblical figure, Joseph, we will find historical roots for the implementation of automatic stabilizers for the economy. We will then turn to the issue of how the Torah society deals with the conflict between full employment and price stability. Finally, we will identify the parameters for the legitimate use of debt creation by the public sector.

Full Employment In The Torah Society

The full-employment goal for the public sector of the Torah society proceeds from two factors: the community's responsibility to initiate antipoverty measures and the principle of *imitatio Dei*

The Antipoverty Responsibility

Judaism's charity obligation consists of both a public and a private component. In talmudic times the public component consisted of a variety of levies for the purpose of attending to the full range of the needs of the poor.[1] Public communal levies were never entirely relied upon to relieve poverty. Evidencing this is the talmudic dictum that if one becomes needy he does not immediately apply for public relief. His relatives and friends must first attend to his needs; only then is the community required to make up the deficiency.[2]

In his analysis of Jewish charity law, R. Ḥayyim Soloveitchik (Russia, 1853–1918) advances the thesis that society as a collective, apart from its individual members, has a responsibility to relieve poverty. The purpose of the coercive levy, he posits, is not to ensure that the individual members of the community qua individuals discharge their charity obligation, but rather to allow the public sector to carry out its own distinctive social welfare responsibility. The theory that the charity obligation consists both of an individual and a collective component is bolstered by its repetition in the Torah. The charity obligation is set out once at Leviticus 25:35 and again at Deuteronomy 15:7–8. The Leviticus passage refers to society's collective responsibility to relieve poverty, while the Deuteronomy passage speaks of the individual's personal charity obligation. Since the reward, "for the Lord your God will bless you for this in all your works and in whatever you undertake," is mentioned in connection with the Deuteronomy passage (Deuteronomy 15:10), coercion cannot be applied to the individual's personal charity obligation. This follows from the general talmudic principle that when a reward is mentioned in connection with a biblical positive precept, the Jewish court will not force compliance, but instead will rely on voluntarism. Since no reward is mentioned in connection with the Leviticus passage, coercion is applied to the individual to force him to finance society's collective charity responsibility.[3]

To be sure, poverty cries out for both an individual and a communal response. But from the standpoint of Judaism's social welfare program, income transfers are not the ideal approach. If the needy individual is capable of engaging in productive labor, offering him a job represents a much-preferred alternative. Relieving poverty by means of job creation, when feasible, is the optimal approach from the standpoint of both donor and recipient. From the standpoint of the donor, offering a job to someone in a precarious financial situation fulfills the charity obligation on the highest level. This is so because the offer of assistance is couched in terms of a quid pro quo proposition, making it devoid of any demeaning or condescending element.[4] From the standpoint of the recipient, engaging in productive labor is an ennobling experience. Evidencing this is R. Shimon b. Elazar's dictum:

> Great is the value of productive labor, for the First Adam ate nothing [from the fruits in the garden of Eden] before he performed work, as it says: "And God took man and placed him in the garden of Eden to work it and to guard it" (Genesis 2:15), and only then: "And God gave the commandment to man: From every tree of the garden may you indeed eat" (Genesis 2:16).[5]

Expanding on this dictum, R. Baruch Epstein (Russia, 1860–1942) finds its message to be that it is improper for man to derive benefit from this world unless he engages in socially useful labor as a quid pro quo for the enjoyment received.[6] Consonant with this notion is Rav's advice to R. Kahana: "Flay carcasses in the marketplace and earn wages, and do not say, I am a priest and a great man, and it is beneath my dignity."

When the economy finds itself in a deep recession, employment opportunities will rapidly shrink. Under these conditions, the private sector's response to the crisis will, for the most part, consist of income transfers to the needy. Given the collapsing demand for labor, society will not be practicing charity on the highest level, regardless of the ingenuity it utilizes to conceal the charitable intent of the income transfers.

In dealing with the malaise of deep economic recession, a modern government enjoys a distinct advantage over the private sector. By means of expansionary fiscal and monetary policies, a modern government is capable of vastly increasing the available employment opportunities. Mechanically, the government substantially reduces taxes and/or increases its spending. The resulting deficit is financed by selling bonds[7] to commercial banks or to the general public. Any initial increase in spending will result in a multiple expansion of income. To see why this happens, we merely need to point out that A's spending is B's income, which, in time, will result in C's income going up. The process will eventually peter out as only a fraction of incremental income is spent. With each successive round of income creation accompanied by some amount of savings, the expansionary process eventually comes to a halt.

The preceding description of the expansionary policy is somewhat overstated. Since the deficit is financed by means of the sale of bonds either to commercial banks or to the public, no increase in the money supply accompanies the expansion in income. But at the higher income levels the demand for money will increase. With the demand for money increasing relative to the supply, interest rates will rise; this, in turn, inhibits spending, which is sensitive to the interest rate, such as investment and housing spending and consumer installment debt.

To ensure that even greater expansionary possibilities will proceed from the deficit-finance operation, the treasury could sell the bonds to the central bank. Since the central bank purchases the bonds by means of crediting the treasury's account with the amount of the deficit, the expansionary policy is accompanied by an increase in the money supply. With the money supply increasing along with the increase in spending, little upward pressure will be exerted on interest rates as the expansionary process unfolds.

Recall R. Ḥayyim Soloveitchik's thesis that society as a collective, apart from its individual members, has a responsibility to relieve poverty. The distinction between what society can accomplish in poverty relief as a collective and what it can accomplish as individuals is highlighted by the technique of deficit finance. Left to its own devices, the free enterprise–oriented economy can do precious little to pull itself out of a depression. But what is an impossibility for individuals, even when joined in cooperative effort, can be accomplished by society as a collective. Deficit finance, as the previous discussion has demonstrated, allows the public sector to transform the depression-ridden economy into one of abundant employment opportunities.

Imitatio Dei

Another rationale for the public sector's full-employment mandate is provided by the principle of *imitatio Dei*. This behavioral imperative applies to the government as well as to the private citizen. The particular dimension of Divine Mercy which compels the full-employment mandate is God's universal goodness. The universal aspect of God's goodness finds expression in the words of the psalmist: "God is good to all; His mercies are on all His works. . . . You open your hand and satisfy the desire of every living thing" (Psalms 145:9, 16). In this regard Rav Judah in the name of Rav taught that during the third quarter of the day, the Almighty is engaged in feeding the whole world, "from the horned buffalo to the brood of vermin."[8]

In making the case for the full-employment policy, one further point should be noted regarding God's provision of human sustenance. God's compassion here, teaches R. Mosheh Ḥayyim Luzzatto (Italy, 1701–1746), manifests itself in bestowing His bounty in a manner that allows man to maximize the potential enjoyment he can derive from it. Since man cannot feel a sense of pride unless he imagines that his achievements are due to his own efforts, the element of Divine grace in his success is not made obvious to him. Despite the inherent danger of leading man to deny the true source of his bounty, God allows this delusion of human independence to persist for the purpose of maximizing for man the joy he derives from the Divine bounty.[9]

What the preceding description of God's universal kindness denotes for human conduct is the obligation for the public sector to foster an economic environment which generates a demand for the services of the entire labor force.

One clearcut application of the full-employment policy requirement is the responsibility the government must assume in a severe economic downturn. If the public sector adopts a laissez-faire attitude amidst a condition of widespread unemployment, it is in violation of *imitatio Dei*. Instead, it must take the lead in propelling the economy to a higher level of employment. Expansionary monetary and fiscal policy, as discussed earlier, is the prescription to accomplish this.

Price Stability And Jewish Law

In this section we will make the case for a price-stability mandate for the public sector of the Torah society. We begin with a definition of inflation and an identification of its costs to society. We will then see that these costs undermine Torah values. Controlling inflationary pressures will be shown to fall within the realm of the proper role of government in the Torah society.

Inflation is a significant and persistent increase in the general price level. However, not all inflations are harmful to social well-being. Creeping inflation, for instance, is quite innocuous.

Even moderate inflation need not be troublesome, provided the price rise is anticipated and balanced, in the sense that all prices, including wage rates, interest rates, and the prices of final goods, increase at the same proportion. But in the real world, inflation is almost never balanced and is always to some extent unanticipated. When these factors interact to produce an accelerated price rise, inflation assumes a particularly virulent form. It is this type of inflation which imposes significant costs on society. These costs consist of an income-redistribution effect and a loss of output for the economy. We begin with the redistribution effect of inflation.

The major distributional impact of inflation arises from differences in the kinds of assets and liabilities people hold. A debtor whose obligation consists of a fixed interest payment gains. Inflation allows him to pay back a debt in a monetary unit which has less purchasing power than it did when the debt was entered into. A creditor, however, loses because inflation effectively drives the real return of his investment below the nominal interest rate he contracted for. What impact inflation has on a household hinges, in part, on whether the family is in a net creditor or net debtor position. It also depends on whether the family's income increases more rapidly or less rapidly than the inflation rate.

Regardless of what inflation does to the distribution of income among different income classes, it generates a substantial redistribution within each income class, since some households are net borrowers and others are net lenders. This type of redistribution is arbitrary. It reflects neither the interplay of the operation of free markets nor the purposeful efforts of government to redistribute income. As a result, inflation undermines society's notion of fairness.

Inflation also affects the tax system adversely. If the tax system is progressive, a higher inflation rate drives people into higher tax brackets more quickly. It thus allows the government to collect more taxes without passing laws. Taxation without legislation does violence to society's basic notion of fairness and justice.

Another source of societal discontent which inflation may bring on is the penalty entailed for saving. Deeply ingrained in society's notion of fairness is the belief that saving is a virtue and should confer the household with greater purchasing power in the future in exchange for the sacrifice of consumption in the present. But if interest rates lag behind the inflation rate, saving is penalized, not rewarded.[10]

Arranging the economic order with the aim, other things being equal, of minimizing societal bitterness, frustration, and discontent is a legitimate concern for the public sector of the Torah society. This goal, discussed in chapter 1, is called *darkhei no'am*..

Given that the income-redistribution consequences of inflation offend society's notion of fairness, it becomes the duty of the public sector to pursue policies which will promote price stability.

The Antipoverty Mandate and Inflation

In his analysis of the income-redistribution effects of inflation, Bach draws a distinction between monetary assets and variable-price assets. Monetary assets consist of assets whose final redemption value is fixed in money terms, such as bank accounts, mortgages, and bonds. Inflation erodes the value of these assets in real terms. Variable-price assets, on the other hand, are assets whose prices can vary freely without having a final, fixed money value, such as land, automobiles, houses, durable goods, and common stocks. These assets have relatively more room to move up in price when inflation occurs, though they do not necessarily do so.

The larger the proportion of its assets a family holds in the form of monetary assets, the more vulnerable it is to inflation. Considering both this ratio and the debtor-creditor position for households along the entire income continuum, Bach concludes that inflation transfers income from the rich and the poor to the middle and upper-middle income classes.

Compared to other income brackets, both the rich and the poor have few debts; but for different reasons. The rich have little need to borrow. No one, on the other hand, will lend money to the poor. In addition, both the rich and the poor tend to hold a relatively large amount of monetary assets. The middle and upper-middle classes, by contrast, are heavily in debt and hold a large portion of their assets in variable-price forms, especially houses, automobiles, and the like.[11]

Given the deprivational impact inflation has on the poor, the public sector would be remiss in its antipoverty function if it did not pursue price stability.

Hakkarat Hatov

Still another redistributional impact of inflation is that it transfers wealth from the elderly to the young in massive amounts. The young are heavily in debt, a condition which, other things being equal, is advantageous in inflationary times. They are setting up households, borrowing heavily to buy houses and consumer durables, and to finance their children's education. The elderly, in sharp contrast, have few debts and hold relatively larger percentages of their assets in monetary form.[12]

The massive transfer of wealth from the elderly to the young which occurs during inflation should be a matter of concern for the Torah society. In the microcosm of the family unit, children are duty bound to honor and render personal service to their parents.[13] Standing as the rationale of these obligations is the duty to express gratitude (*hakkarat hatov*) to parents.[14]

One to whom gratitude is owed should surely be spared from an avoidable harm or loss. Social indifference in the face of the ravages inflation imposes on the elderly not only perverts the gratitude due senior citizens but also undermines the ethical norm of *hakkarat hatov* itself.

Acting alone, the individual can do nothing to spare the elderly from the ravages of inflation. But the control of macroeconomic forces is within the realm of possibility for government. Pointing the economy in the direction of price stability not only spares the elderly from the deprivation effects of inflation, but it goes a long way in promoting the ethical norm of *hakkarat hatov*.

Maximization of Torah Study

One consequence of inflation, which should be of particular concern to the Torah society, is that it forces people to devote more time to the economic sphere of their lives.

Excessive cash management is one aspect of this opportunity cost. People and business firms, as a means of conducting their ordinary business transactions, are forced to hold a portion of their assets in the form of idle cash. But idle cash earns little or no interest for the asset holder. To make matters worse, inflation reduces this rate to a larger and larger negative return. Economizing on one's cash balance represents a strategy to minimize this adverse effect. For the individual, the adjustment takes the form of going to the bank more often; in the case of the corporation, it entails setting up elaborate cash-management schemes.

Similarly, inflation destroys the value of the information that prices ordinarily convey. With the general price level increasing rapidly, consumers are less likely to remain loyal customers of their familiar stores. Instead, they engage in comparative shopping.

Business firms have precisely the same problem with their suppliers. Rising prices force them to shop around more than they are accustomed to, which imposes costs on the firms and, more generally, reduces the efficiency of the whole economy.[15]

In economic terms, the distortions in consumer and business behavior occasioned by inflation are not substantial.[16] We venture to say that this is so because the increase in time spent on cash management and comparative shopping is, in all probability, mainly at the expense of idleness and leisure, rather than at the expense of lost production.

For the Torah society, however, the ideal is to maximize Torah study. Increased time spent on cash management and comparative shopping is at the expense of time that could have been spent on Torah study. Given the inestimable value of Torah study, the distortion in the allocation of time between the spiritual and the mundane that is occasioned by inflation cannot be written off as an insignificant cost.

The Prevention of Poverty and Anti-Inflationary Policies

Unanticipated and unbalanced inflation carries with it the potential to drag the economy down into a recession. One way this can happen is through the effect inflation exerts on replacement costs for firms. Under standard accounting procedures, businesses can only charge depreciation equal to the original cost of their plants and equipment. But when the plant must be replaced, the replacement cost exceeds the depreciation charges if inflation has occurred. The accounting costs which are charged do not cover the real replacement costs. Part of the accounting profits thus must be used to replace the depreciated plant rather than for dividends or net new investment.

Similarly, in inflation, businesses use up inventories purchased when prices were lower. This produces large profits as final-product prices rise. But again, the depleted inventories must be replaced at the higher inflation-period prices. For this reason, standard accounting procedures result in an overstatement of business profits during inflation. This overstatement is concentrated in nonfinancial corporations because they hold large inventories and large amounts of depreciable capital equipment.[17]

Rising replacement costs for business set up the possibility that an expansion will suddenly turn around into an economic downturn. This reversal becomes more likely in the event that wages and other input prices are increasing faster than the prices of final goods and services.

The feeling of uncertainty which prevails in the economic environment of unanticipated and unbalanced inflation may also play a role in driving the economy into a recession. Under creeping inflation, the rate at which prices rise is relatively easy to predict and to take into account in setting interest rates. When prices begin to rise at accelerating rates, the potential redistribution becomes enormous, and as a result, lending and borrowing may cease entirely.

Similarly, any amount of inflation makes it difficult to write long-term contracts. With creeping inflation, the long term may be measured in years. But with accelerating inflation, the long term may be measured in weeks and at the extreme, even in hours. The shorter this time interval, the greater the number of transactions that will be defeated by uncertainty.

Given the possibility that inflation can induce recession, it becomes the duty of the public sector of the Torah society to take timely action to ensure that an inflationary condition does not work to drive the economy into a recession. If the economy is prosperous and healthy, the public sector must do its utmost to ensure that its economic viability does not deteriorate.

This duty proceeds from an aspect of the public sector's anti-poverty responsibility, specifically from its duty to *prevent* poverty. On the individual level, charity in its noblest form consists of aiding an individual from falling into the throes of poverty.

The position of a person in this predicament must be stabilized, and his dignity preserved, by either conferring a gift on him, extending him a loan, entering a partnership with him, or creating a job for him.[18] Preventing him from falling into poverty is given first rank by Maimonides in his eight categories of charity giving.[19] Hence poverty prevention takes precedence over poverty relief.

On a societal level, the poverty-prevention requirement takes the form of ensuring that a healthy and viable economy does not fall into a recession. Taking timely action to ensure that inflation does not turn into recession represents one aspect of the societal obligation to prevent poverty.

Automatic Stabilizers

One aspect of stabilization policy in the modern state is the incorporation of automatic stabilizers into the economic system. An automatic stabilizer is a built-in feature of the economy which provides a stimulus during a recession and a restraint during an economic boom. No discretionary action is needed. The purpose of automatic stabilizers is to soften both the unemployment impact of a recession and the inflationary impact of an expansionary period.

In the United States, the progressive income tax system and the unemployment insurance program constitute the economy's main automatic stabilizers. A progressive tax is structured so that as income rises, a larger fraction of income is taken in the form of taxes. The federal personal and corporate income taxes are both progressively structured. Accordingly, as the economy expands, government taxes increase faster than national income. Thus the tax system works to reduce inflationary pressures during expansionary times. Likewise, when the economy is experiencing a downturn, taxes decrease more than proportional to the drop in national income. With spending a function of disposable income, in a contractionary period the tax system works to moderate the drop in spending from what it otherwise would be.

Unemployment insurance is also an automatic stabilizer. Mechanically, when unemployment is high, government receipts from the unemployment compensation tax will decline because of the reduction in employment. At the same time, government outlays will increase because more workers are now eligible to receive benefits. This government program will thus automatically run a deficit during a business slowdown. In contrast, when the unemployment rate is low, tax receipts from the program will increase because more people are now working. The amount paid in benefits will decline because fewer people are unemployed. Hence the program will automatically tend to run a surplus during good times. So without any change in policy, the program has the desired countercyclical effect on aggregate spending.

Halakhic Aspects

Since automatic stabilizers work to improve the overall health of the economy, it becomes the duty of the public sector of the Torah society to make use of this economic policy tool. This duty is compelled by the public sector's mandate to take action on a macroeconomic level to prevent poverty.

This duty proceeds also from the public sector's *imitatio Dei* mandate. The relevant Divine Attribute here is God's mercy in sparing man a misfortune which otherwise would befall him (*raḥum*).[20] Our perception of the *raḥum* element of God's mercy becomes particularly heightened when a particular misfortune is feared to be in the offing. Macroeconomic instability in the form of inflation and recession is a fact of economic life. Emulating God's conduct requires the public sector to concede the inevitability of macroeconomic instability and to take steps *in advance* to soften the adverse effects of the business cycle.

Another relevant Divine Attribute here is God's compassion in arranging the "cure before the affliction."[21] Since automatic stabilizers smooth out the business cycle, building this feature into the economic system effectively prepares the "cure before the affliction."

Joseph's Automatic Stabilization Policy

The modern economic policy tool of automatic stabilizers finds adumbration in the economic policies of a biblical figure, Joseph.

When called upon to interpret Pharaoh's dreams, Joseph forecasted that Egyptian society would go through a period of seven years of superabundance to be followed by seven years of unprecedented famine.[22] The main feature of his prescription for dealing with the coming crisis was the recommendation "and let him [Pharaoh] appoint officers over the land and *veḥimesh* the land of Egypt in the seven years of plenty" (Genesis 41:34). Most commentators take the word *veḥimesh* to mean a 20 percent tax on the produce of the land. The taxed produce was to be stored in public granaries and subsequently drawn upon to feed the population during the seven years of famine.[23]

In devising this plan, Joseph, as it appears to this writer, hit upon a means of transforming the years of superabundance into the "cure before the affliction." It is easy to see why alternative policies would not have achieved this result. Instead of taxing 20 percent of the country's produce, Joseph could have bought up this amount and had it stored in public granaries for subsequent distribution. But this policy would have greatly increased the money supply during the years of plenty. All this government-created purchasing power would have worked to undermine Joseph's best-laid efforts to prevent profiteering during the years of famine.[24] Besides facing the problem of rationing the food supply during the years of famine, this policy would have compounded the misery by unleashing a skyrocketing price level on the economy.

Voluntarism, consisting of public exhortation to store away part of each year's crop in preparation for the famine, would have fared no better. Most fundamentally, how many people would have given credence to the government's "doomsday" prediction to prepare for a famine amidst current economic conditions of superabundance? Moreover, superabundance works to blunt the work ethic by fostering a climate of indolence and waste. In consequence, voluntarism would surely have run the risk of eliciting too little private savings to avert disaster when famine conditions suddenly arrived for the Egyptian economy.

These pitfalls, however, are avoided by the tax policy Joseph adopted. By withdrawing 20 percent of the annual crop from private consumption, he ensured that the idleness and waste otherwise engendered by superabundance would be minimized. Moreover, by not increasing the money supply during the years of plenty, he prevented the period of superabundance from unleashing massive inflationary forces against a backdrop of economic contraction.

The challenge of elevating the seven years of superabundance to the stature of the "cure before the affliction" was met by Joseph on a psychological level as well. At the outbreak of the famine, the Torah records, "Joseph opened all the storehouses, and he rationed supplies to Egypt" (Genesis 41:56). Since the demands of the moment required him to distribute only a small portion of the total stockpile, what drove him to open all the storehouses? Addressing this issue, R. Ovadiah b. Jacob Sforno (Italy, 1475–1550) and others posit that Joseph's intent was to prevent panic and demoralization from breaking out on the sudden collapse of the economy. By opening all the storehouses, Joseph sent the calming message that the government was well prepared to deal with the crisis.[25]

The Conflict Between Full Employment And Price Stability

In this section we address the issue of how the Torah society mediates between the goals of full employment and price stability. An examination of the "natural rate of unemployment" explains why these goals are in potential conflict. It assumes that as a practical matter the economy cannot achieve full employment. This circumstance comes about because of the effects of the phenomena known as frictional unemployment and structural unemployment.

Frictional unemployment is unemployment due to normal turnover in the labor market. It includes people who are temporarily between jobs because they are moving or changing occupations. Frictional unemployment occurs because labor markets are inherently dynamic. Since information about the characteristics of those searching for work and the nature of the jobs opening up cannot instantly be known or evaluated, it takes time for job matches to be made between unemployed workers and potential employers. Hence, frictional employment will exist even when, in the aggregate, the demand for labor equals the supply.

Structural unemployment occurs when changes in the pattern of labor demand cause a mismatch between the skills demanded and the skills supplied. If wages were completely flexible and the costs of occupational or geographic mobility were low, market adjustments would quickly eliminate this type of unemployment. However, in practice, these conditions may fail to obtain, and structural unemployment may result.

The phenomena of frictional and structural unemployment have led economists to believe that the economy is subject to a natural rate of unemployment. For the United States, this rate is estimated to have risen from 4 percent in the 1960s to 6 percent in the 1980s. At the natural rate of unemployment, price and wage inflation are stable. At this juncture, deficit finance will exert little impact on increasing employment. Instead, such policies will fuel accelerating inflation.[26]

For the Torah society, a case can be made against initiating deficit finance measures as a means of pushing unemployment below the natural rate of unemployment. The goal of full employment is compelled by the public sector's duty to imitate God's universal kindness. But if deficit finance accelerates inflation even as it brings expanded employment opportunities, it loses its character as an act which works to achieve universal kindness.

To be sure, the public sector must also pursue the goal of full employment by dint of its antipoverty mandate. But all public sector antipoverty measures, according to R. Solomon b. Abraham Adret (Spain, ca. 1235–1310), must be financed by imposing a tax proportional to wealth. Achieving gains in employment at the price of accelerating inflation fails this equity benchmark. This is so because inflation, as discussed earlier, does not simply redistribute income from the poor to the middle and upper-middle income brackets, but also redistributes wealth *within* each income bracket.

Guarding society against accelerating inflation, as discussed earlier, is also an aspect of the public sector's antipoverty mandate. While the goal of full employment constitutes a poverty-relief effort, the goal of price stability is intended to prevent poverty. Given the primacy of poverty prevention over poverty relief, sanction cannot be given to a policy initiative which promotes employment but at the same time does violence to poverty prevention. Rejection of deficit finance at this juncture in no way signals an abandonment of the full-employment goal. What the public sector must do is to shift its efforts to expand employment to tax-supported programs. Recall also that the charity obligation is both an individual and a societal responsibility. If the public sector's ability to advance full employment is constrained because it comes into conflict with price stability, voluntarism must step up its efforts to fill the void.

A corollary proceeding from the above analysis is that if the economy finds itself operating below the natural rate of unemployment and is simultaneously faced with accelerating inflation, the government must take decisive action to promote price stability. This objective may be pursued in several different ways. Since price stability is an aspect of the public sector's antipoverty mandate, ideally the cost of accomplishing this goal should be borne by society proportional to wealth. Pursuing the goal of price stability mainly by relying on a restrictive monetary policy fails this criterion. A brief description of restrictive monetary policy will explain why. Restrictive monetary policy is designed to put upward pressure on interest rates which in turn reduces aggregate spending. To implement this policy, the central bank, for example, would sell government securities to the commercial banks. Other things being equal, this selling will depress the price of government bonds and increase their yields. At the same time, this open market sale will soak up the banking system's excess reserves. With the supply of loanable funds decreasing relative to the demand, interest rates can be expected to rise sharply. Higher interest rates will work to depress spending in industries sensitive to interest rates, such as housing, automobiles, consumer durables, and the agricultural sector.

To be sure, the weakness in the aforementioned industries will reverberate throughout the economy in successive rounds of income and spending reduction. Nevertheless, the brunt of the restrictive monetary policy will be borne by the industries that are sensitive to interest rates. Hence this policy is discriminatory, and for this reason it fails R. Adret's proportional-wealth criteria for an antipoverty levy. In light of its discriminatory impact, this policy assaults society's notion of fairness and fails the *darkhei no'am* criterion as well.

Accomplishing a reduction in aggregate spending by relying mainly on a government spending cut, whether across the board or selective, is also discriminatory. Here, government employees will bear the brunt of the cut in aggregate spending.

With the aim of allocating the cost of achieving price stability proportional to wealth, heavy reliance on an increase in taxes is indicated.

Instituting a hiring freeze for government combined with a phasing out of some government programs would also be in line with the equity concerns of an anti-inflationary program for the Torah society.

Within the framework of an austere fiscal policy, there might be some latitude for a simultaneous loosening of monetary policy. Any loosening of monetary policy will, of course, moderate the unemployment effects caused by the government-induced reduction in aggregate spending.

Reducing the Natural Rate of Unemployment

One implication of rationalizing the full-employment goal in terms of imitating God's universal compassion is that this duty must be understood in dynamic rather than static terms. Complacency with regard to progress made toward this goal reflects a disdainful attitude that man's standards of excellence in achieving full employment compare favorably with God's universal kindness. Rather, society must adopt a perfectionist drive in respect to the goal of full employment; no barrier to further progress must be looked upon as impregnable. Accordingly, the natural rate of unemployment should not be viewed as a law of nature. Instead, society should dedicate itself to the task of innovating programs to reduce this rate.

One way of reducing the natural rate of unemployment is to improve the match in the labor market between the positions employers might be willing to fill and the jobs the unemployed are searching for. This matching will prove the most difficult for those whose productivity is perceived to be below that of others competing for the position. Included in this population are the handicapped, individuals of low educational attainments or who lack skills, and those with a background of alcoholism, drug abuse, or a criminal record. Left to their own devices, these job aspirants will encounter substantial bias in the labor market. But if the employer knows in advance that he will receive a government subsidy for each of the targeted individuals he hires, this bias can be reduced significantly.

Taxing society to finance inducements for employers to hire the disadvantaged represents a delicately sensitive manner of imitating God's universal kindness.

In the United States, both general and selective employment tax credits have been tried on a limited scale in recent years.[27]

Increasing the employability of the disadvantaged can also be accomplished by means of the wage-rate subsidy. Instead of subsidizing the employer, this program subsidizes the wages of qualified workers. Details of the wage-rate subsidy concept are taken up in chapter 2.

Government-Engineered Inflation and Halakhah

In the modern era, deficit finance is not merely employed as a means of expanding employment opportunities in a depressed economy. It is also an ordinary means of financing government expenditures. This approach to public finance is not at all surprising. Deficit finance allows the government to finance its expenditures without resort to taxation. If this causes inflation, the government will reap the additional advantage of having its outstanding debt reduced in real terms. Its tax revenues will also be favorably affected. This is because inflation raises the dollar amount of spendable and taxable income. Yields from income, social security, and sales taxes, therefore, increase faster than prices.

Focusing on the Israeli economy in a recent article, Dr. Meir Tamari of Bar-Ilan University puts into question the right of a Jewish government to cause inflation. Tamari buttresses his case by marshaling a number of legal as well as moral arguments.[28]

Several preliminary issues must be explored before the specifics of Tamari's arguments can be evaluated.

One basic issue is the legitimacy of deficit finance as a tool of public finance in the Torah society.

1. In our earlier discussion of the antipoverty role of government, we identified debt creation as a legitimate governmental tool to expand employment opportunities in a depressed economy.

2. Another area of legitimacy for government debt creation is in the financing of its capital projects. In his analysis of the United States federal deficit, Robert Eisner proposes that the government should keep separate current and capital accounts. Outlays whose benefits are confined to the current period should be recorded in the current account. But expenditures which yield long-term benefits belong appropriately in the capital account. A portion of the investment-type outlays, called capital depreciation, however, must be entered in the current account. This is done in recognition that some portion of the current investment outlay benefits the current income stream.

Presenting the budget in the form of separate current and capital accounts is standard practice in the private sector. If the federal government were to adopt the practice, much (all) of the federal deficit, as presently measured, would disappear. This is so because much (all) of the federal deficit is accounted for by investment.[29]

Eisner's argument can be cast in terms of equity theory. Specifically, equity, or fairness, in the financing of a capital project demands that its costs be allocated over the entire benefit stream of the project. If taxation alone were relied upon in the financing of a capital project, the entire burden of the expenditure would be put on the income of the current period. Covering the costs of the project in the current period by means of a combination of taxation and borrowing, however, effectively spreads the financing burden over the entire benefit stream of the project. Intertemporal equity is achieved by equalizing the tax burden of the current period with the taxes which are raised in subsequent periods to cover the interest and amortization costs of the government borrowing.

Halakhah would embrace the above equity benchmark for taxation, according to R. Meir b. Isaac Katzenellenbogen (Italy, 1473–1563). Writing on the financing of a synagogue project, he noted that building a synagogue is by nature a capital project. The benefit stream it generates is not confined to the current year, but extends over many years. Though all members of the community can be regarded as benefiting equally from the synagogue in the current year, the poorer elements of the community cannot reasonably expect to reap the full range of *intertemporal* benefits inherent in the project. This follows from the assumption that what ties an individual to a particular geographic location is his property ownership there. Insofar as the poor are propertyless, the probability of their remaining in the town over the life span of the synagogue is small. This consideration leads R. Katzenellenbogen to propose a proportional property tax as the most equitable means of financing the synagogue project.[30]

What R. Katzenellenbogen's criterion implies for modern public finance is the legitimacy of the use of deficit finance as a means of achieving *intertemporal* equity in the financing of capital projects.

In the Torah society, various functions are mandated on the public sector. These include security measures, water-supply projects, public road repairs, Torah education, and a variety of communal projects of a religious character.[31] Implementing these mandates will perforce involve the public sector in the financing of capital projects.

As Musgrave notes in a different context, capital formation should not be defined only in terms of brick and mortar. Human investment may be equally important to productivity growth. Thus, teachers' salaries are no less an input than classroom space in the production of human capital.[32]

Use of deficit finance for capital formation allows the public sector to achieve equity in allocating the financial burden of these expenditures.

Because borrowing pushes spending above what it otherwise would be, government deficit finance carries with it the potential of exerting an inflationary impact on society. But inflation is a price society is willing to pay in order to achieve intertemporal equity in the financing of government's capital expenditures.

Financing capital projects by means of debt creation may nevertheless impose a considerable tax burden over time. Moderation of this tax burden can be achieved, however, by means of increasing the money supply. Mechanically, a portion of the costs of the project along its entire benefit stream could be financed by means of selling bonds to the central bank. Since the central bank pays for these bonds by simply crediting the government's account with their dollar amount, a portion of the expenditures in the current period as well as a portion of the interest and amortization payments in the future periods is financed by means of money-supply creation. Servicing and retiring debt by means of money-supply creation is, of course, much more inflationary than would be the case if tax revenues were resorted to for this purpose.

The cumulative impact over time of financing a portion of government's capital expenditures by means of increasing the money supply is surely to build into the economy inflationary pressures beyond the benefit stream of the project. If we take it as axiomatic that government may not deliberately shift any portion of its current expenditures onto a future time period which will not benefit from that expenditure, a limitation on the use of money-supply creation to finance a capital project readily suggests itself. This limitation is the inadmissibility of money-supply creation when the capital project is not *mandated* on the public sector. In this instance, if society finds it too burdensome to finance the expenditure by spreading the tax burden over the entire benefit stream, then the project should not be undertaken.

Financing a portion of the capital project by means of money-supply creation over the entire benefit stream amounts, therefore, to a deliberate shifting of the burden of finance beyond the benefit stream of the project. In sharp contrast, when the capital project is mandated, the option of scrapping it does not exist. Financing a portion of the expenditure over the entire benefit stream by means of money-supply creation should, therefore, be legitimate. Any inflationary pressures proceeding beyond the benefit stream should be regarded as an unintended side effect of the government expenditure.

A problem, however, remains. Giving legitimacy to money-supply creation as a means of financing mandated government capital projects amounts to a carte blanche license for government to push inflation on society now and in the future, all in the name of intertemporal tax relief. What is needed is a criterion which will define excessive tax burden for the purpose of legitimizing debt creation by means of money-supply creation.

Suggestive of a guidepost for the purpose at hand is the criterion of financial burden that the sages adopted in relation to charity giving and the performance of positive religious duties. Out of fear that overgenerosity in charity giving could make the donor himself vulnerable to poverty, the sages at Usha (ca. 140 C.E.) enacted an edict against donating more than 20 percent of one's income to charity.[33] Based on this ancient edict, Halakhah excuses an individual from a positive miẓvah duty if its fulfillment would require the expenditure of 20 percent or more of his resources.[34]

Applying the 20 percent rule to the case at hand limits the use of money-supply creation in the financing of mandated government capital projects. Specifically, this method finds legitimacy only when its aim is to keep the tax burden below the 20 percent level along the benefit stream of the capital projects. When the capital expenditures can be allocated along the benefit stream with a tax burden over time of less than 20 percent, money-supply creation must be rejected as a method of financing the capital expenditures.

Inflation redistributes income, and this redistribution, as discussed above, undermines society's notion of fairness. But to a certain degree, inflation, with all its implications, is accepted by society in advance as the price it must pay to secure intertemporal tax relief.

We now turn to a second issue. Tamari's analysis presupposes that government deficit financing ordinarily *causes* inflation. An understanding of the forces behind inflation, however, will show that under ordinary circumstances, government cannot be said to be the cause of inflation.

We begin with the concept of the inertial rate of inflation. At a particular time, the economy has inherited a given rate of inflation—say, for example, 6 percent—and people's expectations have adapted to this rate. This expected or inertial rate is built into the economy's institutions and even into informal arrangements. Labor and management write contracts designed around a 6 percent inflation rate; government planners build the price increase into their monetary and fiscal policies; and interest rates have a 6 percent inflation rate built in. Once built in, the inertial rate can persist for a long time. When a shock occurs, however, the inertial rate moves up or down.

We should note that the inertial rate of inflation is the product of a complex interaction of forces. Government monetary and fiscal policies in the past are just one of these forces. Supply shocks in previous periods, which cause the price of production to rise sharply relative to the demand for goods and services, are, for instance, one major nongovernmental contributing factor to the inertial rate of inflation. Supply shocks include increases in the price of foreign energy, rising labor costs due to increased union power, increased markups resulting from a decline in competition, and pervasive crop failures. On the demand side, the growth over time of consumer installment debt and corporate debt are important nongovernmental factors behind the inertial inflation rate.[35]

This analysis indicates that the government cannot be said to be the cause of the detrimental effects society suffers as a result of inertial inflation. Inherently, deficit finance is merely a method of financing government expenditures and therefore is not a harmful act directed at society. Its side effects and ramifications, however, combine with a complex mosaic of other actions to produce the inertial rate of inflation. Without these other factors, deficit finance itself would normally present no inflationary threat. Moreover, a fully employed economy is impossible without the presence of factors which work to prop up the aggregate spending level. Without such demand-inducing factors as consumer installment debt and corporate debt, government deficit finance would be looked upon as the centerpiece of a strategy to prop up aggregate spending as a means of avoiding a deep recession. Finally, inertial inflation is *anticipated* inflation and is, therefore, in a large measure, adjusted for in advance.

What the government clearly may not do is to initiate deficit finance spending of such huge proportions as to drive the economy above the inertial inflationary rate. Providing a good indication of whether the deficit finance initiative will foster *unanticipated* inflation is the impact it has on the proportion of the government debt to national income. As long as current government policies do not work to increase this fraction, the government cannot be said to be causing unanticipated inflation.

To be sure, inertial inflation may affect society in an unbalanced way; certain groups, such as pensioners and unorganized labor, may find themselves powerless to protect themselves against the general price rise. Unbalanced inflation certainly redistributes income. But given the multiplicity of forces behind the inertial inflation rate, any income redistribution which occurs in its wake should be regarded no differently than the income redistribution which is ascribed to the dynamics of the marketplace and to the structural changes in the economy.

In the Torah society, taking action to make the income distribution "fairer" is not an appropriate role for the public sector.[36] But suppose that inertial inflation not only leaves certain groups worse off in relative terms, but actually pushes them into a state of deprivation. Here, the government must take remedial action. But what compels this action is the government's anti-poverty mandate, and not a responsibility to correct the side effects of its deficit finance policy.

We now turn to the specifics of Tamari's case against government deficit finance: Deficit finance is objectionable because it debases the country's currency. Since this debasement effectively reduces the real return for holders of outstanding bonds, the policy amounts to a tax on government bondholders. This is taxation without legislation.

Moreover, the "inflation tax" fails to meet the equity benchmark Halakhah sets for taxes generally. This consists of setting taxes proportional to wealth and/or in accordance with benefits received from government expenditures. Given the adverse distributional consequences of inflation on the poor, pensioners, and the sick, government-induced inflation violates Halakhah's equity benchmark for taxation.[37]

What the previous discussion points to is the inappropriateness of calling the redistributive effects of inflation a tax. First, society accepts a certain degree of the inflation rate as the price it must pay to achieve intertemporal tax relief. Second, inflation is the product of many forces. Without their combined effect, government deficit finance would not only be an innocuous inflationary factor, but would be regarded as a vital spending stimulant, preventing the economy from falling into the throes of recession. Consequently, even if current government deficit finance results in the economy moving above the inertial inflation rate, the government cannot be said to "cause" inflation.

One caveat should, however, be noted. In the rare historical episodes of hyperinflation, one might very well argue that government policy was the cause of many of the disastrous economic and social consequences. At the height of the German inflation of 1923, for instance, the government's daily output of currency was over 400 quadrillion marks. In the 1945–46 Hungarian hyperinflation, monetary authorities topped this by seeing to it that the average growth rate of the money supply was more than 12,000 percent per month.[38] Since hyperinflation cannot persist without massive increases in the money supply by the government, the government must be held responsible for the accompanying pathologies.

Aside from the instance of hyperinflation, the case against government inflationary policies is not based on the existence of a causative link between these policies and the accompanying objectionable economic conditions. Rather, the halakhic acceptability of government deficit finance must be evaluated in light of the government's mandate to maintain price stability. Provided deficit finance is restricted to its legitimate uses, the government cannot be said to be subverting this mandate.

The Moral Case Against Government Inflationary Policies

In making the moral case against government inflationary policies, Tamari cites a number of morally objectionable conditions associated with accelerating inflation.[39] Here, again, if the case is going to be made by identifying a link between government inflationary policies and the accompanying moral conditions, the link will be even more tenuous than the one we found earlier between government inflationary policies and the accompanying economic environment. To illustrate, Tamari contends that the work ethic dissipates in an inflationary environment. Because wages are eroded by inflation, workers are motivated to put out as little as possible in return for their decreasing real wage rate.[40] But government debt creation does not inherently work to make wages rise less rapidly than the general price level. Accordingly, if the work ethic dissipates in an inflationary environment, this phenomenon cannot be said to be "caused" by the government's inflationary policies.

Relatedly, Tamari contends that in an inflationary environment:

> An escape from money to goods, whether needed or not, is seen as the only way to preserve one's income or wealth. Savings become pointless, further encouraging consumption and waste. Immediate gratification becomes the only way of living.[41]

Tamari's argument here is again unconvincing. Government debt creation works only to encourage the accelerated *purchasing* of commodities. But a shift in wealth from money to commodities is not the same thing as an increase in the rate of *using up* these commodities. If anything, economic forces should bring about the opposite effect. Since workers typically fear that inflation will erode their real wage, anticipated inflation should work to encourage them to reduce the rate at which they *consume* the portion of their wealth stored in the form of commodities. If inflation fosters a life style of immediate gratification and waste, government debt creation, and for that matter, economic forces, cannot be said to be the culprit.

Given the tenuous link between government debt creation and the morally objectionable features of an inflationary environment, the moral case against government debt creation cannot be based on the proposition that government *causes* these morally objectionable features.

In making the moral case against government debt creation, Tamari observes that historically the moral climate of society has always been a legislative concern of the Torah community.[42] Here, Tamari is on the right track. Let us develop his point further.

For the Torah community, concern for the moral climate of society goes beyond legislative prerogative and takes on the character of a mandated government function. This duty is an aspect of the *imitatio Dei* behavioral imperative of the public sector. Specifically, if the economic environment predisposes people to engage in morally objectionable conduct, it behooves government to devise means of neutralizing this tendency toward evil. Accordingly, if society judges that accelerated inflation works to dissipate the work ethic, foster waste, and encourage a life style of immediate gratification and manipulative conduct, then it behooves the public sector to take remedial action in the form of price-stabilization policies.

We should note, however, that the morally objectionable conduct which Tamari describes will first become manifest, in all probability, in the advanced phases of accelerated inflation. Long before the moral decay sets in, inflation will have posed the threat of dragging the economy into a recession. Moreover, the income-redistribution consequences of accelerated inflation, even in its early stages, may already have assaulted society's sense of fairness. Basing the price-stabilization mandate on moral grounds, therefore, works to give the public sector more latitude and maneuverability in delaying price-stabilization initiatives than is warranted.

Glossary of Economic and Legal Terms

ACCELERATING INFLATION. An increasingly sharp rise in the rate of inflation. If government attempts to hold unemployment below the natural rate of unemployment, this will result in accelerating inflation.

AGGREGATE DEMAND. Total spending for consumption, investment, and government goods and services. It increases as the national income increases.

AMORTIZATION. Payments which reduce the principal amount of a debt.

ARBITRAGE. The act of buying a currency or other commodity in one market and simultaneously selling it in another market at a higher price. Arbitrage is an important force in eliminating the price discrepancy, thereby making markets function more efficiently.

ASKED PRICE. Stock market term indicating the lowest price that will be taken by the holder of a security.

ASSET. A physical property or intangible right that has economic value.

AUTOMATIC STABILIZERS. Government spending, taxation, and transfer programs which automatically (i.e., without legislative action) act to increase aggregate spending during economic downturns and decrease aggregate spending during periods of prosperity.

BID PRICE. Stock market term indicating the highest price someone is willing to pay for an issue.

BOND. A promise to pay the holder a fixed sum of money at the specified maturity date and some other fixed amount of interest every year up to the date of maturity.

CAPITAL. Durable goods capable of producing a stream of goods or services over a period of time.

CAPITAL FORMATION. The creation of physical productive facilities, such as buildings, tools, equipment, and roads.

CARTEL. An agreement, often in writing, among manufacturers, dealers, etc., to restrict output or prices or to divide territories.

CENTRAL BANK. A government-established agency (in the United States, the Federal Reserve System) responsible for control over the nation's money supply and credit conditions, and for the supervision of commercial banks.

COMPARABLE WORTH. The doctrine that every job has an intrinsic value, independent of labor supply and demand, and that jobs with equal intrinsic values should be compensated equally.

CONSUL. Abbreviation for "consolidated annuities." Funded government securities or stock which the government need not repay until it wishes. An investor in consuls can, however, sell them at prices reflecting the yield on comparable securities.

CONSUMER PRICE INDEX (CPI). A measure of inflation based on a market basket of goods and services purchased by urban households.

CONSUMER SURPLUS. The difference between the maximum amount a consumer is willing to pay for a given quantity of a good and the amount actually paid.

COST DISEASE OF PERSONAL SERVICES. Tendency of the cost of services to rise faster than the economy's overall inflation rate because it is difficult to increase productivity in the service sector.

CREEPING INFLATION. A slow, but continuous inflation.

DEFICIT FINANCING. A deliberate policy of heavy government spending that is not expected to be offset by increased revenues but is financed by increasing the public debt.

DISEQUILIBRIUM PRICE. A price which is inherently unstable. At the disequilibrium price, supply exceeds demand or demand exceeds supply.

DEPRECIATION. The value of the capital stock that has been consumed or used up in a given year in the process of producing goods and services.

ECONOMIC RENT. The return to a seller of a good or service over and above its opportunity cost when the good is temporarily in fixed supply.

EFFICIENCY. Achieving maximum output value from a given set of inputs, or achieving the desired output with minimum cost of inputs.

FAIR USE DOCTRINE. The principle which entitles a person to use copyrighted material in a reasonable manner, including the use of its theme or idea, without the consent of the copyright owner.

FIDUCIARY. A person or firm acting in a capacity of responsibility for the handling of funds for other persons or firms.

FISCAL POLICY. Government's efforts to use its spending, taxing, and debt-issuing authority to smooth out the business cycle and maintain full employment without inflation. It can occur through variations in the spending and tax rate of the government for the purpose of affecting the level of economic activity, employment, and price level.

FRACTIONAL RESERVE RULE. A regulation in modern banking systems whereby a commercial bank is legally required to keep a specified fraction of its deposits in the form of deposits with the central bank (or in vault cash).

FREE RIDER. Anyone who receives benefits from a good or service without having to pay for them.

FRICTIONAL UNEMPLOYMENT. Unemployment that is due to normal turnover in the labor market. It includes people who are temporarily between jobs because they are moving or changing occupations.

HEDGING. Buying one security and selling another in such a way as to produce a riskless portfolio.

HUMAN CAPITAL. Capital in the form of various investments a worker has made (e.g., education, experience, skill development) that augment his productivity.

HYPERINFLATION. A condition of rapidly accelerating inflation. Under conditions of hyperinflation prices rise tenfold or even a hundredfold in a single month.

INCOME REDISTRIBUTION. Change in the aggregate amount of income which is enjoyed by each of several identified blocs of income recipients.

INDEXING. The process of automatically adjusting wages and prices for the effects of inflation.

INERTIAL INFLATION. A process of steady inflation that occurs when inflation is expected to persist and the ongoing rate of inflation is built into contracts and people's expectations.

INFRASTRUCTURE. The foundation underlying a nation's economy. It includes transportation and communication systems, power facilities, and other public services.

INPUT. Anything that goes into the production of goods and services. Inputs consist of land, labor, capital, and entrepreneurial ability.

KALDOR-HICKS TEST. State A is to be preferred to state B if those who gain from the move to A can compensate those who lose and still be better off. Compensation here is hypothetical, and the Kaldor-Hicks criterion suggests that A is preferable to B even if compensation does not actually take place.

LEVERAGED BUYOUT. When loans are used to finance most of the purchase price. A company is considered highly leveraged when debt far outweighs equity as a percentage of its total capitalization, and most of its cash flow is used to cover debt service.

LIABILITY. Debt owed by an individual or organization.

MACROECONOMICS. Analysis dealing with the behavior of the economy as a whole in respect to output, income, prices, and unemployment.

MARGINAL REVENUE PRODUCT (MRP). The extra revenue that would be brought in if a firm were to buy one extra unit of an input (e.g., labor), put it to work, and sell the extra product it produced.

MONETARY POLICY. The policy of the central bank in exercising its control over money, interest rates, and credit conditions.

MONEY SUPPLY. The "narrowly defined" money supply (M1) consists of coins, paper currency, plus all demand or checking deposits.

MONOPOLY. A market structure in which a commodity is supplied by a single firm.

MULTIPLIER. The number of times by which the change in total income exceeds the size of the expenditure change that brought it about.

NATURAL RATE OF UNEMPLOYMENT. The unemployment rate at which upward and downward pressures on wage and price inflation are in balance, so that inflation neither rises nor falls.

OCCUPATIONAL APPRECIATION. The rate at which new skills are learned on a job.

OCCUPATIONAL DEPRECIATION. The rate at which the skills a job requires depreciate when not in use.

OLIGOPOLY. A market model characterized by a few firms that produce either a homogeneous product or differentiated products and the entry of new firms is very difficult or blocked.

OPPORTUNITY COST. The dollar amount that would be derived from the employment of a resource in its best alternative use.

OPTIONS. A privilege sold by one party to another which offers the buyer the right to buy (call) or sell (put) a security at an agreed-upon price during a specified period or on a specified date.

PARETO OPTIMALITY. A situation in which no reorganization or trade could raise the utility or satisfaction of one individual without lowering the utility or satisfaction of another individual.

PRIMARY FINANCIAL MARKET. Market involving the creation and issuance of new securities, mortgages, and other claims to wealth. It is the market for initial sales of securities.

PROGRESSIVE TAX. A tax whose rate rises as income increases. Thus those with high incomes pay a greater percentage of their incomes as tax than do those with lower incomes.

PURE PUBLIC GOOD. Commodity or service whose benefits are not depleted by an additional user and for which it is generally difficult or impossible to exclude people from its benefits, even if they are unwilling to pay for it.

REAL ASSETS. Assets which include direct ownership of land, buildings, machinery, inventory, and precious metals.

REAL WAGES. The purchasing power of a worker's wages in terms of goods and services. It is measured by the ratio of the money wage rate to the consumer price index.

REGRESSIVE TAX. A tax which falls more heavily on people with low incomes than on those with high incomes.

RESALE PRICE MAINTENANCE. Agreement whereby manufacturers independently or collectively specify minimum prices at which their products may be resold by wholesalers and retailers.

RESTRAINT OF TRADE. Any attempt to restrict competition by combining to create a monopoly, maintain or increase prices, or apportion the available business.

SECONDARY FINANCIAL MARKET. Market involving the transfer of existing securities from old investors to new investors. It is the market for already issued securities.

SELLING SHORT. The act of selling a security that is not owned. Securities belonging to someone else are borrowed and sold. When the short-seller covers, equivalent securities are bought back and restored to the original owner.

SPECIALIST. An exchange member who acts as a broker in the execution of orders, and as a dealer by transacting for his own account. He maintains an orderly market in the limited securities with which he is involved, facilitating execution of odd-lot transactions (stock trades of less than 100 shares).

STREET NAME. Securities held in customer accounts at brokerage houses, but registered in the firm's name.

STRUCTURAL UNEMPLOYMENT. The unemployment that occurs when the skills a worker possesses are no longer in demand, as when industries decline because their product is no longer in demand or is replaced by a lower-cost source.

SUPPLY SHOCKS. In macroeconomics, a sudden change in production costs or productivity that has a large and unexpected impact on the level of output and on the price level.

TAX CREDIT. An amount which is subtracted from the taxes owed to a government.

TOTAL REVENUE. The number of units sold, multiplied by the per unit price charged.

UNJUST ENRICHMENT DOCTRINE. Doctrine that a person should not be allowed to profit or enrich himself inequitably at another's expense.

Glossary of Halakhic and Theological Terms

AMORAIM, AMORAIC. Designation of scholars who were active in the period from the completion of the Mishnah (ca. 200 C.E.) until the completion of the Babylonian and Jerusalem Talmuds (end of the 4th and 5th cent. respectively).

BARAITA. A teaching or a tradition of the Tannaim that was excluded from the Mishnah (ca. 200 C.E.) and incorporated in a later collection compiied by R. Ḥiyya and R. Oshaiah.

BET DIN. Jewish court of law.

DARKHEI NO'AM. Lit. "ways of pleasantness." The goal of achieving harmonious interpersonal relations.

GERAMA. Tortious damage caused indirectly by the tortfeasor's person.

GENEIVAT DA'AT. Conduct designed to deceive or create a false impression.

HAKKARAT HATOV. Gratitude

HALAKHAH. Jewish law.

HETTER ISKA. An elaborate form of the *iska* business partnership wherein conditions are attached with the design of protecting the financier from absorbing a loss on his principal and increasing the probability that he will realize a profit as well. These clauses are structured in such a manner that *ribbit* law is not violated.

ḤINNUKH. Religious training.

IMITATIO DEI. Latin for "imitation of God." Judaism's behavioral imperative consisting of man's duty to emulate God's attributes of mercy in his interpersonal conduct.

ISKA. A form of business partnership consisting of an active partner and a financier who is a silent partner. In the absence of stipulation, half the capital transfer takes on the legal character of a loan, while the remaining half takes on the character of a pledge. The *iska* arrangement may violate *ribbit* law and is therefore subject to regulation.

KABBELAN. A pieceworker hired to perform a specific task, with no provisions regarding fixed hours.

KINYAN. Acquisition of legal rights by means of the performance of a symbolic act.

LASHON HA-RA. Talebearing wherein A delivers a damaging but truthful report regarding B to C, with C being neither the object of B's mischief nor the intended target of his evil designs.

MISHNAH. Compiled and codified by R. Judah ha-Nasi in 200 C.E., it contains the essence of the Oral Law as it had been handed down from the time of the Bible.

ONA'AH. Price fraud involving selling above or below the competitive norm.

ONA'AT DEVARIM. Conduct causing needless mental anguish to others.

PO'EL. Day-laborer hired for a specific period of time or required to work at fixed hours.

REKHILUT. Talebearing wherein A delivers a damaging but truthful report regarding B to C, and C is either the object of B's mischief or the intended target of his evil designs.

RIBBIT. Prohibition against interest.

RISHONIM, RISHONIC. Designation of scholars who were active in the period from the eleventh to the middle of the fifteenth century.

SHELIḤUT. Agency.

SHIKHEḤAH. Forgotten sheaves. This portion of the crop is the entitlement of the poor.

SODOMITIC. Exhibiting the character trait of a citizen of Sodom, i.e., denying a neighbor a benefit or privilege which involves no cost to oneself.

TALMID ḤAKHAM. Rabbinical scholar.

TALMUD. The record of the discussions of scholars on the laws and teachings of the Mishnah. The Babylonian Talmud was codified ca. 500 C.E., the Palestinian Talmud ca. 400 C.E.

TANNA, TANNAIC. Designation of scholars active in the period from the beginning of the common era up to 220 C.E. The period of the Tannaim spans six generations of scholars from Gamliel the Elder and his contemporaries to Judah ha-Nasi (the redactor of the Mishnah).

TENAI KAFUL. Lit. "double condition." A technicality of Jewish contract law which makes a conditional clause unenforceable unless the stipulations expressly spell out the consequences of both fulfillment and nonfulfillment of the clause.

UMDANA. Inferential fact determination.

Notes

NOTES TO CHAPTER 1

1. R. Solomon b. Abraham Adret (Barcelona, 1235–1310), *Responsa Rashba* 3:411; R. Simeon b.Ẓemaḥ Duran (Algeria, 1361–1444), *Tashbeẓ* 2:132 and 239.

2. For sources and discussion of these points see Aaron Levine, *Free Enterprise and Jewish Law: Aspects of Jewish Business Ethics* (New York: Ktav and Yeshiva University Press), p. 135.

3. R. Isaac b. Jacob Alfasi (Algeria, 1013–1103), *Responsa Rif*, ed. Lieter, no. 13; R. Joseph b Samuel Bonfils, quoted by R. Meir b. Baruch of Rothenburg (1215–1293), *Responsa Maharam* 423; R. Ḥayyim (Eliezer) b. Isaac (Germany, 13th cent.), *Responsa Ḥayyim Or Zaru'a*, no. 222; R. Eliezer b. Joel ha-Levi (Bonn, 1140–1225), quoted by R. Mordecai b. Hillel (Germany, 1240?–1298), *Mordecai*, Bava Batra 1:482; Naḥmanides (Spain 1194–1270), *Responsa Rashba* (attributed to Ramban) 280; *Responsa Rashba*, 2:279; 5:126, 270, 242.

4. R. Joseph Colon, *Responsa Maharik*, shoresh 24. See, however, R. Ḥayyim Halberstamm (Zanz, 1793–1876), *Divrei Ḥayyim* 2:60.

5. *Responsa Rashba* 1:788; see also 1:399.

6. For a discussion of the mandated functions for the public sector in the Torah society, see Levine, *Free Enterprise and Jewish Law*, pp. 131–160.

7. For a treatment of the Pareto and Kaldor-Hicks criteria, see Richard A. Posner, *Economic Analysis of Law*, 3rd ed. (Boston: Little, Brown, 1986), pp. 11–15.

8. R. Elijah b. Ḥayyim (Constantinople, 1530?–1610?), Teshuvot ha-Ranaḥ, published in R. Isaac di Leon, *Mayim Amukim* 63; R. Isaac b. Sheshet Perfet (Spain, 1326–1408), *Responsa Ribash* 228.

One aspect of political authority in the Torah society, referred to in the text earlier, is the functions Halakhah mandates on the public sector. Among these functions is the security-tax levy. In talmudic times, this tax took the form of a levy imposed on the townspeople to construct a town wall (Mishnah, Bava Batra 1:2). Analysis of the rationale behind this mandated function lends support to the agency concept of political authority. Elsewhere, we have argued that economic efficiency provides the rationale for this levy. What follows is the essential elements of our thesis: We begin with the premise that security measures represent a preferred item in the budget of each permanent resident of the town. Notwithstanding this effective demand for security measures, the emergence of defense projects, in the absence of a coercive levy, could very well be frustrated. Since once the defense project is completed (e.g., the construction of the town wall), everyone residing in the town, contributors and noncontributors alike, benefits from it, each resident is motivated to rely on the collective efforts of his fellow townspeople to bring the defense measures to fruition. Paradoxically, the vital nature of the town's defense project works to strengthen the "free-rider" motive, as each resident reasons that the importance of the project guarantees its completion without his own efforts. To the extent that the free-rider motive is pervasive, the defense project will not be completed within the framework of a voluntary exchange system. Economic goods, such as local security projects, which are characterized by an inability to exclude nonpayers, are referred to in the economic literature as pure public goods. We have argued elsewhere that public road-repair and water-supply projects also fall into this category. Introduction of a coercive levy in respect to such projects amounts, therefore, to nothing more than eliminating the free-rider phenomenon and allowing a preferred expenditure to take place. See Levine, *Free Enterprise and Jewish Law*, pp. 136–150.

Within the framework of the efficiency rationale for the pure-public-good case, the role of government is merely that of a collecting agent for each individual who harbors a demand for the expenditure at hand. Hence political authority in the pure-public-good case clearly rests on the agency concept.

9. Cf. Kiddushin 42b, Ketubbot 85a, 95b.

10. Baraita, Bava Meẓia 51a; Rif, ad loc.; Maimonides (Egypt, 1135–1204), *Yad*, Mekhirah 12:1; Rosh (R. Asher b. Jeḥiel, Germany, 1250–1327), Bava Meẓia 4:17; R. Jacob b. Asher (Germany, 1270–1343), *Tur*, Ḥoshen Mishpat 227:1; R. Joseph Caro (Safed, 1488–1575), Shulḥan Arukh, Ḥoshen Mishpat 227:1; R. Jeḥiel Michel Epstein (Belorussia, 1829–1908), Ḥoshen Mishpat 227:1.

11. Bava Batra 78a and Rashi (R. Solomon b. Isaac, Troyes, 1040–1105), ad loc.; Rif, ad loc.; *Yad*, Mekhirah 27:5; Rosh, Bava Batra 5:7; *Tur*, Ḥoshen Mishpat 220:5; Shulḥan Arukh, Ḥoshen Mishpat 220:8; Arukh ha-Shulḥan, Ḥoshen Mishpat 220:7.

12. Bava Meẓia 50b; Rif, ad loc.; *Yad*, op. cit., 12:4; Rosh, Bava Meẓia 4:15; *Tur*, Ḥoshen Mishpat 227:6; Shulḥan Arukh, Ḥoshen Mishpat 227:4; Arukh ha-Shulḥan, Ḥoshen Mishpat 227:3.

13. Bava Meẓia 50b; Rif, ad loc.; *Yad*, Mekhirah 12:2; Rosh, Ḥoshen Mishpat, 4:15; *Tur*, Ḥoshen Mishpat 227:3; Shulḥan Arukh, Ḥoshen Mishpat 227:2; Arukh ha-Shulḥan, Ḥoshen Mishpat 227:3.

14. Bava Meẓia 50b; Rif, ad loc.; *Yad*, Mekhirah 12:3; *Tur*, Ḥoshen Mishpat 227:4; Shulḥan Arukh, Ḥoshen Mishpat 227:2; Arukh ha-Shulḥan, Ḥoshen Mishpat 227:3.

15. Rava, Kiddushin 42b; Rif, ad loc.; *Yad*, Mekhirah 13:9; *Tur*, Ḥoshen Mishpat 227:48; Shulḥan Arukh, Ḥoshen Mishpat 227:30; Arukh ha-Shulḥan, Ḥoshen Mishpat 227:36.

16. Though the *ona'ah* claim is rooted in the presumption of imperfect knowledge on the part of the complainant, the claim is not automatically invalidated by certainty that he was aware of the market norm at the time he entered into the *ona'ah* transaction. For the development of this point, see Levine, *Free Enterprise and Jewish Law*, pp. 108–109.

17. R. Solomon b. Abraham Adret (Spain, 1235–1310), *Responsa Rashba* 1:729, 3:411, 5:126; R. Israel b. Pethahiah Isserlein (Germany 1390–1460), *Terumat ha-Deshen*, Pesakim u-Khetavim, no. 214; R. Ben-Zion Meir Ḥai Ouziel, *Mishpetei Uziel*, Ḥoshen Mishpat, no. 4.

18. *Terumat ha-Deshen*, loc. cit.

19. Shulḥan Arukh, Yoreh De'ah 256:3.

20. *Mishpetei Uziel*, loc. cit.

21. Rav Naḥman, Kiddushin 42b; Rif, ad loc.; *Yad*, Mekhirah 13:12; Rosh, Kiddushin 2:3; *Tur*, Ḥoshen Mishpat 227:37; Shulḥan Arukh, Ḥoshen Mishpat 277:37; Arukh ha-Shulḥan, Ḥoshen Mishpat 227:37.

22. Rava, Kiddushin 42b; Rif, ad loc.; *Yad*, loc. cit., Rosh, loc. cit.; *Tur*, Ḥoshen Mishpat 227:38; Shulḥan Arukh, Ḥoshen Mishpat 227:38; Arukh ha-Shulḥan, loc. cit.

23. R. Abraham Isaac Kook (Israel, 1865–1935), quoted in R. Menachem Elon, *Ha-Mishpat ha-Ivri* (Jerusalem: Magnes Press, 1973), vol. 2, p. 46. See also R. Sol Roth, Halakhah and Politics: The Jewish Idea of a State (New York: Yeshiva University Press, 1988), p. 131.

24. R. Aaron ha-Levi (Barcelona, 1235–1300), *Sefer ha-Ḥinnukh* 502.

25. *Yad*, Sekhirut 13:7; *Tur*, Ḥoshen Mishpat 337:20; Shulḥan Arukh, Ḥoshen Mishpat 337:20, Arukh ha-Shulḥan, Ḥoshen Mishpat 337:26.

26. *Yad*, Sekhirut, loc. cit.; *Tur*, Ḥoshen Mishpat 337:20; Shulḥan Arukh, Ḥoshen Mishpat 337:20; Arukh ha-Shulḥan, Ḥoshen Mishpat 337:26.

27. R. Moses Isserles (Rema), Shulḥan Arukh, Ḥoshen Mishpat 163:1.

28. Gittin 59b.

29. Cf. Mishnah, Gittin 5:8. For a extensive treatment of the *darkhei no'am* principle, and especially of its role in the interpretation of scriptural rules and rabbinical enactments, see Aaron Kirschenbaum, *Equity in Jewish Law* (Hoboken: Ktav and Yeshiva University Press, 1991), pp. 151–183.

30. Mishnah, Gittin 5:8. Tannaic authorities ad loc. argue about whether the ordinance went so far as to call for the courts to uphold the property right of the minor. Adopting the position of the *tanna kamma*, decisors define the enforcement element of the enactment as consisting of voluntary compliance. The Jewish court, however, will not intervene to uphold the property right of the minor. See *Yad*, Gezeilah ve-Avedah 17:12; *Tur*, Ḥoshen Mishpat 270:1; Shulḥan Arukh, Ḥoshen Mishpat 270:1; Arukh ha-Shulḥan, Ḥoshen Mishpat 270:1.

31. Tosafot, Pesaḥim 91b; Rosh, Kiddushin 1:25; R. Nissim b. Abraham Gerondi (Barcelona, 1310–1375), Gittin 39a; Kiddushin 19a; Rema, Shulḥan Arukh, Ḥoshen Mishpat, 243:15

32. Rashi, Bava Meẓia 8a.

33. Rashi, Sanhedrin 25b.

34. Gittin 61a; Rif, ad loc.; *Yad*, Gezeilah ve-Avedah 6:13; Rosh, Gittin 5:22; *Tur*, Ḥoshen Mishpat 273:16; Shulḥan Arukh, Ḥoshen Mishpat 273:16; Arukh ha-Shulḥan, Ḥoshen Mishpat 273:20.

35. Mishnah, Gittin 5:8. The enforcement procedure for the enactment, as in the previous case, is left to voluntary compliance. See *Yad*, loc. cit; *Tur*, loc. cit.; Shulḥan Arukh, loc. cit.; Arukh ha-Shulḥan, loc. cit.

36. R. Mordecai b. Hillel, *Mordecai*, Kiddushin 524.

37. Sotah 14a.

38. Sifrei, ad loc.

39. Ibid.

40. Maimonides, *Sefer ha-Mizvot*, miẓvat aseh, no. 8; *Yad*, De'ot 1:6.

41. Yiẓḥak Twersky, "On Law and Ethics in the *Mishneh Torah*: A Case Study of Hilkhot Megillah II:17," *Tradition* 24, no. 2 (Winter

1989): 142–143. See also Lawrence Kaplan, "Hilkhot Megillah 2:17 Revisited: A Halakhic Analysis," *Tradition* 26, no. 1 (Fall 1991): 14–21.

42. R. Naftali Ẓevi Yehudah Berlin, *Emek Neẓiv*, Sifrei at Deuteronomy 10:2, piska 13.

43. Ibid.

44. R. Joseph B. Soloveitchik, *Shiurim le Zekher Abba Mori*, vol. 2 (Jerusalem, 1986), pp. 170–171.

45. Maimonides, *Guide of the Perplexed*, trans. S. Pines (Chicago: University of Chicago Press, 1963), chap. 54, pp. 126–127.

46. For the development of this point, see R. Norman Lamm, "Notes on the Concept of *Imitatio Dei*," in *Rabbi Joseph H. Lookstein Memorial Volume*, ed. R. Leo Landman (New York: Ktav, 1980), pp. 227–229.

47. Yoma 75a.

48. Mekhilta at Exodus 15:2.

49. Exodus Rabbah 21:7 and R. Samuel Jaffe b. Isaac Ashkenazi (Constantinople, 16th cent.), *Yefeh To'ar*, Exodus Rabbah, ad loc.; R. Jacob Culi (Constantinople, ca. 1685–1732), *Me-Am Lo'ez*, Exodus 14:19.

50. Yoma 38b.

51. Song of Songs Rabbah 5:2.

52. Kiddushin 30b.

53. Sanhedrin 107a.

54. Berakhot 60b.

55. Sanhedrin 43b.

56. R. Menaḥem b. Solomon Meiri, Beit ha-Beḥirah, Sanhedrin 44a.

57. Rashi at Bava Meẓia 75b.

58. R. Joel Sirkes, Baḥ to *Tur*, Ḥoshen Mishpat 70, n. 1; R. Joshua b. Alexander ha-Kohen Falk, *Perishah* to *Tur*, Ḥoshen Mishpat 70, n. 1.

59. R. Abraham b. Moses di Boton, Leḥem Mishneh to *Yad*, Malveh 2:7; R. Jacob Moses Lorberbaum, *Netivot ha-Mishpat* 70, n. 1.

60. Leḥem Mishneh, loc. cit.

61. Rashi, at Leviticus 19:14. The Torah makes use of the phrase "And you shall fear your God" in connection with the following moral imperatives: (1) the prohibition against offering ill-suited advice (Leviticus 19:14); (2) the duty to bestow honor upon a talmudic scholar (Leviticus 19:32); (3) the injunction against causing someone needless mental anguish (Leviticus 25:17); (4) the interdict against charging interest (Leviticus 25:36); and (5) the prohibition against working an Israelite slave oppressively (Leviticus 25:43).

62. Leviticus 19:32, Kiddushin 32b.

63. Kiddushin 32b–33a.

64. In the event the defendant admits the indebtedness but pleads ignorance of whether the debt was repaid, the plaintiff is entitled to recover his claim in full. See Mishnah, Bava Kamma 10:7; Rif, ad loc.; *Yad,* To'en ve-Ni-tan 1:9; Rosh, Bava Kamma 10:32; *Tur,* Ḥoshen Mishpat 75:9; Shulḥan Arukh, Ḥoshen Mishpat 75:9; Arukh ha-Shulḥan, Ḥoshen Mishpat 75:13–14.

65. Ibid. In defending his interpretation of Rav's dictum, R. Boton adduces a reductio ad absurdum argument: If the dictum is rooted in concern about the willful denial of a lawful debt, then by force of the *lifnei iver* interdict, even a properly witnessed loan should be prohibited. This follows from the fact that Jewish law does not require a debt to be repaid with the formality of witnesses (see Ketubbot 18a). Consequently, even if the loan was entered into by means of witnesses, the debtor could escape payment by denying the obligation.

The difficulty is, however, resolved with the recognition that a witnessed loan transaction does not generate a setting of hidden misconduct for the debtor. In the latter instance, a plea of ignorance will not be sufficient to allow the debtor to escape liability (see Shulḥan Arukh, Ḥoshen Mishpat 75:12). Here, the debtor can escape payment only by claiming outright that he paid off the debt. Provided that the debt was not entered into by means of *kinyan,* taking an oath that he repaid the debt enables the debtor to evade responsibility (see Ḥoshen Mishpat 70:1). Since a witnessed loan transaction does not generate a situation wherein the debtor can escape responsibility by engaging in hidden misconduct, the making of the loan cannot entail violation of the *lifnei iver* interdict.

66. Deuteronomy 8:16.

67. Aaron Levine, "The LBO and Jewish Law," *Sh'ma,* 20/381, November 10, 1989, pp. 1–3; idem, "Getting the Economics and Ethics Straight," *Sh'ma,* 20/385, January 5, 1990, pp. 39–40.

NOTES TO CHAPTER 2

1. Baraita, Bava Batra 8b.

2. *Torat Kohanim,* Be-Har; Maimonides (Egypt, 1135–1204), *Yad,* Mattenot Aniyyim 10:7; R. Jacob b. Asher (Toledo, 1270–1340), *Tur,* Yoreh De'ah 249:7; R. Joseph Caro (Safed, 1488–1575), Shulḥan Arukh,

Yoreh De'ah 249:6; R. Jeḥiel Michel Epstein (Belorussia, 1829–1908), Arukh ha-Shulḥan, Yoreh De'ah 249:15.

3. *Yad*, loc. cit.

4. Rema, Yoreh De'ah 249:7; Arukh ha-Shulḥan, Ḥoshen Mishpat 163:1. For a description of these levies, see Aaron Levine, *Free Enterprise and Jewish Law: Aspects of Jewish Business Ethics* (New York: Ktav and Yeshiva University Press, 1980), p. 155.

5. Nedarim 65b; R. Asher b. Jeḥiel, *Perush ha-Rosh*, ad loc.; Shulḥan Arukh, Yoreh De'ah 257:8.

6. Cf. Avot de-Rabbi Natan, chap. 11.

7. R. Shimon, Mishnah Ketubbot 5:5.

8. Pesaḥim 113a.

9. Bava Batra 90a; Rif, ad loc.; *Yad*, Mekhirah 14:1; Rosh, Bava Batra 5:2; *Tur*, Ḥoshen Mishpat 231:27; Shulḥan Arukh, Ḥoshen Mishpat 231:20; Arukh ha-Shulḥan, Ḥoshen Mishpat 231:20.

10. R. Joshua b. Alexander ha-Kohen Falk (Poland, 1555–1614), *Sefer Me'irat Einayim*, Shulḥan Arukh, Ḥoshen Mishpat 231, n. 43.

11. John C. Goodman and Edwin G. Dolan, *Economics of Public Policy: The Micro View*, 3rd ed. (New York: West Publishing Co., 1985), pp. 176–182.

12. Marvin Kosters and Finis Welch, "The Effects of Minimum Wages on the Distribution of Changes in Aggregate Employment," *American Economic Review* 62 (June 1972): 30.

13. Richard Burkhauser and T. Aldrich Finegan, "The Minimum Wage and the Poor: The End of a Relationship," *Journal of Policy Analysis and Management* 8 (Winter 1989): 53–71; Edward Gramlich, "Impact of Minimum Wages on Other Wages, Employment, and Family Incomes," *Brookings Papers on Economic Activity* (1976), pp. 409–51; William Johnson and Edgar Browning, "The Distribution Efficiency Effects of Increasing the Minimum Wage," *American Economic Review*, March 1983, pp. 204–211.

14. Masanori Hashimoto, *Minimum Wages and On-the-Job Training* (Washington, D.C.: American Enterprise Institute for Public Policy Research, 1981).

15. Goodman and Dolan, *Economics of Public Policy*, pp. 178–180.

16. Ibid., p. 181.

17. *Responsa Rashba* 3:38, quoted in *Beit Yosef*, Yoreh De'ah 250:5; Rema, Yoreh De'ah 250:5.

18. *Tur*, Ḥoshen Mishpat 231; Shulḥan Arukh, Ḥoshen Mishpat 231:20; Arukh ha-Shulḥan, Ḥoshen Mishpat 231:20.

19. Ibid.

20. Ibid.

21. For a detailed discussion of the law of *ona'ah* as it pertains to modern markets, see Aaron Levine, *Economics and Jewish Law: Halakhic Perspectives* (Hoboken: Ktav and Yeshiva University Press, 1987), pp. 64–68.

22. R. Menaḥem b. Solomon Meiri (Perpignan, ca. 1249–1306), Beit ha-Beḥirah, Bava Meẓia 40b; Rosh, Bava Meẓia 3:16; *Tur*, Ḥoshen Mishpat 231 and comment of *Perisha*, n. 26. R. Joel Sirkes (Poland, 1561–1650), however, interpreting Maimonides' position on this matter, posits that the one-sixth profit rate is the return the owner receives for his labor services (Baḥ to *Tur*, loc. cit., n. 26).

23. Bava Batra 91a; Rif, ad loc.; *Yad*, Mekhirah 14:4; Shulḥan Arukh, Ḥoshen Mishpat 231:23; Arukh ha-Shulḥan, Ḥoshen Mishpat 231:23.

24. Arukh ha-Shulḥan, loc. cit.

25. See Marcus Arkin, *Aspects of Jewish Economic History* (Philadelphia: Jewish Publication Society, 1975), pp. 22–33.

26. R. Simeon b. Samuel of Joinville (12th–13th cent.), quoted in Tosafot, Bava Batra 91a.

27. *Yad*, Genevah 8:20, Mekhirah 14:1.

28. Baḥ to *Tur*, Ḥoshen Mishpat 231, n. 26.

29. *Yad*, Mekhirah 14:9.

30. Goodman and Dolan, *Economics of Public Policy*, pp. 181–182.

31. Rema, Shulḥan Arukh, Yoreh De'ah 246:21.

32. Kiddushin 29b; Rif, ad loc.; Rosh, Kiddushin 1:42; *Yad*, Ishut 15:2; *Tur*, Even ha-Ezer 1:3; Shulḥan Arukh, Even ha-Ezer 1:3; Arukh ha-Shulḥan, Even ha-Ezer 1:3.

33. Kiddushin 29a; Rif ad loc.; *Yad*, Talmud Torah 1:1; *Tur*, Yoreh De'ah 245: Shulḥan Arukh, Yoreh De'ah 245; Arukh ha-Shulḥan 245:1–13.

34. R. Shneur Zalman of Liadi (1745–1813), Shulḥan Arukh ha-Rav, Hilkhot Talmud Torah 1:6.

35. Ibid. 1:3.

36. For detailed discussion of this point, see, R. Moshe Meiselman, *Jewish Woman in Jewish Law* (New York: Ktav and Yeshiva University Press, 1978), pp. 34–42; R. Menachem M. Brayer, *The Jewish Woman*

in Rabbinic Literature, vol. 2 (Hoboken: Ktav and Yeshiva University Press, 1986), pp. 83–125.

37. Bava Batra 22a.

38. Maimonides, commentary at Mishnah Avot 4:5.

39. Rosh, Bava Batra 2:13.

40. John Bishop and Robert Lerman, "Wage Subsidies for Income Maintenance and Job Creation," in Job Creation: What Works?, ed. Robert Taggart (Salt Lake City: Olympus Publishing Co., 1977), pp. 39–71; John Bishop, *The Administration of a Wage Rate Subsidy* (Madison: University of Wisconsin, Institute for Research on Poverty, 1977), pp. 1–36; John Bishop and Robert Haveman, *Targeted Employment Subsidies: Issues of Structure and Design SR 24* (Madison: University of Wisconsin, Institute for Research on Poverty), pp. 1–65.

41. See Levine, *Economics and Jewish Law*, pp. 133–135.

42. Bishop, *Administration of a Wage Rate Subsidy*, p. 3.

NOTES TO CHAPTER 3

1. Walter Fogel, *The Equal Pay Act* (New York: Praeger, 1984), p. 59.

2. *Hodgson* v. *Brookhaven General Hospital*, 436 F2d 719 (CA 5, 1970).

3. *Hodgson* v. Robert Hall Inc., 473 F2d 589 (CA 3, 1973).

4. *AFSCME* v. *State of Washington*, no. C82-465 T (E.D. Washington, 1983).

5. *AFSCME* v. *Washington*, 1985 (CA 9 Washington, 1983).

6. R. Meir b. Baruch of Rothenburg (1215–1293), *Responsa Maharam* 477; R. Isaac b. Moses of Vienna (ca. 1180–1250), *Or Zaru'a* 3, Bava Meẓia, piska 242; R. Meir ha-Kohen (end of 13th cent.), *Haggahot Maimuniyyot*, Sekhirut 9:4.

7. R. Jekuthiel Asher Zalman Zausmir (d. 1858), *Responsa Mahariaz*, siman 15, amud 14, tur 1.

8. Maimonides, *Yad*, Mekhirah 8:15.

9. The Talmud (Megillah 23b) explicitly states only that heathen slaves are assimilated to land. Commentators, however, take the assimilation to apply to Israelite slaves as well. See R. Israel b. Pethahiah Isserlein (Germany, 1390–1460), *Responsa Terumat ha-Deshen* 318; R. Elijah b. Solomon Zalman (Vilna, 1720–1797), *Gera* at Shulḥan

Arukh, Ḥoshen Mishpat 227, n. 48; see also R. Joshua b. Alexander ha-Kohen Falk (Lemberg, 1555–1614), *Sma* to Shulḥan Arukh, Ḥoshen Mishpat 227, n. 60.

10. Baraita, Bava Meẓia 56b.

11. Ibid.

12. R. Joshua b. Alexander ha-Kohen Falk, *Sma* to Shulḥan Arukh, Ḥoshen Mishpat 227, n. 59.

13. R. Israel b. Pethahiah Isserlein, *Terumat ha-Deshen* 318.

14. *Yad,* Mekhirah 13:8.

15. R. Eliezer b. Samuel of Metz, *Sefer Yere'im* 127; R. Moses Isserles on interpretation of R. Shabbetai b. Meir ha-Kohen in *Siftei Kohen* to Shulḥan Arukh, Ḥoshen Mishpat 227, n. 17.

16. R. Jacob Tam, quoted in *Responsa Rosh,* kelal 102, and in *Tur,* Ḥoshen Mishpat 227:40; R. Joshua b. Alexander ha-Kohen Falk on interpretation of R. Moses Isserles, *Sma* to Shulḥan Arukh, Ḥoshen Misphat 227, n. 49.

17. "Some authorities" quoted in Rif, Bava Meẓia 56b and in Rosh, Bava Meẓia 4:21.

18. Naḥmanides at Leviticus 25:14.

19. *Siftei Kohen,* loc. cit.

20. Aaron Levine, *Free Enterprise and Jewish Law: Aspects of Jewish Business Ethics* (New York: Ktav and Yeshiva University Press, 1980), pp. 105–109.

21. Ketubbot 105a, 106a.

22. *Yad,* Shekalim 4:7; R. Mosheh Sofer (Hungary, 1762–1839), *Responsa Ḥatam Sofer,* Ḥoshen Mishpat 166; R. Leopold Winkler (Hungary, b. 1844), *Levushei Mordekhai,* Ḥoshen Mishpat 15.

23. Tosafot, Ketubbot 105a.

24. Implicit in R. Judah's reasoning is the modern analytical tool of consumer surplus. This concept is concerned with the relationship between market price and subjective value. Market price is today understood to be the result of the interplay of aggregate supply-and-demand forces. Price is determined outside the influence of the individual producer or consumer. The price an individual consumer would be willing to pay to obtain a given product may not coincide with the market price. When the consumer's subjective evaluation of the product falls below this price, he obviously rejects the product. When his subjective evaluation of the product either coincides with or exceeds the market price, he will buy the product. In the latter instance, he will enjoy a

windfall as well. The difference between the maximum price the consumer would willingly pay to obtain the product rather than do without it and the actual transaction price provides a measure of this windfall, or consumer surplus. Market price affords the purchaser a consumer surplus when the commodity generates for him complementarities in consumption. Subjective equivalence is therefore realized by the purchaser at the above-market price he paid for the commodity.

25. Decisors ruling in accordance with the sages' view include R. Hai b. Sherira of Pumbedita (939–1038), quoted in Rif, Bava Meẓia 58b and in Rosh, Bava Meẓia 4:21; *Yad*, Shekalim 13:13; *Tur*, Ḥoshen Mishpat 227:15; Shulḥan Arukh, Ḥoshen Mishpat 227:15; Arukh ha-Shulḥan, Ḥoshen Mishpat 227:16. R. Ḥananel b. Hushi'el (11th cent.), Bava Meẓia 59b, and *Sefer Yere'im* 259 follow R. Judah's view.

26. R. Yom Tov Ishbili (Ritva), Kiddushin 8a.

27. See R. Aryeh Loeb b. Joseph ha-Kohen, *Keẓot ha-Ḥoshen*, Ḥoshen Mishpat 227, n. 1.

28. R. Aaron Walkin, *Zer Saviv li-Yere'av*, Sefer Yere'im 259, n. 4.

29. R. Samuel b. Meir (Rashbam, ca. 1060–ca. 1130), Bava Meẓia 51b; *Yad*, Shekalim 13:5; *Tur*, Ḥoshen Mishpat 227:37; Shulḥan Arukh, Ḥoshen Mishpat 227:27; Arukh ha-Shulḥan, Ḥoshen Mishpat 227:28. For a varient view of what constitutes selling on trust, see R. Israel of Krems (ca. 1375), *Haggahot Asheri*, Bava Meẓia 4:17. This view is quoted in *Tur*, loc. cit.

30. Arukh ha-Shulḥan, loc. cit.

31. R. Moses Isserles (Rema), Shulḥan Arukh, Ḥoshen Mishpat 163:1.

32. Paula Englard, "The Sex Gap in Work and Wages," *Society* (July/August 1985): 70–71.

33. Fogel, *Equal Pay Act*, p. 12.

34. *Wetzel* v. *Liberty Mutual Insurance Company*, 449 F Supp. 397 (W.D. Pa. 1978).

35. *Schultz* v. Wheaton Glass Co., 421 F2d 259 (CA 3, 1970).

36. Fogel, *Equal Pay Act*, pp. 42–48.

37. Mark R. Killingsworth, "Economics of Comparable Worth: Analytical, Empirical, and Policy Questions," in Comparable Worth: New Dimensions for Research, ed. Heidi I. Hartmann (Washington, D.C.: National Academy Press, 1985), pp. 93–97.

38. "Paying Women What They're Worth," *Report from the Center for Philosophy and Public Policy* 3 (1983): 1–2.

39. Solomon Polachek, "Occupational Self-Selection: A Human Capital Approach to Sex Differences in Occupational Structure," *Review of Economics and Statistics* 58 (1981).

40. Edward G. Dolan and John C. Goodman, *Economics of Public Policy*, 3rd ed. (New York: West Publishing Co., 1985), p. 152.

41. Walter Block, "Economic Intervention, Discrimination and Unforseen Consequences," in *Discrimination, Affirmative Action and Equal Opportunity*, ed. W. E. Block and M. A. Walker (Vancouver: Fraser Institute, 1982), pp. 105–113.

42. Elaine Sorensen, "Equal Pay for Comparable Worth: A Policy for Eliminating the Underevaluation of Women's Work," in *Journal of Economic Issues* 18, no. 2 (June 1984): 465–471.

43. Dolan and Goodman, *Economics of Public Policy*, pp. 153–157.

44. Robert L. Simon, "Comparable Pay for Comparable Work," in *Ethical Theory and Business*, ed. Tom L. Beauchamp and Norman E. Bowie, 3rd ed. (Englewood Cliffs, N.J.: Prentice-Hall, 1988), pp. 370–371.

45. R. Abraham b. David (Posquières, 1125–1198), introduction to his *Ba'al ha-Nefesh*.

46. Yevamot 63a, Sanhedrin 22b.

47. Mishnah, Yevamot 6:6; Rif, Yevamot 65b; *Yad*, Ishut 15:2; Rosh, Yevamot 6:20; *Tur*, Even ha-Ezer 1:1; Shulḥan Arukh, Even ha-Ezer 1:1; Arukh ha-Shulḥan, Even ha-Ezer 1:1.

48. *Tanna kamma*, Mishnah, Yevamot 6:6; Rif, loc. cit.; *Yad*, loc. cit.; Rosh, loc. cit.; *Tur*, Even ha-Ezer 1:13; Shulḥan Arukh, Even ha-Ezer 1:13; Arukh ha-Shulḥan, Even ha-Ezer 1:2.

49. R. Samson R. Hirsch, *The Pentateuch* (Gateshead: Judaica Press, 1982), commentary at Genesis 2:18.

50. R. Moshe Meiselman, *Jewish Woman in Jewish Law* (New York: Ktav and Yeshiva University Press, 1978), pp. 22–25.

51. Ibid., pp. 9–34.

52. Berakhot 17a, Sotah 21a, Arukh ha-Shulḥan, Even ha-Ezer 246:20.

53. Naḥmanides, commentary at Deuteronomy 4:12.

54. R. Baḥya b. Asher, commentary at Deuteronomy 4:12.

55. Ibid.

56. Mekhilta at Exodus 19:3.

57. Meiselman, *Jewish Woman in Jewish Law*, pp. 26–33.

58. R. Ahron Soloveichik, "The Fire of Sinai," in *Building Jewish Ethical Character*, ed. Joseph Kaminetsky and Murray I. Friedman (New York: Fryer Foundation, 1975), p. 12.

59. Ray Marshall and Beth Paulin, "The Wages of Women's Work," *Society*, July/August 1985, p. 28.

60. Brigette Berger, "At Odds With American Reality," *Society*, July/August 1985, p. 77.

61. Dolan and Goodman, *Economics of Public Policy*, p. 155.

62. Simon, "Comparable Pay for Comparable Work," pp. 364–365.

NOTES TO CHAPTER 4

1. *FTC* v. *Universal Battery*, 2 FTC 95 (1919).

2. *Gelb* v. *FTC*, 144 F 2d 580 (2d cir. 1944), following *Gelb*, 33 FTC 1450 (1941).

3. *Heinz W. Kirchner*, 63 FTC 1282 (1963).

4. Ibid. at 1290.

5. Ivan L. Preston, *The Great American Blow-Up: Puffery in Advertising and Selling* (Madison: University of Wisconsin Press, 1975), pp. 162–174.

6. R. Jonah b. Abraham Gerondi, *Sha'arei Teshuvah*, sha'ar 3, ot 184.

7. R. Yom Tov Ishbili (Ritva) at Ḥullin 94a.

8. R. Solomon b. Isaac (Rashi) at Ḥullin 94b.

9. The Mishnah is divided into six orders (*sedarim*). These are (1) Zera'im ("seeds"), (2) Mo'ed ("festivals"), (3) Nashim ("women"), (4) Nezikin ("damages"), (5) Kodashim ("holy things"), and (6) Toharot ("purities"). The various tractates of the Babylonian Talmud fit into these orders. For the Jerusalem Talmud, the Kodashim and Toharot orders are missing.

10. R. Jeḥiel Michel Epstein (Belorussia, 1829–1908), Arukh ha-Shulḥan, Ḥoshen Mishpat 81:10.

11. Sanhedrin 29a; R. Isaac b. Jacob Alfasi (Algeria, 1013–1103), ad loc.; Maimonides (Egypt, 1135–1204), *Yad*, To'en venit'an 67:6; R. Asher b. Jeḥiel (Rosh; Germany, 1250–1327), Sanhedrin 3:25; R. Jacob b. Asher (Germany, 1270–1343), *Tur*, Ḥoshen Mishpat 81:1; R. Joseph Caro (Safed, 1488–1575), Shulḥan Arukh, Ḥoshen Mishpat 81:1; Arukh ha-Shulḥan, Ḥoshen Mishpat 81:1.

12. Sanhedrin 29b; Rif, ad loc.; *Yad*, To'en venit'an 6:6; Rosh, loc. cit.; *Tur*, loc. cit.; Shulḥan Arukh, loc. cit.; Arukh ha-Shulḥan, loc. cit.

13. R. Saadiah Gaon (Egypt, 882–942), quoted by Rosh, loc. cit.; *Tur*, loc. cit.; Shulḥan Arukh, loc. cit.; Arukh ha-Shulḥan, loc. cit.

14. Rif, loc. cit.; Yad, loc. cit.; 6:8; Rosh, loc. cit.; *Tur*, loc. cit.; Shulḥan Arukh, Ḥoshen Mishpat 81:3; Arukh ha-Shulḥan, loc. cit.

15. *Tur*, loc. cit.; Shulḥan Arukh, loc. cit.; Arukh ha-Shulḥan, loc. cit.

16. Sanhedrin 29a; Rif, ad loc.; *Yad*, To'en venit'an 6:6; Rosh, loc. cit.; *Tur*, loc. cit.; Shulḥan Arukh, Ḥoshen Mishpat 81:6; Arukh ha-Shulḥan, loc. cit.

17. *Tur*, loc. cit.; Shulḥan Arukh, Ḥoshen Mishpat 81:7; Arukh ha-Shulḥan, loc. cit.

18. Sanhedrin 29b; Rif, ad loc.; *Yad*, To'en venit'an 7:1; Rosh, loc. cit.; *Tur*, loc. cit.; Shulḥan Arukh, Ḥoshen Mishpat 81:14;Arukh ha-Shulḥan, Ḥoshen Mishpat 81:3.

19. R. Moses Isserles (Rema; Poland, 1525 or 1530–1572), Shulḥan Arukh, Ḥoshen Mishpat 81:14; Arukh ha-Shulḥan, Ḥoshen Mishpat 81:3.

20. R. Joshua ha-Kohen Falk (Poland, 1565–1614), *Sma* to Shulḥan Arukh, Ḥoshen Mishpat 81, n. 31; Arukh ha-Shulḥan, Ḥoshen Mishpat 81:3.

21. Rosh, loc. cit.; Rema, Ḥoshen Mishpat 81:14; Arukh ha-Shulḥan 81:5. For a contrary view, see *Yad*, To'en venit'an 6:8; R. Joseph Ḥabiba (early 15th cent.), *Nimmukei Yosef* at Rif, Sanhedrin 29b; R. Shabbetai b. Meir ha-Kohen (Poland, 1621–1662), *Sifte Kohen* to Shulḥan Arukh, Ḥoshen Mishpat 81, n. 39.

22. Arukh ha-Shulḥan, Ḥoshen Mishpat 81:5.

23. R. Joseph Ḥabiba (at Rif, Sanhedrin 29b) finds the practice rooted in the desire to distance oneself from the "evil eye."

24. Mishnah, Bava Meẓia 4:12; Rif, ad loc.; *Yad*, Mekhirah 18:7; Rosh, Bava Meẓia 4:24; *Tur*, Ḥoshen Mishpat 228:16; Shulḥan Arukh, Ḥoshen Mishpat 228:16; Arukh ha-Shulḥan, Ḥoshen Mishpat 228:12.

25. Rashi to Mishnah, Bava Meẓia 4:12; *Tur*, loc. cit.; Shulḥan Arukh, loc. cit.; Arukh ha-Shulḥan, loc. cit.

26. Baraita, Bava Meẓia 60b; Rif,. ad loc.; *Yad.*, Mekhirah 18:3; Rosh, Bava Meẓia 4:24; *Tur*, Ḥoshen Mishpat 228:9; Shulḥan Arukh, Ḥoshen Mishpat 228:9; Arukh ha-Shulḥan, Ḥoshen Mishpat 228:5.

27. *Sma* to Shulḥan Arukh, Ḥoshen Mishpat 228, n. 16; Arukh ha-Shulḥan, loc. cit.

28. Baraita, Bava Meẓia 51a; Rif, ad loc.; *Yad*, Mekhirah 12:1; Rosh to Bava Meẓia 4:17; *Tur*, Ḥoshen Mishpat 227:1; Shulḥan Arukh, Ḥoshen Mishpat 227:1; Arukh ha-Shulḥan, Ḥoshen Mishpat 227:1.

29. For the development of this thesis, see Aaron Levine, *Free Enterprise and Jewish Law* (New York: Ktav and Yeshiva University Press, 1980), pp. 105–109.

30. See Shulḥan Arukh, Ḥoshen Mishpat 227.

31. Bava Batra 78a and Rashi ad loc.; Rif ad loc.; *Yad*, Mekhirah 27:5; Rosh to Bava Batra 5:7; *Tur*, Ḥoshen Mishpat 220:5; Shulḥan Arukh, Ḥoshen Mishpat 220:8; Arukh ha-Shulḥan, Ḥoshen Mishpat 220:7.

32. Rashi to Ḥullin 94a.

33. Ibid.

34. Tosafot to ibid.

35. Rashi to ibid.

36. Beẓah 16a.

37. Rashi to ibid.

38. Illustrating the phenomenon of cognitive dissonance is the Kassarjian and Cohen study which investigated the effect the Surgeon General's Report had on smokers' attitudes and behavior. The findings showed that 36.5 percent of the surveyed smokers did not believe that the report had established a linkage between smoking and cancer. Moreover, the figure among heavy smokers was 41 percent, suggesting that the more committed one is to a product, the greater the dissonance and the less likely one is to admit the product's adverse effects. Study cited in Richard L. Oliver, "An Interpretation of the Attitudinal and Behavioral Effects of Puffery," *Journal of Consumer Affairs* 13, no. 1, (March 1979): 8–27.

39. In Re Thompson Medical Co., Inc., 103 FTC 648 (1984).

40. In *Virginia State Board of Pharmacy* v. *Virginia Citizens Consumer Council*, 425 U.S. 748 (1976), the Supreme Court extended constitutional protection to commercial speech.

41. *FTC* v. Colgate-Palmolive Co., 380 U.S. 374, 391–92 (1965).

42. Roger E. Schechter, "The Death of the Gullible Consumer: Towards a More Sensible Definition of Deception at the FTC," *University of Illinois Law Review* 1989, no. 3, pp. 571–623.

43. Bava Batra 89a; Rif, ad loc.; *Yad,* Genevah 8:20; Rosh, Bava Batra 5:22; *Tur,* Ḥoshen Mishpat 231:2; Shulḥan Arukh, Ḥoshen Mishpat 231:2; Arukh ha-Shulḥan, Ḥoshen Mishpat 231:3.

44. *Yad,* Maakhalot Asurot 11:25.

45. Arukh ha-Shulḥan, Yoreh De'ah 119:2.

46. Ḥullin 94a.

47. R. Aryeh Judah b. Akiba, *Lev Aryeh,* Ḥullin 94a.

48. R. Mosheh Mordecai Epstein, *Levush Mordecai* 24.

49. R. Eliezer Meir Preil, *Ha-Me'or* 1:26–27.

50. R. Mosheh Feinstein (New York, 1895–1986), *Iggerot Mosheh,* Yoreh De'ah 2:61.

51. 133 FTC 676 (1944).

52. 133 FTC 679 (1944).

53. *Goodman* v. *FTC,* 244 F 2d 584 (9th Cir. 1957).

54. Preston, *Great American Blow-Up,* pp. 90–119.

55. Richard L. Oliver, "Interpretation of the Attitudinal and Behavioral Effects of Puffery," *Journal of Consumer Affairs* 13, no. 1 (March 1979): pp. 8–27.

56. Exodus 34:6.

57. Ibid.

58. Micah 7:20; Makkot 24a; *Yad,* Sekhirut 13:7.

59. Genesis 30:32–33 and commentaries ad loc.

60. Marginal gloss to Tosafot, Rosh ha-Shanah 17b.

61. See Yevamot 65b.

62. R. Solomon Luria (Rashal), Yevamot 63a. For another approach to reconciling Yevamot 63a with the general permissibility of altering the truth for the purpose of promoting domestic harmony, see R. Jacob b. Joseph Reicher (Austria, d. 1733), *Iyun Yaakov,* commentary on *Ein Yaakov,* Yevamot 63a.

NOTES TO CHAPTER 5

1. Sotah 36b.

2. In midrashic literature, Joseph is pointed up as the exemplar of the miẓvah of honoring and respecting parents. Cf. Mekhilta deRabbi Shimon bar Joḥai, BeShalaḥ; Seder Eliyahu Rabbah 24; Yalkut Shimoni, Vayeshev 141; Pesikta Rabbati 12 (Zakhor).

3. The father's moral-educational role proceeds most directly from the miẓvah of *ḥinnukh*. This rabbinically mandated miẓvah requires the father to train his children in the performance of miẓvot which they will be subject to when they reach adulthood (Ḥagigah 4a). Relatedly, this miẓvah assigns the father an interventionist role whenever he observes his children engaged in wrongdoing, with the additional duty to remonstrate them for their misconduct. Cf. R. Joseph Caro, Shulḥan Arukh, Oraḥ Ḥayyim 343:1. The father's role of remonstrator continues, of course, even after his children reach adulthood by dint of the pentateuchal miẓvah of *tokhaḥah* (reproof; Leviticus 19:17).

The *ḥinnukh* a son receives in normative conduct is potentially reinforced by dint of the father's pentateuchal obligation to teach him Torah (Kiddushin 29a). This obligation requires the father to teach his son the entire *Torah She-bikhtav* (Written Law; cf. Shulḥan Arukh, Yoreh De'ah 246:6 and comments ad loc. of *Taz*, n. 2, and *Shakh*, note 5).

For a glimpse at how the moral-educational role of the father worked itself out in practice, see R. Israel Ibn Al-Nakawa (Spain, 14th cent.), *Menorat ha-Maor*, ed. H. G. Enelow, vol. 4 (New York: Bloch, 1932), p. 145.

For the mother's role as enabler in connection with the miẓvah of *Talmud Torah*, see Berakhot 17a. For the mother's obligation to transmit the experience of Sinai to her children, see R. Ahron Soloveichik, "The Fire of Sinai," in *Building Jewish Ethical Character*, ed. Joseph Kaminetsky and Murray I. Friedman (New York: Fryer Foundation, 1975), p. 12.

Authorities dispute whether the sages imposed the miẓvah of *hinnukh* on the mother. For opposing views, cf. R. Abraham Abele b. Ḥayyim ha-Levi Gombiner (Poland, ca. 1637–1683), *Magen Avraham* to Shulḥan Arukh, Oraḥ Ḥayyim 343, n. 1, and R. Samuel b. Nathan ha-Levi Kolin (Bohemia, 1720–1806), *Maḥaẓit ha-Shekel* to Shulḥan Arukh, Oraḥ Ḥayyim 343, n. 1. In any case, Halakhah assigns a vital role to the mother as a moral educator of her children. One manifestation of this role is the mother's responsibility to remonstrate her children for wrongdoing. In this regard many authorities assign greater responsibility to the mother than to the father. Cf. R. Isaiah ha-Levi Horowitz (Poland, 1565–1630), *Shelah*, Sh'ar ha-Otiot, ot Derekh Ereẓ.

For a description of the vital role mothers historically assumed in the moral education of their daughters, see R. Moses b. Hanoch, *Sefer Brontshpiegel*, quoted and translated by Solomon Schimmel, "Ethical Dimensions of Traditional Jewish Education," in *Studies in Jewish Education*, ed. Barry Chazan, vol. 1 (Jerusalem: Magnes Press, 1983), pp. 94–95.

4. Bava Batra 21a; For the obligation of an educator to inculcate habits of truth in his students, see Maimonides (Egypt, 1135–1204), *Yad*, Shevu'ot 12:8.

5. Mekhilta, Exodus, parsha 8.

6. Ibid.

7. R. Ahron Soloveichik, *Logic of the Heart, Logic of the Mind* (Jerusalem: Genesis Jerusalem Press, 1991), pp. 92–98.

8. Exodus 20:12.

9. Leviticus 19:3.

10. Kiddushin 31b.

11. Cf. Shulḥan Arukh, Yoreh De'ah 242.

12. Beẓah 16a; Shabbat 10b.

13. Rashi, Beẓah 16a.

14. R. Baḥya Ibn Pakudah (Spain, 11th cent.), *Ḥovot ha-Levavot*, introduction to Sha'ar Avodat ha-Elokim.

15. Relative abundance works, other things being equal, to reduce price.

16. *Ḥovot ha-Levavot*, Sha'ar ha-Beḥinah.

17. *Sefer ha-Ḥinnukh* 33.

18. Sukkah 56b.

19. Ibid. and Rashi, ad loc.

20. *Sefer ha-Ḥinnukh*, loc. cit.

21. R. Abraham Danzig (Vilna, 1748–1820), *Ḥayye Adam* 67:2.

22. Midrash Rabbah, Exodus 1:8.

23. Genesis 41:39–46.

24. Genesis 49:22.

25. Genesis 45:17–20, 47:5–6.

26. Exodus 1:8–22.

27. Genesis 47:14, Pesaḥim 119a.

28. Sotah 11a, and see Rabbi Samson R. Hirsch (Germany, 1808–1888) at Exodus 1:8.

29. R. Ze'eb Wolf Einhorn (d. 1862), MHRZW at Exodus Rabbah 1:8.

30. Cf. R. Judah Loew b. Bezalel (Prague, ca. 1525–1609), *Gur Aryeh* at Exodus 1:8; R. Baruch ha-Levi Epstein (Russia, 1868–1942), *Torah Temimah* at Exodus 1:8.

31. Genesis 41:37–39, 47:45.

32. Targum Jonathan at Genesis 41:34; Midrash Sekhel Tov at Genesis 41:34; Ibn Ezra, Rashbam, and Redak ad loc.

33. Genesis 47:20–26.

34. Support for this attitude can be found in the language of Joseph's proposal to Pharaoh: "And the food shall be for a store (*lepikkadon*) for the land for the seven years of famine which shall come to the land of Egypt, that the land perish not through the famine" (Exodus 41:36). Since the Hebrew word *lepikkadon* literally means "something held in trust," Joseph's words can be taken to impart that the 20 percent tax will constitute the means of implementing forced private saving.

35. Rashi, at Genesis 41:55.

36. Bereshit Rabbah 79:6.

37. Exodus 7:19, 8:1.

38. Shemot Rabbah 9:10.

39. Exodus 8:12.

40. Shemot Rabbah 10:7.

41. William J. Baumol and Alan S. Blinder, *Economic Principles and Polices*, 5th ed. (New York: Harcourt Brace Jovanovich, 1991), pp. 623–627.

42. For an international comparison of the treatment of this issue and other policies relating to the family, see Sheila B. Kameron and Alfred J. Kahn, eds., *Child Care, Family Benefits, and Working Parents: A Study in Comparative Policy* (New York: Columbia University Press, 1981).

43. For sources, see above, n. 3.

44. R. Jeḥiel Michel Epstein (Belorussia, 1829–1908), Arukh ha-Shulḥan, Yoreh De'ah 245:9, 27.

45. For a description and efficiency analysis of several variants of the voucher system, see Aaron Levine, "Economic Analysis of Education Vouchers" (Ph.D. diss., New York University, 1973).

46. For an innovative curriculum proposal for moral education in yeshiva high schools, see R. Morris Sosevsky, "Incorporating Moral Education into the Jewish Secondary School Curriculum" (Ph.D. diss., Yeshiva University, 1980).

NOTES TO CHAPTER 6

1. *SEC* v. Texas Gulf Sulphur Co., 258 F. Supp. 262 (S.D. N.Y. 1966), aff'd in part, rev'd in part, 401 F. 2d 833 (2nd Cir. 1968), cert. denied, 394 U.S. 976 (1969); 312 F. Supp. 77 (S.D. N.Y. 1970), aff'd in part, rev'd in part, 446 F. 2d 1301 (2d Cir.), cert. denied, 404 U.S. 1005 (1971).

2. *SEC* v. Texas Gulf Sulphur Co., 401 F. 2d 833, 843–848 (2nd Cir. 1968).

3. R. Abraham David Wahrmann, *Kesef ha-Kedoshim,* in R. Joseph Caro (Safed, 1488–1575), Shulḥan Arukh, Ḥoshen Mishpat 227:9.

4. Tosafot, Ketubbot 47b.

5. Ḥullin 51a; R. Isaac b. Jacob Alfasi (Rif; Algeria, 1012–1103), ad loc.; Maimonides (Egypt, 1135–1204), *Yad,* Mekhirah, 15:6; R. Asher b. Jeḥiel (Rosh; Germany, 1250–1327), Ḥullin 3:34; R. Jacob b. Asher (Germany, 1270–1343), *Tur,* Ḥoshen Mishpat 232:11; Shulḥan Arukh, Ḥoshen Mishpat 232:11; R. Jeḥiel Michel Epstein (Belorussia, 1829–1908), Arukh ha-Shulḥan, Ḥoshen Mishpat 232:17.

6. Tosafot, Ketubbot 47b.

7. R. Moses Sofer, *Responsa Ḥatam Sofer,* Ḥoshen Mishpat 70.

8. For the development of this thesis, see Aaron Levine, *Free Enterprise and Jewish Law: Aspects of Jewish Business Ethics* (New York: Ktav and Yeshiva University Press, 1980), pp. 105–109.

9. R. Abraham David Horowitz, *Responsa Kinyan Torah* 1:14.

10. Mishnah Erkhin 6:5.

11. Naḥmanides (Ramban; Spain, 1194–1270), Kiddushin 12a.

12. R. Yom Tov Ishbili (Ritva; Spain, ca. 1250–1330), Kiddushin 12a.

13. For an example of delusive disclosure which fails the halakhic standard, see Shulḥan Arukh, Ḥoshen Mishpat 232:8.

14. The disclosure obligation does not extend to an openly visible defect. See *Sma* to Shulḥan Arukh, Ḥoshen Mishpat 245, n. 16.

15. R. Yom Tov Lipmann b. Nathan ha-Levi Heller (Moravia, 1579–1654), *Divrei Ḥamudot*, commentary on *Piskei ha-Rosh*, Ḥullin 7, n. 80; *Sma* to Shulḥan Arukh, Ḥoshen Mishpat 228, n. 7.

16. Ibid.

17. See Shulḥan Arukh, Ḥoshen Mishpat 232:6.

18. See Aaron Levine, *Economics and Jewish Law* (Hoboken: Ktav and Yeshiva University Press, 1987), pp. 17–21.

19. *Torat Kohanim,* Leviticus 19:14; *Yad,* Roẓeaḥ 12:14.

20. R. Mordecai Jacob Breisch (Israel, 1896–), *Responsa Ḥelkhat Ya'akov* 3:136.

21. R. Shmuel de Medina (Turkey, 1506–1589), *Responsa Maharash-dam*, Ḥoshen Mishpat 379.

22. Avodah Zarah 14a.

23. *Yad*, Roẓeaḥ 12:14.

24. R. Isaiah b. Mali di Trani the Elder (Italy, ca. 1180–1260), *Tosafot Rid*, Avodah Zarah 14a.

25. R. Ahron Soloveichik (Chicago, 1918–), "Teshuvah be-Inyan Mikvah," *Hadarom* 55 (1987): 15–30.

26. Cicero, *De Officiis*, bk. III, chap. iii (W. Miller trans., 1968). For an analysis of Cicero's case as it relates to the ethics of insider trading, see Gary Lawson, "The Ethics of Insider Trading," *Harvard Journal of Law and Public Policy* 2, no. 3, pp. 737–783.

27. R. Eliezer b. Joel ha-Levi and R. Jacob Tam, both quoted by R. Israei of Krems (fl. mid-14th cent.), *Haggahot Asheri* gloss to *Piskei ha-Rosh*, Bava Meẓia 2; R. Isaac b. Asher ha-Levi (Speyer, late 11th–early 12th cent.) and R. Eliezer b. Joel ha-Levi quoted by R. Mordecai b. Hillel ha-Kohen (Germany, 1240?–1298), *Mordecai*, Bava Meẓia 2:258; Rema, Shulḥan Arukh, Ḥoshen Mishpat 232:18.

In the actual incident, as quoted in both *Haggahot Asheri* and *Mordecai*, A is identified as a non-Jew. In recording this law, *Rema* (ad loc.) fails to identify A as a non-Jew.

28. R. Mordecai b. Abraham Jaffe (Prague, ca. 1535–1612), *Levush*, Ir Shushan, 233; *Responsa Avodat ha-Gershuni* 94. See, however, R. Jacob Moses Lorberbaum (Poland, ca. 1760–1832), *Netivot ha-Mishpaṭ*, Ḥoshen Mishpat 232, n. 23.

29. *Levush*, Ir Shushan 233.

30. See Shulḥan Arukh, Ḥoshen Mishpat 233:1.

31. Frederic Morton, *The Rothschilds: A Family Portrait* (New York: Atheneum, 1962), pp. 48–50.

32. For an overview of the prohibition against acting in the manner of the inhabitants of Sodom, see Levine, *Economics and Jewish Law*, pp. 36–41.

33. Bava Kamma 21a.

34. *Mordecai*, Bava Kamma 2:16; R. Joseph Ḥabiba (Spain, early 15th cent.), commentary on Rif, *Bava Kamma* 21a; Rema, Shulḥan Arukh, Ḥoshen Mishpat 363:6; Arukh ha-Shulḥan, Ḥoshen Mishpat 363:16. Other authorities vest the landlord with the right to object to

the squatter's presence even when he could not theoretically rent out the apartment; see R. Abraham Hirsch b. Jacob Eisenstadt (Bialystok, 1813–1868), *Pitḥei Teshuvah* to Shulḥan Arukh, Ḥoshen Mishpat 363, n. 3.

35. 17 Code of Federal Regulations 10b; 17CFR 240.10b-5.

36. *SEC* v. Texas Gulf Sulphur Co., 401 F. 2d 833, 843–847 (2nd Cir. 1968).

37. Ibid. at 848.

38. *Yad*, Mekhirah, 22:13 and R. Vidal Yom Tov of Tolosa (Spain, second half of 14th cent.), *Maggid Mishneh*, ad loc.; *Tur*, Ḥoshen Mishpat 212:1; Shulḥan Arukh, Ḥoshen Mishpat 212:1; Arukh ha-Shulḥan, Ḥoshen Mishpat 212:1.

39. R. Hai Gaon (Babylonia, 938–1038), *Sefer ha-Mikkah ve-ha-Mimkar*, sha'ar 2.

40. R. David b. Solomon ibn Abi Zimra (Radvaz), quoted by R. Moses b. Joseph Trani (Safed, 1500–1580), *Responsa Mabit* 132. For an opposing view, see Arukh ha-Shulḥan, Ḥoshen Mishpat 212:2.

41. Arukh ha-Shulḥan, Ḥoshen Mishpat 212:3.

42. Nicholas Wolfson, "Trade Secrets and Secret Trading," *San Diego Law Review* 25, no. 95 (1988): 110.

43. R. Solomon b. Joseph Ganzfried (Hungary, 1804–1886), *Kiẓẓur Shulḥan Arukh* 65:28; R. Mosheh Feinstein (New York, 1895–1986), *Iggerot Mosheh*, Oraḥ Ḥayyim 1:90; R. Shelomoh Zalman Aurebach, *Ha-Ne'eman*, Tishri 5723 (1963), pp. 6–10, 12; R. Menasheh Klein, *Mishneh Halakhot*, vol. 6, no. 277; R. Ezra Basri (Israel, contemp.), *Dinei Mamonot*, vol. 1, chap. 3, fn. 16.

Following the above line, R. Yiẓḥak Ya'akov Weisz (Israel, contemp.), Teshuvot Minḥat Yiẓḥak, 3, no. 1, draws a distinction between voting and nonvoting shareholders. Only voting shareholders, in his view, should be regarded as owners; nonvoting shareholders are to be regarded merely as creditors of the voting shareholders. Disputing R. Weisz, R. Mosheh Sternbuch (Israel, contemp.), *Mo'adim u-Zemanim* 3:269, pp. 160–163, treats both classes of shareholders alike, regarding them as partners in the business.

A minority position in this matter holds that the Halakhah regards the corporation as a legal personality, separate and distinct from the shareholders. See R. Joseph Rozin (Dvinsk, 1858–1936), Ẓofnat Pa'aneaḥ 184; R. Saul Weingurt, *Yad Sha'ul*, pp. 35–49; R. David Hoffmann (Germany, 1843–1921), *Melamed le-Ho'il*, Oraḥ Ḥayyim 91.

44. *Dinei Mamonot,* loc. cit.
45. Bava Meẓia 34b and Rashi ad loc.
46. Rosh, Bava Meẓia 3:5.
47. Rif, Bava Meẓia 34b; *Yad,* Sekhirut, 1:6; Rosh, Bava Meẓia 3:5; *Tur,* Ḥoshen Mishpat 307:5; Shulḥan Arukh, Ḥoshen Mishpat 307:5; Arukh ha-Shulḥan, Ḥoshen Mishpat 307:5.
48. Rashba, Bava Kamma 21a.
49. Rashba quoted in *Nimmukei Yosef,* Bava Meẓia 8.
50. R. Joseph Ḥabiba, *Nimmukei Yosef,* Bava Kamma 2.
51. R. Ya'akov Yesha'yahu Bloi (Israel, 1929–), *Pitḥei Ḥoshen,* Hilkhot Genevah Ve-Ona'ah, p. 218.
52. R. Ephraim b. Aaron Navon, *Maḥaneh Efrayim.*
53. For a general description of the function specialists play in the operation of the stock exchange, see Richard J. Teweles and Edward S. Bradley, *The Stock Market*, 5th ed. (New York: John Wiley, 1987), pp. 165–175.
54. See William K. S. Wang, "Trading on Material Non-Public Information on Impersonal Stock Markets: Who Is Harmed, and Who Can Sue Whom Under SEC Rule 10b-5?" *Southern California Law Review* 54 (1981): 1230–1240.
55. Tosafot, Avodah Zarah 15b; Ritva, Avodah Zarah 15b; R. David b. Samuel ha-Levi (Poland, 1586–1667), *Turei Zahav* to Shulḥan Arukh, Yoreh De'ah 151, n. 1. For an extensive discussion of this point, see R. Ḥayyim Ḥezekiah Medini (Russia, 1832–1904), *Sedei Ḥemed,* vol. 2, pp. 305–306.
56. *Maḥaneh Efrayim.*
57. 445 U.S. 222 (1980).
58. Ibid. at 224.
59. 588 F. 2d 1358 (2d Cir. 1978), rev'd, 445 U.S. 222 (1980).
60. 445 U.S. at 231–235.
61. R. Solomon Leib Tabak, *Responsa Erekh Shai* 183:1.
62. *Pitḥei Ḥoshen,* Hilkhot Sekhirut, pp. 163–164.
63. 463 U.S. 646 (1983).
64. 681 F. 2d 842 at 829–831; 463 U.S. 646 at 648–649.
65. 681 F. 2d at 829.
66. 463 U.S. at 651.
67. Ibid. at 658–659.
68. R. Israel Meir ha-Kohen Kagen, *Ḥafeẓ Ḥayyim*, Be'er Mayim Ḥayyim, Hilkhot Issurei Rekhilut 9:1.

69. Leviticus 19:16.

70. *Ḥafeẓ Ḥayyim*, Lavin 1–17, Essin 1–14.

71. Ibid., Hilkhot Issurei Lashon ha-Ra K'lal 10:1–17; Hilkhot Rekhilut K'lal 9:1–15.

72. *Dirks* v. *SEC*, 463 U.S. (1982) 646 at 669.

73. Tosafot, Bava Meẓia 31b.

74. Rosh, Sanhedrin 8:2.

75. Bava Meẓia 31b; Rif ad loc.; *Yad*, Gezelah ve-Avedah, 12:3–4; Rosh, Bava Meẓia 2:28; *Tur*, Ḥoshen Mishpat 265; Shulḥan Arukh, Ḥoshen Mishpat 265; Arukh ha-Shulḥan, Ḥoshen Mishpat 265. For a detailed analysis of the monetary claims which may arise in conjunction with a rescue operation, see R. Aaron Kirschenbaum, "The Good Samaritan: Monetary Aspects," in *Journal of Halacha and Contemporary Society* 17 (Spring 1989): 83–92.

76. 463 U.S. 646, 655–662.

77. *SEC* v. *Switzer*, 590 F. Supp. 756 (W.D. Okla. 1984).

78. 590 F. Supp. 756, 761–764.

79. Ibid. at 764–767.

80. Ibid. at 766.

81. Henry Mann, "Insider Trading and the Law Professors," *Vanderbilt Law Review* 23 (1970): 565–566.

82. Office of the Chief Economist, Securities and Exchange Commission, "Stock Trading Before the Announcement of Tender Offers: Insider Trading or Market Anticipation?," pp. 3, 32–34.

83. Iman Anabtawi, "Toward A Definition of Insider Trading," *Stanford Law Review* 41 (January 1989): 394–396.

84. Ibid., pp. 396–399.

85. Henry Mann, *Insider Trading and the Stock Market* (New York: Free Press, 1966), pp. 138–145.

86. Richard A. Posner, *Economic Analysis of Law*, 3rd ed. (Boston: Little, Brown, 1986), p. 392.

87. Saul Levmore, "In Defense of the Regulation of Insider Trading," *Harvard Journal of Law and Public Policy* 11, no. 1, pp. 104–105.

88. See R. Solomon b. Abraham Adret (Barcelona, 1235–1310), *Responsa Rashba* 3:411; R. Simeon b. *Ẓemaḥ* Duran (Algeria, 1361–1444), *Tashbeẓ* 2:132 and 239.

89. Frank H. Easterbrook, "Insider Trading as an Agency Problem," in Principles and Agents: *The Structure of Business*, ed. John W. Pratt

and Richard J. Zeckhauser (Boston: Harvard Business School Press, 1985), pp. 91–94.

90. Insider Trading Sanctions Act of 1984, Pub. L. no. 98-376, 98 Stat. 1264 (1984).

91. Pub. L. no. 100-704, 102 Stat. 4677 (1988).

92. Sec. 3(a)(2), 21A(e), 102 Stat. at 4679.

NOTES TO CHAPTER 7

1. Kenneth Kelly, "The Role of the Free Rider in Resale Price Maintenance: The Loch Ness Monster of Antitrust Captured," *George Mason University Law Review* 10, no. 2 (1988): 330–335.

2. For a bibliography of the various positions on this matter, see ibid., fnn. 28–31.

3. One example of such an argument may be found in Pitofsky, "In Defense of Discounters: The No Frills Case for a Per Se Rule Against Vertical Price Fixing," *Georgia Law Journal* 71 (1983): 1487.

4. Frank H. Easterbrook, "Vertical Arrangements and the Rule of Reason," *Antitrust Law Journal* 1, pt. 11 (March 21–23, 1984): 141–142.

5. Ibid., p. 142.

6. L. G. Telser, "Why Manufacturers Should Want Fair Trade," *Journal of Law and Economics* 3 (October 1960): 96–105.

7. Ibid., pp. 91–96.

8. Richard A. Posner, Antitrust Law: An Economic Perspective (Chicago: University of Chicago Press, 1976), pp. 149–150.

9. Telser, "Why Manufacturers Should Want Free Trade."

10. Kelly, "Role of the Free Rider," p. 329.

11. Ibid., pp. 344–361.

12. Ibid., pp. 357–361.

13. R. Meir b. Samuel, quoted in Tosafot, Kiddushin 59a.

14. Cf. R. Moses Sofer (Hungary, 1762–1839), *Responsa Ḥatam Sofer*, Ḥoshen Mishpat 79; R. Yaakov Y. Bloi (Israel, 1929–), *Pitḥei Ḥoshen*, Hilkhot Genevah ve-Ona'ah, chap. 9, n. 27.

15. Leviticus 25:17, Mishnah Bava Meẓia 4:10; R. Isaac b. Jacob Alfasi (Rif; Spain, 1012–1103), Bava Meẓia 58b; Maimonides (Egypt, 1135–1204), *Yad*, Hilkhot Mekhirah 14:12; R. Asher b. Jeḥiel (Germany, 1250–1327), Bava Meẓia 4:22; R. Jacob b. Asher (Germany, 1270–1343), *Tur*, Ḥoshen Mishpat 228:1; R. Joseph Caro (Safed,

1488–1575), Shulḥan Arukh, Ḥoshen Mishpat 228:1; R. Jeḥiel Michel Epstein (Belorussia, 1829–1908), Arukh ha-Shulḥan, Ḥoshen Mishpat 228:1.

16. R. Menaḥem b. Solomon Meiri (Perpignan, ca. 1249–1306), Beit ha-Beḥirah, Bava Meẓia 59a. Pricing an article with no intention to buy it, according to R. Samuel b. Meir (Rashbam; France, ca. 1080–1174), Pesaḥim 114b, is prohibited on account of the possible financial loss this might cause the vendor. While the vendor is preoccupied with the insincere inquiry, serious customers may turn elsewhere.

17. See commentary by Rashi (R. Solomon b. Isaac; Troyes, 1040–1105) at Leviticus 25:17.

18. Avodah Zarah 6b; Rif ad loc.; *Yad*, Roẓeaḥ 12:4; *Tur*, Yoreh De'ah 151:1; Shulḥan Arukh, Yoreh De'ah 151:1.

19. Robert Springer and H. E. Frech III, "Deterring Fraud: The Role of Resale Price Maintenance," *Journal of Business* 59, no. 3 (1986): 433–449.

20. Samuel, Ḥullin 94a; Rif, ad loc.; *Yad*, Genevah 18:3; Rosh, Ḥullin 7:18; *Tur*, Ḥoshen Mishpat 228:6; Shulḥan Arukh, Ḥoshen Mishpat 228:6; Arukh ha-Shulḥan, Ḥoshen Mishpat 228:3.

21. Rosh, Bava Meẓia 4:23; *Tur*, Ḥoshen Mishpat 228:2; Shulḥan Arukh, Ḥoshen Mishpat 228:10; Arukh ha-Shulḥan, Ḥoshen Mishpat 228:6. These are based on Mishnah Bava Meẓia 4:11. For a different understanding of this Mishnah, see Rashi, ad loc.; Ran, commentary on Rif, Bava Meẓia 59b; *Yad*, Mekhirah 18:5.

22. Aaron Levine, *Free Enterprise and Jewish Law: Aspects of Jewish Business Ethics* (New York: Ktav and Yeshiva University Press, 1980), pp. 4–32; idem, "Minimum Wage Legislation: A Halakhic Perspective," *Tradition* 24, no. 1 (Fall 1988): 17–18.

23. Easterbrook, "Vertical Arrangement and the Rule of Reason," pp. 147–150.

NOTES TO CHAPTER 8

1. *Encyclopaedia Britannica* (15th ed., 1981), 5:156.

2. Thomas R. Leavens, "In Defense of Unauthorized Use: Recent Developments in Defending Copyright Infringement," *Law and Contemporary Problems* 44, no. 4 (Autumn 1981): 5.

3. 17 U.S.C. 107, "Limitations on Exclusive Rights; Fair Use," Pub L, 653, Title I, 101, Oct. 19, 1976, 90 Stat 2546.

4. 17 U.S.C. 107 (1982).

5. 487 F. 2d 1345 (Ct. Col. 1973), aff'd by an equally divided court, 420 U.S. 376 (1975).

6. 17 U.S.C. 108 (f) 4 (1976); Cong. Rec. House, at H10878.

7. The act of Dec. 31, 1976, Pub. L. No. 93-573, 201, 88 Stat. 1873, established in the Library of Commerce a National Commission on New Technological Uses of Copyrighted Works.

8. H.R. Rep. No. 1733, 94 Cong. 2d Sess. 72-74, 108 (1976).

9. H.R. Rep. No. 1476, 94th Cong., 2d Sess. 66 (1976) at 67-72.

10. 758 F. Supp. 1522 (S.D. N.Y. 1991)

11. Act of Oct. 15, 1971, Pub. L. No. 92-140, 1, 85 Stat. 39.

12. H.R. Rep. No. 487, 92d Cong., 1st Sess. 5.

13. For various aspects of Jewish copyright law, see Arthur Jay Silverstein, "Copyright in Jewish Law," *Tradition* 14, no. 3 (Spring 1974): 23–36; Rabbi J. David Bleich, *Contemporary Halakhic Problems* (New York: Ktav and Yeshiva University Press, 1983), pp. 121–130; R. Israel Schneider, "Jewish Law and Copyright," in *Journal of Halacha and Contemporary Society* 21 (Spring 1991): 84–96

14. R. Moses Sofer, *Responsa Ḥatam Sofer*, Ḥoshen Mishpat, no. 79. See also no. 41 and 6:57. Disputing R. Sofer's view, R. Mordecai Banet (Moravia, 1753–1829), *Perashat Mordecai*, no. 8, argues, in effect, that the decree described in the text could not have been promulgated. Drawing an analogy from Ezra's decree, R. Banet posits that promoting the widest dissemination of religious works calls for a free-entry rather than a protectionist approach.

15. For the parameters of communal Jewish legislation, see Aaron Levine, "Minimum Wage Legislation: A Halakhic Perspective," *Tradition* 1 (Fall 1988): 11–13.

16. Sukkah 18a.

17. See Shulḥan Arukh, Oraḥ Ḥayyim 307:16; Arukh ha-Shulḥan, Oraḥ Ḥayyim 307:9–10.

18. *Encyclopedia Talmudit*, 15:64–66; see also R. Moshe Weinberger, "On Studying Secular Subjects," *Journal of Halacha and Contemporary Society*, Spring 1986, pp. 105–106.

19. R. Joseph Saul ha-Levi Nathanson, *Sho'el u-Meshiv*, Mahadura Kamma, I, no. 44.

20. R. Yiẓḥak Yehudah Schmelkes, *Bet Yiẓḥak*, Yoreh De'ah 2:75.

21. Ibid., Ḥoshen Mishpat 80.

22. Ibid., Yoreh De'ah 1:75.

23. R. Meir b. Samuel, quoted in Tosafot, Kiddushin 59a.

24. *Responsa Ḥatam Sofer,* Ḥoshen Mishpat 79. See also Ḥoshen Mishpat 41 and 6:57.

25. R. Yaakov Yesh'yahu Bloi, *Pitḥei Ḥoshen,* Hilkhot Genevah ve-Ona'ah, chap. 9, n. 27.

26. R. Ḥayyim David ha-Levi, *Aseh Lekha Rav* 6:77.

27. Ibid.

28. See hearing on S. 1739, serial no. J-99-69, Oct. 30, 1985; March 25 and Aug. 1, 1986, at pp. 4–5

29. Baraita, Bava Meẓia 78b.

30. Mishnah Bava Meẓia 6:3.

31. Bava Meẓia 78a.

32. For the *tenai kaful* condition, see *Yad,* Ishut 6:1–7; Rosh, Gittin 6:9; *Tur,* Even ha-Ezer 38:2; Shulḥan Arukh, Even ha-Ezer 38:2; Arukh ha-Shulḥan, Even ha-Ezer 38:26–27.

33. See Tosafot Kiddushin 59b.

34. R. Zalman Nehemia Goldberg, "Haatakat mi-Cassette le-lo Reshut ha-Bealim," *Tehumin* 6 (1984): 185–207.

35. *Sho'el u-Meshiv,* loc. cit.

36. Shulḥan Arukh, Ḥoshen Mishpat 111:3.

37. R. Joshua b. Alexander ha-Kohen Falk, *Sma* to Shulḥan Arukh, Ḥoshen Mishpat 111:3, n. 7.

38. R. Naftali Bar-Ilan, "Haatakat Sefarim o Cassetot," *Tehumin* 7 (1985): 360–367. See also R. Goldberg's response to R. Bar-Ilan's rejoinder in the same issue: "Tenai ve-shiyyur be-Hiskemim," pp. 368–380.

39. R. Ezekiel b. Judah ha-Levi Landau, *Noda bi-Yehudah,* Ḥoshen Mishpat 24.

40. Goldberg, "Haatakat mi-Cassette le-lo Reshut ha-Bealim," pp. 194–198.

41. Bar-Ilan, "Haatakat Sefarim o Cassetot," pp. 366–367.

42. *Pitḥei Ḥoshen,* Hilkhot Genevah ve-Ona'ah, loc. cit.

43. R. Israel Joshua Trunk, *Yeshu'ot Malko,* Ḥoshen Mishpat 22.

44. *Pitḥei Ḥoshen,* loc. cit. A variant of the case dealt with in the text is the issue of whether it is permissible to copy a tape without the owner's express consent. Addressing this issue, R Mosheh Feinstein (New York, 1895–1986) disallows the practice. Since the owner is en-

titled to charge a fee for the use of his tape, denying someone the privilege of making use of it gratis does not reflect a Sodomitic character. Hence, copying the tape without the owner's express consent amounts to unlawful use of someone else's property.

Given the duty to disseminate Torah, it is apparently illegitimate for a Torah lecturer to ask his audience to refrain from taping his talk. Dismissing this assertion, R. Feinstein avers that various legitimate motives could underlie the request; e.g., concern that the conclusions might be incorrect. Since various legitimate concerns may underlie the request, the audience is bound by it. Violating the request is tantamount to making someone work against his will, but does not constitute an act of theft. Nonetheless, copying a tape from a tape which was recorded against the wishes of the Torah lecturer is an act of theft. *Iggerot Mosheh,* Oraḥ Ḥayyim, vol. 4, no. 40:19.

45. *Aseh Lekha Rav* 6:94.

46. Hearing on S. 1739, pp. 23–.

47. Ibid., p. 6.

48. S. J. Liebowitz, "Copyright Law, Photocopying and Price Discrimination," in *Research in Law and Economics*, ed. John Palmer, vol. 8 (JAI Press, 1986), pp. 194–197.

49. *Academic Permission Service Newsletter* (Salem, Mass: Copyright Clearance Center, 1991).

50. Liebowitz, "Copyright Law," p. 195.

51. Hearing on S. 1739, pp. 1–2.

52. For a comparison of legislation in countries imposing royalties or taxes on blank tapes or recording equipment, see ibid., appendix III.

53. Statement of Prof. Albert P. Blaustein, Rutgers University School of Law, to the Committee on the Judiciary, U.S. Senate, and its Subcommittee on Patents, Trademarks and Copyright, hearings on S. 1361, serial no. JLE-74-2293, July 1973, pp. 573–575

54. S. J. Liebowitz, "Copying and Indirect Appropriability: Photocopying of Journals," in *Journal of Political Economy* 93, no. 5.

55. Bernard M. Fry and Herbert S. White, *Publishers and Librarians: A Study of Scholarly and Research Journals* (Lexington, Mass.: Lexington, 1976); S. J. Liebowitz, *The Impact of Reprography on the Copyright System* (Ottawa: Dept. of Consumer and Corporate Affairs, 1981).

NOTES TO CHAPTER 9

1. For a description of these levies, see Aaron Levine, *Economics and Jewish Law: Halakhic Perspectives* (Hoboken: Ktav and Yeshiva University Press, 1987), pp. 125–126.

2. Nedarim 65b.

3. R. Hayyim Soloveitchik, quoted in the name of R. Joseph Soloveitchik by R. Daniel Lander, "Be-Inyan Dei Maḥsoro," in *Kavod ha-Rav* (New York: Student Organization of Yeshiva Rabbi Isaac Elchanan Theological Seminary, 1984), pp. 202–206.

4. See Maimonides (Egypt, 1135–1204), *Yad*, Mattenot Aniyyim 10:7, and Levine, *Economics and Jewish Law*, p. 114.

5. Avot de R. Natan, chap. 11.

6. R. Baruch Epstein (Russia, 1860–1942), *Torah Temimah* at Genesis 2:15.

7. Predicating the existence of a capital market in the Torah society, e.g., in the State of Israel, is not inconsistent with Halakha's prohibition against *ribbit* (interest payments) on inter-Jewish debt instruments.

One consideration is that the prohibition of *ribbit* applies only to the interest payments of a debtor. Debtor status, as it pertains to the *ribbit* interdict, obtains only when the transaction confers upon the lender or the creditor a lien on the property of the obligator in the event of default. In respect to government debt, the holder of a government bond enjoys no lien on the property of the government in the event of default. Interest payments on government debt should therefore not be regarded as a *ribbit* violation.

In a similar vein, R. Mosheh Feinstein (*Iggerot Mosheh*, Yoreh De'ah 2:62–63) ruled that a corporate debtor is free of the *ribbit* constraint. Standing as the basis of this point of leniency is the limited-liability feature of the corporate entity. Since a corporate bondholder only enjoys a lien on the business assets of the corporation but not on the personal assets of the shareowners, the shareowners do not assume the halakhic status of debtors. This point of leniency, however, is sharply disputed by many other authorities. They maintain that holding a personal lien on the debtor (*shi'abud ha-guf*) is not critical in creating the halakhic status of debtor (cf. R. Isaac Jacob Weisz, *Minḥat Yiẓḥak* 3:1; and R. Mordecai Jacob Breisch, *Ḥelkat Yaakov* 3:190). But these disputants could possibly agree that the government does fall short of the halakhic definition of debtor. While a corporate borrower obligates the assets of the corporation in the payment of the debt, no such commitment is made by government in respect to its debt instruments. Rather, the government bondholder must rely entirely on the "good faith" promise of his government to make payment on interest and principal. Interest payments on government debt, therefore, do not violate *ribbit* law.

In the State of Israel, the revenue of government bonds is used to absorb immigrants and develop the infrastructure of the economy. For this reason, government debt can be viewed as a mechanism to bring together land, labor, capital, and technology in a cooperative effort to fulfill the mizvah of settling of the land of Israel. The government bondholder is no more a *creditor* of the state than the capitalist or the worker in the joint venture of investing in human capital and developing the infrastructure of the economy. Each resource owner is entitled to compensation for the role it plays in this partnership venture (cf. R. Ben Zion Meir Ḥai Ouziel, quoted in R. Shmuel Tuvia Stern, *Ha-Shavit*, vol. 4, pp. 53–55).

In the text, reference is made to Robert Eisner's work. His research on the U.S. government deficit found a close correspondence between the deficit and government investment-like spending for the same year. In consequence, government borrowing should be viewed as a *mechanism* for matching the benefit streams of the investment projects with the corresponding income streams. Interest and amortization payments over the lifetime of the investment projects amount to no more than the "fair price" society pays each period for the *services* of the capital projects.

In respect to private capital markets, we note that when A transfers capital to B for business purposes, the transaction need not be structured in the form of a loan. The *ribbit* constraint can be avoided by structuring the transaction in the form of a business partnership between A and B, with the financier assuming the role of silent partner and the recipient assuming the role of active partner. Provided that the financier assumes the same percentage of the losses as of the profits, the agreement can call for any symmetrical division of profits and losses. With the aim of ensuring that the agreement will be free of *ribbit* violation as well as to safeguard the financier's desired return, various clauses are added to the basic agreement. This type of agreement is called *hetter iska*. For details of *hetter iska* as it pertains to modern financial markets, see Levine, *Economics and Jewish Law*, pp. 185–213.

Within the framework of the *hetter iska* mechanism, a capital market emerges in the Torah society, notwithstanding the *ribbit* prohibition.

One final observation regarding the capital markets of the Torah society. Given that it is only inter-Jewish transactions that are subject to the *ribbit* prohibition, Jewish participation in non-Jewish capital markets presents no problem. The rate of return obtainable in these markets serves as a measure of the opportunity cost the Jewish investor incurs both for making capital available for *hetter iska* purposes and for purchasing debt instruments issued by the Jewish state. If inflationary pressures push up the relative real return in the non-Jewish bond markets, the supply of Jewish capital for *hetter iska* ventures as well as the demand for bonds issued by the Jewish state will decrease. Hence, price instability in the non-Jewish world can be expected to raise the cost of capital in the Torah society. Since the Torah society cannot insulate itself from the world financial community, it has a vested interest in price stability in the non-Jewish world.

8. Avodah Zarah 3b.

9. R. Mosheh Ḥayyim Luzzatto (Italy, 1701–1746), *Da'at Tevunot*, siman 18. For an elaboration of this concept, see R. Shelomo Harkavi, *M'Imrei Shelomo*, pp. 3, 16.

10. For an elementary discussion of the costs of inflation, see William J. Baumol and Alan S. Blinder, *Economics: Principles and Policy*, 5th ed. (New York: Harcourt, Brace, Jovanovich, 1991), pp. 99–111.

11. G. L. Bach, "The Economic Effects of Inflation," *Proceedings of the Academy of Political Science* 31 (1975): 25–28.

12. Ibid., p. 28.

13. For a detailed discussion of these laws, see *Shulḥan Arukh*, Yoreh De'ah 240.

14. R. Aaron ha-Levi (Barcelona, 1235–1300), *Sefer ha-Ḥinnukh* 33.

15. Paul A. Samuelson and William D. Nordhaus, *Economics*, 12th ed. (New York: McGraw-Hill, 1985), p. 236, fn. 5.

16. Ibid.

17. Bach, "Economic Effects of Inflation," pp. 28–29.

18. *Torat Kohanim*, B'har; *Yad*, Mattenot Aniyyim 10:7; *Tur*, Yoreh De'ah 249:7; *Shulḥan Arukh*, Yoreh De'ah 249:6; *Arukh ha-Shulḥan*, Yoreh De'ah 249:15.

19. *Yad*, loc. cit.

20. Marginal gloss to *Tosafot*, Rosh haShanah 17b.

21. Megillah 13b.

22. Genesis 41:15–33.

23. Rashi (R. Solomon b. Isaac; 1040–1105), at Genesis 41:34, on interpretation of *Siftei Ḥakhamim* and Mizraḥi; R. Shmuel b. Meir (Rashbam; Ramerupt, 1060–ca. 1130), ad loc.; R. Ḥizkiyah Ḥizkuni (Provence, ca. 1250), ad loc.; R. Ḥayyim Ibn Attar (Jerusalem, 1696–1743), *Or ha-Ḥayyim*, ad loc.; R. Meir Loeb b. Jeḥiel Michel (Malbim; Russia, 1809–1880), ad loc.

Taking a minority position, R. Abraham Ibn Ezra (Spain, 1089–ca. 1164) understands *veḥimesh* to mean that Joseph purchased one-fifth of the national crop each year of the seven years of prosperity. This government reserve was then sold to the populace during the years of famine.

24. For a description of the measures Joseph took to prevent profiteering during the years of famine, see Genesis Rabbah 91:4.

25. R. Ovadiah b. Jacob Sforno at Genesis 41:56; R. Ḥayyim Ibn Attar, *Or ha-Ḥayyim*, ad loc..

26. For a discussion of the natural rate of unemployment, see Samuelson and Nordhaus, *Economics*, pp. 217–222.

27. For a description of these wage-subsidy programs, see Ronald G. Ehrenberg and Robert S. Smith, *Modern Labor Economics: Theory and Public Policy*, 4th ed. (New York: Harper Collins, 1991), pp. 121–124.

28. Meir Tamari, "May a Jewish Government Cause Inflation?" *Diné Israel* 12 (1984–85): 39–48.

29. Robert Eisner, *How Real Is the Federal Deficit?* (New York: Free Press, 1986), pp. 26–32.

30. R. Meir b. Isaac Katzenellenbogen, *Responsa Maharam of Padua*, no. 42.

31. For a discussion of the mandated functions the Torah society imposes on the public sector, see Aaron Levine, *Free Enterprise and Jewish Law: Aspects of Jewish Business Ethics* (New York, Ktav and Yeshiva University Press, 1980), pp. 131–160.

32. Richard A. Musgrave and Peggy B. Musgrave, *Public Finance in Theory and Practice*, 5th ed. (New York: McGraw"Hill, 1989), p. 536.

33. Ketubbot 50a; Rif, ad loc.; *Yad*, Arakhim 8:3; Rosh, Ketubbot 4:15; *Tur*, Yoreh De'ah 249:1; *Shulhan Arukh*, Yoreh De'ah 249:1; *Arukh ha-Shulhan*, Yoreh De'ah 249:1.

34. R. Moses Isserles (Rema; Poland, 1525 or 1530–1572), *Shulḥan Arukh,* Oraḥ Ḥayyim 656:1. Avoidance of the infringement of a negative commandment requires an individual, if necessary, to go to any expense (Rema, ad loc.).

Disputing Rema's view, R. Mosheh Sofer (Hungary, 1762–1839), ad loc., extends the one-fifth rule to negative commandments. To be sure, the leniency applies only if the negative commandment would be violated passively (*shev ve-al ta'aseh*). Avoidance of an active violation of a negative commandment requires an individual, if necessary, to go to any expense.

35. For a discussion of the inertial rate of inflation, see Samuelson and Nordhaus, *Economics,* pp. 242–247.

36. For the development of this point, see Aaron Levine, "The Negative Income Tax: A Halakhic Perspective," *National Jewish Law Review* 3 (1988): 100–106.

37. Tamari, "May a Jewish Government Cause Inflation?" pp. 42–44.

38. Baumol and Blinder, *Economics,* p. 110.

39. Tamari, "May a Jewish Government Cause Inflation?" pp. 44–48.

40. Ibid., p. 46.

41. Ibid., pp. 45–46.

42. Ibid., pp. 47–48.

Subject Index

Geneivat da'at,
and agreement concluded in error, 129
and diversionary tactics, 123-124, 132
and insider trading, 123
and misleading markups, 169-170
and puffery, 89-90
and self-assessment, 84-88
and self- deception, 70-73
and trading on superior information, 122-124
biblical source, 69
definition, 69
Government subsidy,
educational enterprise, 107-109
family, 109-110
for disadvantaged, 218
invisible misconduct, 20
religious education of the indigent, 110
Hakkarat hatov,
and filial responsibility to parents, 104, 103-104
and government policies to strengthen, 112-113
and price stabilization policy, 208
and submission to God's moral code, 100-101
as a personality trait, 100
as an ethical norm, 103-106
standards for in Judaism, 106-107
Heinz W. Kirchner case (1963), 68-69
Hetter iska, 267-268
Ḥinnukh, (religious ed.), 253-254
Hodgson v. Brookhaven General Hospital (1970), 40
Hodgson v. Robert Hall (1973), 40
Hostile takeover, 113
Humphrey-Hawkins Act (1978), 201
Hyperinflation, *See* inflation

Imitatio Dei,
and economic public policy, 12-16
and *emet*, 89-92
and prohibition against inciting the evil inclination, 180
and insider trading, 20, 156-157
and interpersonal conduct, 12-13
and legalizing insider trading, 156
and long-run time frame, 19
and *raḥum*, 89-91, 212
and resale price maintenance, 20, 170
and social component, 14
and standard for human conduct, 12-13
and the full employment mandate, 20, 204-205
and the moral climate of society, 15-16
and the moral personality, 19, 95
and unauthorized copying and dubbing, 20
arranging the cure before the affliction, 212-214
as the rationale for the FTC, 19, 89-92
definition, 3
universal kindness, 204-205
weakening the power of the evil inclination, 15-16
Indirect appropriation, 196-198

Name Index

Simeon b. Samuel of Joinville, R., 244 n.26
Simon, Robert, 248 n.44
Sirkes, R. Joel, 17, 32, 241 n.58, 244 n.22, n.28
Sma, See Falk, R. Joshua b. Alexander ha-Kohen
Smith, Robert, 269 n.27
Sofer, R. Mosheh, 120, 181, 182, 246 n.22, 256 n.7, 261 n.14, 264 n.24, 270 n.34
Solomon b. Isaac, R., 17, 18, 45, 71, 78-82, 100, 238 n.11, 240 n.32, n.33, 241 n.57, n.61, 249 n.8, 250 n.25, 251 n.31, n.32, n.35, n.37, 254 n.13, n.19, 255 n.35, 259 n.45, 262 n.17, n.21
Soloveichik, R. Ahron, 60, 98, 125, 126, 140, 254 n.7, 257 n.25
Soloveitchik, R. Ḥayyim, 202, 204, 266 n.3
Soloveitchik, R. Joseph B., 13, 241 n.44, 266 n.3
Sorensen, Elaine, 57, 248 n.42
Sosevsky, R. Morris, 255 n.46
Springer, Robert, 168, 169, 262 n.19
Stern, R. Shmuel Tuvia, 267 n.7

Tabak, R. Solomon Leib, 143, 259 n.61
Tam, R. Jacob, 42, 44, 257 n.27
Tamari, Meir, 218, 222, 224-227, 269 n.28, 270 n.37, n.39
Tashbeẓ, See Duran, R. Simeon b. Ẓemaḥ
Telser, L.G., 164, 165, 168, 170, 261 n.6, n.9
Terumat ha-Deshen, See Isserlein, R. Israel b. Pethahiah
Teshurat Shai, See Tabak, R. Solomon Leib
Torah Temimah, See Epstein, R. Baruch
Tosafot, 78-82, 119, 120, 251 n.34, 252 n.60, 256 n.6, 264 n.23, n.33, 269 n.20
Tosafot ha-Rosh, See R. Asher b. Jeḥiel
Tosafot Rid, See Trani, Isaiah b. Mali di, R.
Trani, Isaiah b. Mali di, R., 125, 126, 257 n.24
Trunk, R. Israel Joshua, 189, 264 n.43
Tur, See R. Jacob b. Asher
Turei Zahav, See R. David b. Samuel ha-Levi
Twersky, R. Yiẓḥak, 13, 240 n.41

Wahrmann, R. Abraham David, 119, 256 n.3
Walkin, R. Aaron, 45, 46, 247 n.28
Wang, William K.S., 259 n.54
Wasner, R. Shmuel ha-Levi, 182, 183
Weinberger, R. Moshe, 263 n.18
Weisz, R. Yiẓḥak Ya'akov, 258 n.43, 266 n.7
Welch, Finis, 243 n.12
White, Herbert, 265 n.55
Wolfson, Nicholos, 258 n.42

Yad, See Maimonides
Yakhin u-Vo'az, See Duran, R. Ẓemaḥ b. Solomon
Yere'im, See R. Eliezer b. Samuel of Metz

Zausmir, R. Jekuthiel Asher, 245 n.7